RUTH'S RECORD

The Diary of an American
in Japanese-Occupied
Shanghai
1941-1945

Ruth Hill Barr

Ruth's Record

By Ruth Hill Barr

ISBN-13: 978-988-8422-00-5

Cover Design: Magic Wang

This book has been reset in 10pt Book Antiqua. Spellings and punctuations are left as in the original edition.

BIOGRAPHY & AUTOBIOGRAPHY / Historical

EB076

Published by Earnshaw Books Ltd. (Hong Kong)

CONTENTS

ABBREVIATIONS

AAUW	American Association of University Women
AC	American Club
ADC	Amateur Dramatic Club
Am As	American Association
AMT	Associated Mission Treasurers
ARC	American Red Cross
ARP	Air Raid Precautions
BRA	British Residents' Association
BWA	British Women's Association
CAC	Civil Assembly Centre
CCC	Columbia Country Club
CIM	China Inland Mission
CP	Communist Party
CRB	Central Reserve Bank
DC	District Committee (of the LMS)
DSC	Distinguished Service Cross
HMS	His Majesty's Ship
ILO	International Labor Organization
IRC	International Red Cross
LCH	Lester Chinese Hospital
LMS	London Missionary Society
OC	Officer Commanding
NCC	National Christian Council
NY	New York
PM	Prayer Meeting

PO	Post Office
POW	Prisoner of War
PWD	Public Works Department
RAS	Royal Asiatic Society
SAS	Shanghai American School
SMC	Shanghai Municipal Council
SMU	Southern Methodist University
SS	Sunday School
SVC	Shanghai Volunteer Corps
TB	Tuberculosis
UNA	United Nations Association
UNRRA	United Nations Relief and Rehabilitation Association
U. of S.	University of Shanghai
UP	United Press
USA	United States of America
USS	United States' Ship
USSR	United Soviet Socialist Republics
YMCA	Young Men's Christian Association
YWCA	Young Women's Christian Association (also 'YW' or 'Y')
YW Int. Br.	YW International Branch

Note on illustrations:

The provenance of the photographs of the Lunghwa camp included in this book is unknown. They must have been taken just after the end of the war as cameras were not allowed in the camp before VJ Day. The drawings / paintings are by Deirdre Fee, an Irish internee who was a friend of Ruth Barr. The map of Shanghai was created by George Wang.

BRIEF HISTORICAL TIMELINE

September 1931	Japan invades and occupies Manchuria
July 1937	Outbreak of Sino-Japanese War
August 1937	Japanese bomb Shanghai, take over Chinese parts of the city
September 1939	Outbreak of European War
December 7, 1941	Japanese attack Pearl Harbor
December 8	Japanese enter foreign concessions in Shanghai
October 1942	Enemy aliens in Shanghai required to wear red armbands
January 1943	Japanese begin to intern enemy aliens
April 10, 1943	Barr family enters Lunghwa internment camp
May 1945	German surrender
August 1945	US atomic bomb attacks on Hiroshima and Nagasaki; Japanese surrender
September 26, 1945	Ruth and Betty Barr leave Lunghwa for an American hospital ship, *USS Refuge*
October 22, 1945	Ruth and Betty arrive in San Francisco
October 28, 1945	Ruth and Betty arrive in Dallas, Texas

Ruth Barr
Jan 1 1941
to
Dec. 31, 1945

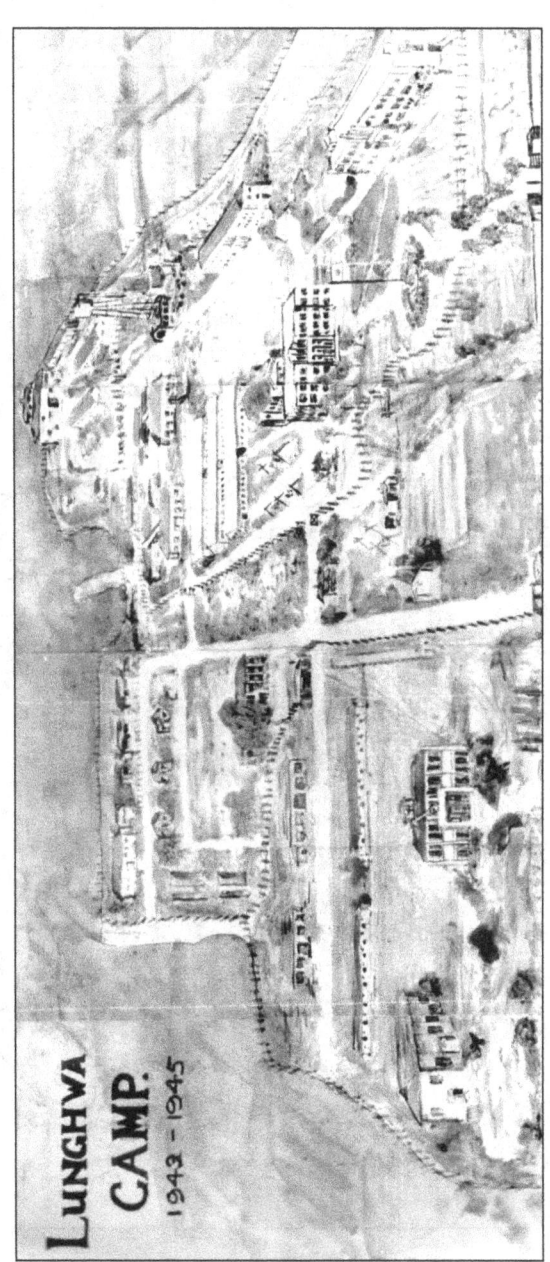

LUNGHWA CAMP.
1943 - 1945

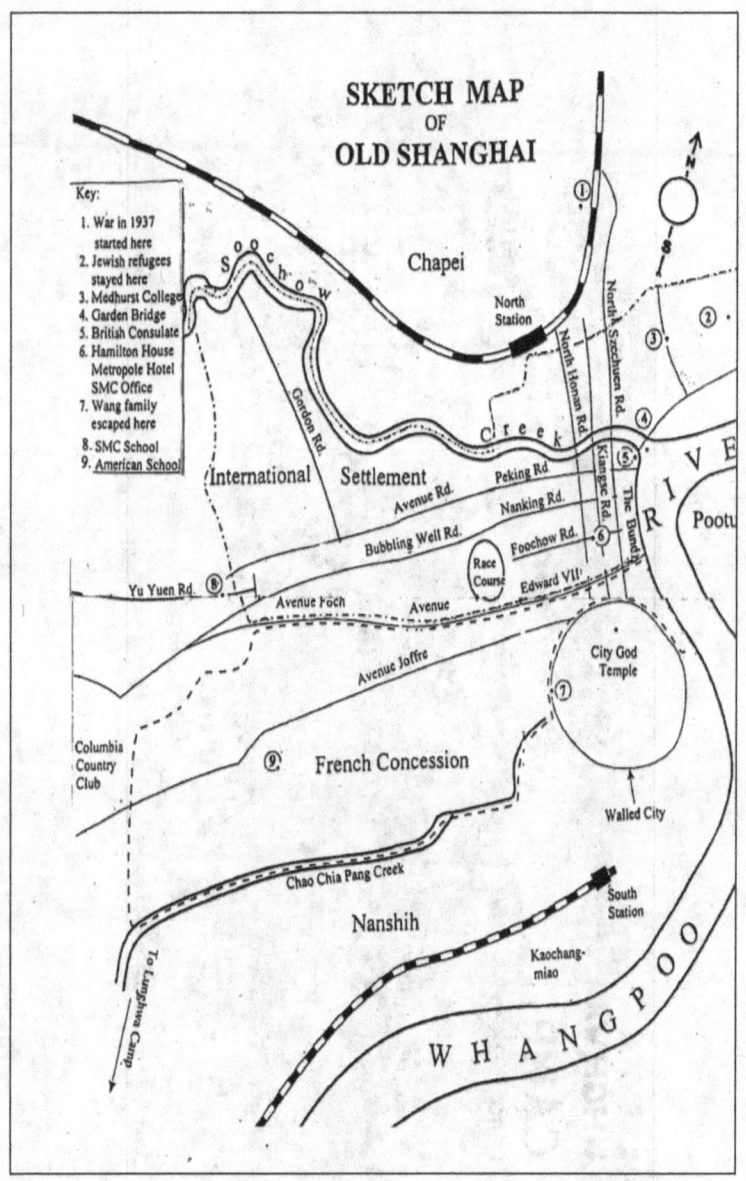

FOREWORD

By Betty Barr, Ruth's daughter

WHEN THIS DIARY BEGINS, I was nearly eight years old, living in a flat on Yu Yuen Road in Shanghai with my parents and my brother, Dick. Today, I am in my early eighties, living in the Hongkou (formerly Hongkew) District of Shanghai with my husband, Wang Zhengwen (George.) I have had the privilege of living in Shanghai for fifty of those eighty-plus years.

In 1941 we lived on Yu Yuen Road because it was near the temporary location of Medhurst College, where my father was teaching. Mother also taught there as well as at the University of Shanghai.

Dick and I went to primary schools founded by the Shanghai Municipal Council for foreign children. Our parents encouraged us to be independent and to go to school by public bus. One of my earliest memories is of not being able to get off the bus at the right stop. At the next stop I stood there, crying, because I was lost. A kind British policeman took me by the hand and once we had rounded the corner I could see my school. I thanked him profusely but, to my embarrassment, he insisted on taking me all the way into my classroom.

It was only when Mother died at the age of 87 in Scotland in 1990 that I found a small parcel labelled "Record—1941-1945 (During the War)." Before that, I had not known that she had kept this meticulous record. To my knowledge, at no other time in her life did she keep such a journal.

The diary itself was printed in the U.S.A. complete with lists of American "Legal Holidays" and "The States of the Union." We can gather that it may have been a fashionable thing to do in those days when the pace of life was so different from the present.

Mother began writing the diary on January 1, 1941, in a Shanghai already tense because the Japanese army was in control of the Chinese parts of the city. Only the International Settlement and the French Concession were still, nominally, under foreign control. This history has been extensively covered by many writers. Readers who are interested in finding out more about it can consult the list of books given For Further Reading at the end of this book.

My parents "stayed on," I think, when many other foreigners were leaving — mainly sailing away on American President Lines ships — because they hoped they could be of assistance to their Chinese colleagues. (They did the same in 1949.)

When she began writing the diary, Mother had no way of knowing that by the end of the five years, half of that time would have been spent in a Japanese internment camp. I never saw her writing it in our one small room in the camp. Perhaps she wrote it under her mosquito net after I had gone to bed. She of course kept it hidden in the daytime; it was brave of her to write it at all.

Readers will find some cryptic remarks in the diary such as "Story of..." but we will never know what the story was. Some sentences are left unfinished. On Oct. 29, 1942, she wrote "Mr H. taken." and we are left to guess that he was probably taken to the infamous Bridge House where many men who were suspected of being spies were tortured by the Japanese.

...In the small parcel labelled 'Record,' I found not only the five-year diary but also three other small notebooks. The smallest one, a paper notepad, begins on Dec. 8, 1941. I call it Notebook 1. I presume that, realizing the historical significance of the day, she began writing it that very evening. It gives an almost hourly

MOTHER

LET ME INTRODUCE my mother to you. She was a feisty Texan who lived most of her life in Shanghai, China, and, latterly, in Scone, a small village in central Scotland.

Her own mother, Pearl Porter Hill, my grandmother, was the eldest of nine siblings in a large Southern family. Pearl was a strong believer in the importance of education and I, at the age of twelve, lived with her for a year while she was the Superintendent of a large Sunday School in a nearby Southern Methodist Church.

When it was time for a meal she would shout down to the basement where her husband, James Hill, was pottering about, "Mr. Hill! Dinner's ready!" That formal Southern mode of address must have influenced me because for the whole of my life I called my maternal parent "Mother," never the British "Mummy" or "Mum" or the American "Mom."

Ruth was born in Dallas on July 17, 1903, and a sister, Esther, was born two years later. I know little about my mother's childhood. Like most of us, I wish now that I had asked her more questions.

She attended Southern Methodist University in Dallas and then went to Columbia University in New York City to study for an MA; not many women had such strong qualifications in the 1920s. At Columbia she took a course in the History of Chinese Civilization; her well-known professor was Carrington Goodrich. My mother always said that she came to China not as a missionary but because she admired Chinese civilization.

She came with the YWCA, an organization then in its heyday.

The "Y" sent her first to Beiping (as Beijing was then called) for a year of language study. The language was, of course, Mandarin. I have now in my possession several photograph albums of black-and-white photos showing how much she enjoyed that year.

On arrival in Shanghai, Ruth began her work with the International YWCA, work she thoroughly enjoyed. All her life she kept in close touch with friends, both Chinese and foreign, she made in Shanghai at that time.

Before long, however, she met and married in Community Church on Avenue Petain (now Hengshan Lu) a Scottish widower, John Snodgrass Barr. Their wedding photo shows them standing outside the church with Juanita Byrd, an American Southern Baptist missionary who was my mother's close friend.

John Barr was a missionary teacher whose first (American) wife, Marie Raffo, had died in childbirth on July 1, 1930. Ruth became the stepmother of John Richard (Dick), and I was born on April 8, 1933, in the then Country Hospital (now Huadong Hospital.) Dick and I were brought up together as brother and sister.

In the early 1930s we lived in a large house in the London Missionary Society (LMS) compound in Hongkew (now Hongkou) next door to Medhurst College, a secondary school founded in 1899, where my father was a teacher. In addition to looking after the children, with the help of three servants — a cook, an amah and a gardener — Ruth also did some teaching in the school.

It happened that in 1937 my father was due to go on furlough and so we sailed across the Pacific Ocean, a month-long journey, in the President Wilson. (I have to admit that the family photograph albums are an aid to my own memories.) Ruth was going to introduce her husband and family to her own parents and friends.

While we were in Dallas, news came that Medhurst College and our house had been bombed by the Japanese. On our return to Shanghai a year later, my parents found small pieces of their wedding china in the rubble. My mother later said that the experience taught her that material possessions are not the most important thing in life.

The school moved to temporary accommodation on Tifeng Road (now Wulumuqi Lu) and so the Barr family moved to Yu Yuen Road, outside the International Settlement. We lived in a ground floor flat in a three-storied building in Lane 749, a building and lane which still exist.

Dick and Betty in Dallas, 1937

Dick and I attended Shanghai Municipal Council primary schools for foreign children; the buildings now house a middle school and the fire station beside them on the corner of the present Yu Yuan Lu and Wulumuqi Lu is a landmark of my childhood.

We have now reached 1941, the year when my mother decided to begin to keep a five-year diary. I will let the diary speak for those years.

After the war, Mother took me to Dallas where I had my freshman year in Adamson High School—a huge culture shock, coming, as I had, straight from a Japanese internment camp in Shanghai. The following summer we sailed across the Atlantic to join my father and brother. It was decided that Dick should stay in Scotland and go to a boarding school in Perthshire, the same school that my father had attended. The LMS wanted me, too, to stay to attend a boarding school, like the other British missionary children. My feisty mother would have none of it, pointing out that I had just had a year of American-style education. She did not want me to be more mixed-up than I already was!

Thus, we returned to Shanghai in the fall of 1946 and our home was now back in Hongkew in an LMS house that had survived the Japanese bombing. Shanghai American School (SAS), which I was to attend, was, however, far across the city on Hengshan Lu, across the street from Community Church where my parents had married. I therefore became a boarder at the school.

As a teenager, it did not occur to me to ask how my parents managed to pay the high fees. Only later did I realize that my mother came to teach several days a week at the school for that purpose. At SAS Reunions, schoolmates have told me that my mother was the best English teacher they ever had. One of them recently wrote to me:

> I'm sure I've told you probably several times, that
> your mother was the most long range helpful teacher
> I ever had in school because she made us write every
> week and then read to classmates what we had written.
> Reading out loud teaches a lot about tuning into one's
> own writing.

In 1949, when many other foreigners, both business people and missionaries, left China, my parents stayed on, just as they had at the onset of the war. I think their purpose was to be with their Chinese colleagues as long as they could be of help.

I myself left Shanghai in the spring of 1950 to go to Wellesley College near Boston. I well remember Christmas Day 1951 when I was back in Dallas with my grandmother. Feeling homesick for China, I wondered whether it would be possible to phone my parents who were still in Shanghai — at the height of the Korean War. When I asked the Dallas telephone operator whether it would be possible to telephone Shanghai, she said briskly, "Yes. What number, please?" Fortunately, I remembered. My parents were having a Christmas morning breakfast with a Chinese friend.

Since my father was the last of the LMS missionaries in Shanghai to leave, they had to wait some time for their exit visa, there being properties and other matters to deal with. Finally, in late 1952 they departed China via Hong Kong and went to the US on their way back to the UK.

Like quite a number of former China missionaries, my father was sent in 1953 to Hong Kong, where he taught at Chung Chi College, later part of the Chinese University of Hong Kong. My mother enjoyed living on the beautiful campus in the New Territories, where they continued their tradition of inviting both Chinese and Western friends to their home, just as they had done in Shanghai.

In 1965, they retired to Scotland. Perthshire, where my father had gone to school, is a beautiful part of Scotland and at first they rented a house in Scone, a historic village near the town of Perth. Mother loved living there. She rose to the occasion and learned from the neighbors how to grow different kinds of vegetables — to supplement my father's mission pension. Both of them went to the Village Institute to do Scottish Country Dancing.

Sadly, my father died of lung cancer in 1970, just five years after his retirement. But Mother continued living in Scone for another twenty years. She loved the village itself but she also found that from Perth it was easy to travel by train to either Edinburgh or Glasgow.

In her later years she had many interests. Ever an internationalist, she played an active part in the United Nations Association. Even in her eighties, she could be found on street corners in Perth on Saturday mornings selling flags to raise money for the UNA.

She took up yoga seriously and in her eighties was still standing on her head. Alternative medicine was another interest;

she regularly consulted an acupuncturist. I once went with her to a Reflexology Weekend at a hotel in Perthshire.

When I told Mother in 1984 that I was returning to Shanghai to marry a widower, George Wang, she took it in her stride. After all, she too had married a widower unknown to her family in a far-away country.

Many retired teachers enjoy the lectures given at the University of the Third Age (U3A) and so did my mother. She grew away from the church, joining the Humanist Society in Edinburgh. That led her to join the Voluntary Euthanasia Society of Scotland (VESS.)

She even wore in her lapel the VESS badge, a white dove flying upwards, and was happy to give an explanation to anyone who asked about it. She and I discussed the subject many times; her explanation was simple but deep—she thought voluntary euthanasia benefitted the individual, the family and society. In July 1990, she acted on her principles.

I am proud of my beloved mother. I am only sorry that it has taken me twenty-five years since her death to share this diary of hers with you.

1941

Working and Playing

MOTHER'S FIRST ENTRY in the diary, on January 1, 1941, sets the scene for most of that year:

> New Year's Eve—dinner with Juanita on Kinnear Rd: turkey, roses, mints. Movie afterward. New Year reception at Community Church attended by 150+. Harriet & Hoovers leave on Coolidge. Betty—bronchitis.

One main impression of her life gained from the diary is of the many social activities in which she was engaged and of her many friends of many nationalities. The names of a few of her friends and some information about them are given in the section entitled 'People,' beginning on p. 287.

It must be remembered that in that era, all foreign residents in Shanghai usually had servants—a cook and an amah at the very least—and thus it was relatively easy for them to entertain their friends in their homes. Mother sometimes writes of two or three such activities within one day.

It seems they went to a movie after dinner. Hollywood movies were very popular in those days. Mother mentions "The Thief of Baghdad" and "Citizen Kane" (Orson Welles.) Some of the movie theaters, like the Grand and the Majestic, still exist in Shanghai today, though others, like the Roxy, have disappeared. She also went to see Chinese movies such as "Chia" (Family) (Oct.6.) And, in those long-ago days before TV, a primary reason for going to the movie theaters was to see Newsreels.

Many of Mother's social activities centered on Community Church, the church where she and my father had married. It is amusing to me to see that even in this first entry she has given an approximate figure for the number of people present. Throughout her life she was a very orderly and organized person. I can remember my parents sitting together at the end of the day to write down how much money each of them had spent that day.

On January 1, 1941, she mentions the names of friends who were leaving on the Coolidge. It is difficult in this era of air travel to imagine the importance of the American President Lines ships to foreigners in Shanghai at that time. Frequently in the diary, Mother writes not only about friends arriving and departing but also about the incoming and outgoing mail carried by the ships.

Finally, in her January 1, 1941, entry, she mentions B, her daughter, having bronchitis. I do not remember that particular illness but to this day I have had ear trouble, an ailment which appears frequently in these pages. I do remember, with embarrassment the incident when, on February 13, 1941, Mother had to take me to see Dr. Dunlap because, liking the smell, I had stupidly put a mothball up my nose—and could not get it out. I could not, of course, have told you the date without having read this diary.

Naturally enough, in these pages we often read about her activities and her many friends. Besides meals in friends' homes, Mother went to restaurants, both Chinese and foreign. Sun Ya (January 23,) a Cantonese restaurant, was a favorite as well as the Chocolate Shop for Western drinks and snacks (January 9.)

Mother uses the Shanghai term "tiffin" as well as the American "lunch" and "luncheon."

Shanghai, then as now, was a cultural center and Mother enjoyed going to plays performed by various associations or school groups. On February 8, she records, my father took me to the Russian ballet and in May they both came to see me perform as "Mr. Woodpecker" in a ballet titled "Who Killed Cock Robin?" (I am proud to say that I attended the same School of Dancing in Shanghai as Dame Margo Fonteyn.)

In the summer the Shanghai Symphony Orchestra, under Maestro Mario Paci, gave evening concerts in Jessfield Park. I can remember being woken up at what seemed like midnight to go and sit in a deckchair under the stars to listen to Dvorak's New World Symphony.

One surprise which awaited me when I read the diary was the frequency with which my parents played bridge! In the 1940s this was a favorite pastime and they played with a variety of friends from many countries. My parents also opened their home to people of varying backgrounds, such as German Jews then living in the Hongkew ghetto, Japanese friends, the Danish parents of my good friend, Stine, and my father's former Chinese students and their wives.

One of my mother's activities which must be mentioned in addition to all the above is her great love of reading. At the end of the whole diary is a list of books read during the five years; this list is included near the end of this book. It can be seen that on the whole she chose rather serious nonfiction: *Testament of Friendship* by Vera Brittain, *The American Presidency* by Harold Laski and *Dawn Watch in China* by Joy Homer, for example.

Another activity carried out at home was handwork. She liked needlepoint (January 9) and throughout 1941 she mentions going to friends' homes for knitting bees for the war effort. On June 17 she was knitting the neckband of her first air force sweater. I am proud to say that on our bed in Hongkou now is a patchwork quilt made by my mother out of my childhood dresses.

It should not be thought that my mother spent all her time 'playing.' She taught English at Medhurst College and also at the University of Shanghai, both part-time. This work, however, is not mentioned very often in the diary except at exam time, perhaps because of its rather routine nature. She also continued to be involved with the YWCA which had sent her to China. On January 10 she was campaigning for the YW and on January 20 she attended a meeting of the National Executive Committee.

In amongst all these activities she was a mother. Apart from taking Dick and me to doctors and to visit our friends, she spent time trying to educate us. Roland van den Berg, Dick's good friend and later Dutch Ambassador to China and then Japan, has told me that he, like me, remembers sitting on cushions on the floor (I think) while listening to, say, Beethoven's Fifth Symphony being played on a 78 rpm record on our gramophone.

Mother's diary is full of her daily activities, some of which, such as shopping and washing her hair, were mundane. But they, too, reveal the quality of her life. In the summer of 1941 she several times mentions the bad floods after heavy rains which kept her in the house for several days at a time. When she writes about moving around the city, we learn that she either took a tram or a pedicab—or walked. We did not own a car.

From time to time there is mention of the larger environment, i.e. the political situation. On January 23 she mentions briefly an incident well known in the annals of Shanghai history, a Ratepayers Meeting which "was broken up when Hayashi shot Keswick upon failure of the Japanese amendment." The Japanese ratepayers were opposing higher taxes. On February 10 she writes, "The lane was full of Ta Tao police. Wang Chingwei party, says cook. On

February 19, "More Americans leaving."

Even though more Americans were leaving, the American marines were still in place in Shanghai in early 1941. Mother writes on May 11 about a "Mother's Day Dinner for the marines" at the church! However, on November 14, the story has changed: "Marines ordered to leave China."

In November there were other unsettling signs: (November 3) "Tailor's prices went up 80% on November 1. Postage abroad doubled." And on November 17, "The cook spent all day trying to get permit for bag of rice." On the morning of December 8, everything changed.

JANUARY 1941

1, Wednesday: New Year's Eve—dinner with Juanita on Kinnear Rd.—turkey, roses, mints. Movie afterward. New Year reception at Community Church attended by 150+. Harriet & Hoovers leave on Coolidge. Betty—bronchitis.

2, Thursday: Spent quietly at home. Read *Testament of Friendship*. Sent games and books to Friends' Home. Baxters' wedding anniversary.

3, Friday: Luncheon and tea with Nita on Kinnear Rd. Dinner with the Baxters on their 32nd wedding anniversary (really Jan. 2)—and bridge with Scotts and Beynons.

4, Saturday: Guests to dinner and bridge: Myrna and Floyd O'Hara, Einar Edwards, Phil Sullivan, Maynard Guss, George Greene. Myrna sailing on the Pierce, Jan. 5. Jeanne's birthday.

5, Sunday: A Sunday at home. Went to look at the Wilson house on Jessfield Road and were not very favorably impressed.

6, Monday: A visit to Dr. Dunlap and then a session with *The Family*. Nita came to supper and went with us to see the British News Reels.

7, Tuesday: To Barbara's after school. AWC Executive. Tea with Nita. Music program with Katherine Gordon playing.

8, Wednesday: After school, a day at home writing letters. Tram strike. Signed 3 months lease on Apt. 10 at $30 US.

9, Thursday: Afternoon spent with Nita. After a visit to the Sea Gull Studio to purchase needlepoint, we walked to the Chocolate Shop for tea and then home. She left me the Dec. *Atlantic* with articles on attitude to war.

10. (Fri) To town after school to finish YW campaigning and take typewriter for overhauling. Took Betty to Dunlap for check up.

11. **(Sat)** At home all day sending out a mimeographed letter. Betty was at Moira Charters', John and Dick at Race Course watching games.

12. **(Sun)** Walked to church. At 4:00 walked to the Edwards where church campaign canvassers had tea and received instructions.

13. **(Mon)** Church Auxiliary (40) went to visit Nantao Institute & have lunch there. Average 750 people a day. 300 in school using only old paper. All green vegetables grown. Dr. Ly came to dinner and we saw *This Man Reuter* at the Nanking.

14. **(Tues)** Gave term exam at school. Nita and I walked to the AWC where Mourne Hudspeth had tea with us and Nell spoke on "Cost of Living." We walked home again. Nita and Miss Lanneon (?) came round after supper.

15. **(Wed)** Joe Hardie came to help set up Creighton's electric train. Semi-annual dinner at the Church. 122 present.

16. **(Thurs)** Wave set at home while reading the "Support-the-War" articles in *Christian Century*. Afternoon spent grading term papers. 9:30 pm *The Dover Road* (Milne) produced at the Country Club to aid British War Fund.

17. **(Fri)** Finished *The Family*. Went to Report Reading at the Lester Hospital. Purchased a transformer for Dick's train. "World Settlement" proposed by Brit. League of Nations Union doesn't seem realistic.

18. **(Sat)** Took Betty to Barbara's. Nita and I went to the Sea Gull for needlepoint and on to her house on Ave. du Roi Albert. Ernest came for lunch; Joe Hardie to work on the train. To dinner at the Edwards — Kings, Barnetts, Phil, George, Jack, Carleton.

19. **(Sun)** Church in the morning. After lunch to see church members about contributions, with a short visit to Nita. Then games with Betty. Read Laski's *Where Do We Go From Here?*

20. **(Mon)** With Mrs Baxter to see Foncim about a house.

International Branch Com. meeting at noon. $201,000 for all purposes raised by Shanghai YW in 1940. Nat'l Ex. Com. at YW. Ruth Woodsmall coming.

21. **(Tues)** Dick at home with a cold. Betty took the doctor set to Moira's for the afternoon. House tailor making blouses. J to DC. I went to AWC where Helen Ling spoke on "Joys and Trials of an Art Collector." Lois Hendry's rickshaw accident. Read *Unser Kampf.*

22. **(Wed)** M. Hoenigsfeld came for the day. Bacharachs wrote to ask who would buy their silver. Read *War-Time Letters to Peace Lovers* (Brittain.)

23. **(Thurs)** Chinese tiffin with Juanita at Sun Ya. Ratepayers' Meeting at Race Course where great excitement was caused and the meeting broken up when Hayashi shot Keswick upon failure of the Jap. amendment. AAUW Meeting at AWC (50 present) "Shanghai 40 yrs ago."

24. **(Fri)** Took Betty to Dr. Dunlap who dismissed her at last. Went to dinner at the Beynons—30 of us to celebrate their silver wedding anniversary.

25. **(Sat)** Visits to dentist and oculist followed by afternoon at home reading, playing games, hearing music. To dinner with the Mains (Carleton, Wallines, Tuttle) where discussion turned to whether the world is getting better or worse.

26. **(Sun)** Quiet Sunday at home. Read *Victories without Violence* by Ruth Fry, Quaker. American mail held up in Hong Kong for censorship. Church budget campaign over the top: $29,500 in one week. Goal was $26,000.

27. **(Mon)** Chinese New Year. A delightful day with Nell, V., Nita. In the car out Minghong way, Hungjao, Monument Rd. to Kiangwan. Picnic lunch outside on U. of Shanghai campus. To V.'s to see jade treasures. On to Nita's on Kinnear for the night.

28. **(Tues)** In the afternoon walked over to see Lois Hendry. Read

Faith for Living (Lewis Mumford). American mail arrived. What grand holidays!

29. (Wed) Barbara came in with Martin to get some books on the Peace-War question. Mildred Owen & Lucile Oliver to lunch, it being Mildred's birthday. Rosa May Butler and Ernest came to tea. We helped Betty construct her *Rubber Gatherer's Hut on the Amazon.*

30, Thursday: Devoted the morning to getting a new permanent. Walked round after lunch for a last visit with Nita on Kinnear Rd. Guests to dinner & bridge: Barnetts, Wise, Lacy, Smith, Sullivan. Ernest's paper suggests S.M.C. should yield to some J. requests and should act without Land Regulations.

31, Friday: Played bridge with Cozy, Mary Brown, Helen King at AWC (80 present.) Went on to the YMCA to a dinner given by the 1937 Medhurst class. Nita moved to Roi Albert. Betty became a Brownie.

FEBRUARY 1941

1, Saturday: Dick and Betty to Hunter, the dentist. Lunch at Sincere's with Dr. Miao & son, who exchanged stamps with Dick. Dinner at the Olivers with Lil, Milly, Haigs, Phil, Jack. Read *Mrs. Miniver*.

2, Sunday: Dr. Rankin at Community Church. Guests lunch: Blacks, N. Murray, Miss Howard. Guests to supper: 2 Chens, Miss Wong. Nanking money forced on people for change in this area. Gambling dens forced to use "local" cigarettes & candies.

3, Monday: A day at home writing letters. Two Japanese attempted to burn the matshed enclosure put up for the ratepayers' meeting.

4, Tuesday: Lunch at Sun Ya with Bobby, Rosie, Louise, Olive. On to the AWC for executive and program. Brought *Mein Kampf* from the library.

5, Wednesday: Walked to Winling to play bridge and have lunch with Mary Edward, Mary Brown, Helen Scott of Peking. With Nita to the Ratepayers' Meeting 2:30 – 5:30 and then on to see *New Moon* at the Roxy. Taxes are increased. Next Japanese move?

6, Thursday: Took Betty for a permanent wave and bought a white beret. To dinner at the McGavins with Ernest, Barbara, A.E.,Luther, Lucy, Bernard. Sent typed letter – 14 copies. Burnet writes that he may stand for Parliament. Was awarded DSC.

7, Friday: Christmas cards and letters from home. To the PO to buy stamps for John Estes. Bought the Emperor Concerto. To the Roxy to see *Pride & Prejudice*. It's not so easy for John when the school principal threatens to resign.

8, Saturday: Betty and I had lunch with Nita on Roi Albert. Dick with Roland, John at school. John took Betty to see the Russian ballet. I had the afternoon with Nita. Much mail including hymn books and Brittain book from Elise.

9, Sunday: Walked to church with Rosie & Sue. Called on Miss Howard with book etc for Brenda. Chinese church men to tea. Took Dick to Symphony Concert at Lyceum with Nita. Beethoven, Bach, Brahms Concertos.

10, Monday: Back to school and on to the YWCA & shops. The lane was full of Ta Tao police. Wang Ching-wei party says cook. Delicious dinner at the Damsgaard's with the Caugheys. Read *The Defenders* (Franz Hoellering.)

11, Tuesday: Spent some time in the kitchen making a new dessert and candy. At the AWC (27 present) Miss England spoke on dinner menus. Guests to dinner and bridge: Mansfield Freeman, the Edwards, Maynard Guss, Phil Dunbar, Jack Service.

12, Wed John's birthday. G. Hoenigsfeld came for the day. We had dinner at the Mayflower with Dick, Betty, Nita, Ernest. Snow. Read Willa Cather's *Sapphire and the Slave Girl* sent by Miss Aduddell.

13, Thursday: A joyous day at home reading. Had to take Betty for Dr. Dunlap to extract a mothball from her nose.

14, Friday: Icy cold at school. The rest of the day spent at home on odds and ends. Walked to Roma to order corsages for Sat. guests. Nance divulged that Mary Small has an enlarged heart and too rapid a pulse.

15, Saturday: Nita's birthday. Took Betty to the dentist. Guests to dinner: Nita, Beibeng and Paul Feng, Catherine Gordon and Maurice, Floyd. Corsage bouquets and music after dinner. Nita stayed the night.

16, Sunday: Spoke at church for the YWCA. Employment Bureau — Benevolence Contribution. Miss Tsai and Nita for lunch. All the family went to the Symphony Concert at the Lyceum.

17, Monday: To Barbara's after school, where Martin has bronchitis. YWCA Committee at noon and on to town for shopping and new passport. Out of 1483 missionaries, 329 have gone and 75 more due to leave by May.

18, Tuesday: Mrs. Young, Dick's teacher, and Jimmy Sutcliffe came to lunch. Took Dick's engine to the Caters' for repair and went on to the AWC where Mabel Smith reviewed *The Family*. About 35 there.

19, Wednesday: Lunch with Nita at the Chocolate Shop and then shopping. M. Hoenigsfeld came and Olive to visit (very pessimistic.) Nell, V. and O. Hall came to supper. More Americans leaving.

20, Thursday: To tea at Lelia Boynton's.

21, Friday: Lunch with Pat Barnett at the American Club and with Nita. Shopping and on to tea at the Hotel Pacific with Dr. Ly. Dinner at the LCH with sisters and Baxters.

22, Saturday: Spent the day planning and preparing and executing Washington's Birthday party for the children, using red, white, blue decorations from Jo Tucker: Moira, Billy,, Eliz. Chris, Paul, Michaela, Betty Brown, Christine, Roland. Dinner at the Nash's for Ernest with Barbara & A.E.

23, Sunday: Guests to lunch: Ernest, the Hudspeths, the Smalls. Eloise Bradshaw came to tea. The No. 2 in the Wang police force has moved into our lane. Great doings with squads of police in attendance.

24, Monday: A day at home with the tailor. Wrote letters to go on the Coolidge. Mr Wu Shipao, the Wang man, is having a 3 day celebration of his 60th birthday. Cars and people passing all night till 6 a.m. No sleep.

25, Tuesday: A leisurely day at home. Finished *The Defenders* by Hoellering.

26, Wednesday: Saw Ernest before the Coolidge left. Mary Brown & Lois Hendry went. Mrs. Chun came in the mornning. M. Hoenigsfeld came at noon. Bought Betty new shoes. She was sick at night.

27, Thursday: Read *My Name is Aram*. To the wedding reception at the Blackstone of Nettie Bain & Leonard Tomlinson after a Quaker wedding at the McGavins. On to the AAUW where J.B. Powell spoke on "America's Defense Measures."

28, Friday: To the Church for World Day of Prayer meeting with Jap., Chinese, Russian, French, Ger., Korean, Brit etc. taking part. On to Nat'l YW where Ruth Woodsmall spoke on World's YW, France, Germany etc. Supper there. To see *Northwest Passage*.

MARCH 1941

1, Saturday: With Dick to his music lesson. Nita came for the day – a leisurely one at home sewing, talking, reading, playing *The Mikado*. Children went to a war benefit at the Lyceum organized by Scouts.

2, Sunday: To church. In the afternoon paid a call at McTyeire. Tea at home and songs. Called on A.E. to talk over the house problem.

3, Monday: To town for shopping and house hunting in the pm. To see Stanley Gregory about his house and about the Austrian refugee's problems.

4, Tuesday: To AWC for executive and meeting. F. McLorn spoke on "Back Stage." Sid and Olive came to talk about using the new church building for the Methodist Conference.

5, Wednesday: Spoke to the boys at Medhurst. The white furniture arrived from Mansfield Freeman. Went with Nell to see *The Thief of Baghdad* – beautiful color. Power Co. reports only 3 months' coal supply. May be shortage of electricity.

6, Thursday: Wave set at home. Quiet day reading and writing. Such days are gems to be valued.

7, Friday: To the American Club to have lunch with Pat Barnett and help her buy luggage. Nita's student came to hear *The Mikado*. Nita stayed to supper. German agents are buying leather and other supplies here.

8, Saturday: At home writing letters and reading *Thrice a Stranger* (Brittain.) Dinner with Bei-tseng and Paul Feng on Edinburgh Rd. Nita & Inabelle Coleman were there and Lucile Fong Wu & husband.

9, Sunday: At 3 pm service and dedication of new Church building. More than 300 there. John presiding.

10, Monday: To the Auxiliary at Com. Church for tiffin and dedication of the new room. To the American Club to have tea with Pat Barnett. Nell says serious times in factories. They are studying how to conserve power.

11, Tuesday: A wet, sleety, snowy day spent at home reading *Thrice a Stranger* & *Pilgrim's Way* (Tweedsmuir.) Purchased $300 worth of kitchen supplies, thinking prices may go up.

[March 11, 1942: a rare comment on the year before: "They did. And how!"]

12, Wednesday: Holiday for Sun Yat-sen's birthday—a quiet, gentle day. After lunch J and I walked in the Park and on to St. John's for books. Letter from Clare. Read more of *Pilgrim's Way*. Robert & Pat Barnett sailed on the Pierce.

13, Thursday: A visit to Dunlap and a hair wave at home. Dinner and bridge—another excellent party at the Dunbar-Service house. Came home with a box of Lilly's Peppermints and a book called *Here I Stay* (Coatsworth.)

14, Friday: After school to Mrs Ottewell's (?) to plan tea for Jeanne. On to Lucile Oliver's to plan lunch for Jeanne. Much walking on a fine day. Oranges purchased for marmalade. Read *Here I Stay* (Coatsworth.) Cold flat. Boiler broken.

15, Saturday: Took Betty to Dunlap, one ear opened. On to Stine's where she had lunch. I had lunch with Nita. To St. John's for Medhurst teachers' outing. Moira came to spend the night with Betty. Daylight time began.

16, Sunday: To church. Lunch—the whole family—at the Boyntons. He has 16,000 maps, besides records, coins, books, etc. other hobbies. Eloise came in to see about her prophet plays. John went to see Tsao Leung.

17, Monday: Class 30 minutes later!! To Ethel Hylbert's with salad for 18, committee meeting, Jeanne's last. Bei-tseng called with small son, 6 months old. David. Burnet's pudding & shortbread arrived. With Mo-li How to 4C dinner at Community Church.

18, Tuesday: Lunch at AWC where Mrs White read *The White Cliffs* (Alice Duer Miller.) Excellent. Took Betty to Dr. Dunlap & he opened the right ear. Went to the Mardens' flat in Grosvenor House where he spoke on "Ivories" & exhibited his collection. Electric signs off.

19, Wednesday: Bus strike. Walked to the dance studio to bring Betty home. Dick went to the Husi Club for lunch with Roland.

20, Thursday: Hair Wave at home. Made fudge for Nellie's birthday. Had dinner at Sun Ya with Phil, Olive, Sid, Bobby, Rosie, John.

21, Friday: Holiday at school. At home reading & writing. Walked around to McTyeire for books at noon. Their flowering trees are magnificent and the willows oh! so lacy and graceful.

22, Saturday: Took Betty from dancing to see Dunlap & Hunter. Visited Nell's office and the Chocolate Shop for a Coffee Ring. Nita and Nell came for the afternoon. We read "My America" from *Pilgrim's Way*. Nita stayed to supper.

23, Sunday: After church to lunch with the Caugheys. Old boys and wives to tea. Finished *Tragedy of France* by Maurois. Ruth's father has sent a $50 check.

24, Monday: Shopping tour to get bedspreads for Betty and leave her watch for repairs. Collected my new green American passport. Bomb outrages on gov. banks.

25. Tue Round to Barbara's. They've joined a glee club. Stine came home with Betty and we visited Dr. Dunlap (final, we hope). Stericker showed colored round-the-world films at Betty's school. Excellent. How memories warm the heart!

26, Wednesday: Spoke to junior boys at school on Grenfell. Spent the rest of the day reading and working on lecture on "Vera

Brittain and Winifred Holtby." Wrote to U.B. Letters from Elise, Harriet, Cath'n.

27, Thursday: To YWCA to plan tea for Jeanne. On to AAUW at Mayflower Restaurant (30 there.) Chinese tea and Town Meeting of the Air on Lend-Lease bill. More letters from America.

28, Friday: Spoke to English Literary Club of US at Nita's and had dinner with her. Yugoslavia revolts. King Peter to the throne. Against axis! Matsuoke in Berlin.

29, Saturday: A day in a thousand — time for reading at home and some Tschaikowsky on the gramophone and preparations for dinner-bridge: Mabel, Ivor, George Carver, B. Read, F. O'Hara, P.N. Dunbar.

30, Sunday: Barriers up for a Wang Ching-wei anniversary. After church to lunch at the Hudspeths with the Blacks and Nan Smith. Dinner for Ruth Woodsmall: Olive, Suensons, Jack Service, Mansfield Freeman.

31, Monday: School holiday. John breakfasted in the park with students. Purchased copper for Louise. Tea for Jeanne at YWCA, Wedding dinner — Chen Pi-yao — at the YMCA. Bride in pink & silver. Barbara decided to go to Australia.

APRIL 1941

1, Tuesday: Needlepoint finished for chair-bottom and back. AWC Executive and then a visit to see new Cater baby—but didn't see it. W.Y. Chen spoke at Missionary Ass: "Developments in the West." Dwelt on Kuomintang-Com, Friction. Christians should help.

2, Wednesday: Spent most of the day grading test papers. Looked at fur coats. We took Nita and Miss Tsai to see the British News Films. Nita and I talked in the Chocolate Shop about what contributions we could make to the war and to the peace.

3. Thursday Nita came and we read *There Shall be No Night* (Sherwood.) Jeanne and Van came calling in the evening.

4, Friday: Fetched out summer clothes. Dinner with Floyd O'Hara, and bridge: McCrackens, Greiner, BW Smith, Phil Dunbar. Letter from Louise Theune. Carleton Lacy elected bishop.

5, Saturday: Tiffin with Nellie Murray—and Hardie, Frame, Baxter, Betty, Christine. Dick at cub picnic. Dinner with Nita and on to *Merry England*, war benefit. The program auctioned brought $10,500.

6, Sunday: A day of rest and gladness. Tea with Jeanne, Lydia, Nita in the garden. Brought home the white lilac & thought of Kew and wrote to Brenda. A good time singing with the children. Yugoslavia—Germany at war.

7, Monday: Cashed P.O. order for $160 from Mrs Stacey—$100 for teachers' rice. Typhoid inoculation. Went to Nell's where Mrs McLorn discussed *There Shall Be No Night*. Nita was there and Dr. Lawney.

8. Tue Betty's birthday. Packages from Barbara, Nellie, Mrs Nash,

Milly, Catherine, Keith, Mother, the family, et al. Went to Mrs Stacey's to knit. Betty was in the play *Sweet Winter* at school. Groggy with typhoid shot.

9, Wednesday: While shopping met Olive & we had tea at the Chocolate Shop. Bought Easter eggs for Betty's party and knitting needles. Back to Betty's school for the play. Lyman Hoover returned.

10, Thursday: Four girls came home with Betty for the day—her birthday celebration: Elizabeth, Stine, Moira, Christine. They made Perky Prill dolls (sent by Ruth) and colored Easter eggs. Nita sent a big basket. Too much Chinese food for B. She lost it at 10 pm.

11, Friday: Took my class to see *Tale of Two Cities*. Betty and I went to Mildred's to color Easter eggs. To the annual dinner of the Chinese Art Council at the American Club with Dr. Ly & Mr Eisenbeiss.

12, Saturday: Took Betty for typhoid shot and eye examination. Went to the War Fund Bazaar at the Days'. At night with Nita saw the German news films. Such organization, efficiency, power can belong only to the conquering side, they would have you know.

13, Sunday: Betty was feverish from typhoid shot so I stayed at home with her. Guests to lunch: Mrs Chun (Miss Yang), Mrs & Mr T.T. Chang, and Eric. Easter gifts to children from Jeanne & Lydia, Edwards, Charters. Flowers from Bobby.

14, Monday: Took Betty to Dr. Tsang for eye exam. We priced skates but they were $39.50. A fine day for the cub Rally. 9th pack won again. To the tea at church to farewell the Caugheys. The school won't change to new time: very awkward. 19 dresses from Nancy.

15, Tuesday: War knitting after school. Visit from Dr. Spitzer in afternoon. He's trying to get his children here from Paris. Called to see the Pai baby.

16, Wednesday: To YW Nat'l Executive meeting and tiffin for Jeanne. Bridge at Mary Edwards' with Mrs Steinbeck and Dorothy Wong. Nita came to supper and we went to see the Senior play at SAS – *The Importance of Being Earnest.*

17, Thursday: Ratepayers' Meeting with Jeanne. This is no doubt the last for a provisional Council has been voted in. Back to Jeanne's for Van's birthday tea. At night the Commencement of the American School. The last? Hope not.

18, Friday: Physical Exam. Spent the afternoon and night with Nita.

19, Saturday: Tea for Kate & Ronald. Dinner and bridge for Lyman, Carleton, Maynard, Dwight, Eddie. Many Jap. planes overhead. 300 German airmen said to be here training the Japanese.

20, Sunday: Off to Sunday school with the children to learn how to conduct the Primary Dep't. Luncheon party for the Caugheys – Hart Westbrook, Miss Li, Miss Tsai, Dr. Nance.

21, Monday: YWCA Int. Branch meeting at noon. Rehearsal for class dramatic contest. J dined at the Church with the Men's Brotherhood, 1st meeting 1938, this time in London at Whitelands College.

22, Tuesday: Wrote letters for the Coolidge. AWC tea with Nita. Dju Yu-pao spoke on "Street Children." Called on Miss Jones for points on women's work. News from Europe is depressing, except the spirit of the English people.

23, Wednesday: Margaret Hoenigsfeld came to lunch, bringing a pastry. Olive is to go on the Coolidge Apr. 25. This house has been sold to a Polish Jew who is moving in upstairs. Rents likely to soar.

24, Thursday: Barbara came to tea with Martin. Went to Jeanne's to see Ruth Woodsmall and Polly Babcock. Coolidge in port. Jeanne says a Pole has bought Neil's and the Washington Apt.

25, Friday: Shopping for fur coats with Mrs Wm (Polly) Babcock of Manila & Jeanne. Mrs Hughes (of Hong Kong) and Mrs Baxter came to lunch. Saw Olive, Kate, Ronald, Caugheys, Keswick et al off. Dinner with M. Frame & L. Lyon: Stanley Smiths, M. Gordon, Fahs of Pomona.

26, Saturday: Medhurst teachers (24) and families had a jaunt to the Buddhist garden which we attended. Financed by Mrs Stacey's money. Dinner with Eddie Wise, Mr Kay and the Olivers & Howes. Saw *Philadelphia Story*.

27, Sunday: Took over the Primary Department at Sunday school. Frank Short arrived from the North after Standing Com. meeting.

28, Monday: Nita came to lunch. Dinner for Barbara, A.E., Nellie, Nettie, Mac, Leonard, Frank. All the LMS folk came to coffee afterward.

29, Tuesday: Knitting at Mrs Stacey's. To AWC to rehearse play. Took Betty to Tsang for eye exam and bought her a new hat. Letters from USA. Mother, F.A.S., Lisabeth, Ruth Hill.

30, Wednesday: Called in to see Barbara. Then to Yates Road to try on dresses. Frank Short left for Hong Kong. Went to see *100 Men & a Girl*. Students came to rehearse *Roast Pig*.

MAY 1941

1, Thursday: Barbara, Martin, Mary left on the Hanyang for Australia. Mail from: U.S., England, Germany.

2, Friday: Rehearsed *The Lovely Meeting* at the AWC. Tiffin Club with Jeanne at the BWA. Purchased fur coat at Chan Kee. Settled with the new landlord (A. Loonis & Co.) for 6 mo lease at $28 U.S. + taxes + heat.

3, Saturday: Play contest at school with Nita, Paul Feng, Joe Hardie to judge. They came to lunch afterward, Bei-tseng, too. Got B's new glasses. Saw *Haensel & Gretel* at McTyeire. Had dinner and bridge with Mabel & Ivor, along with Lyman, Phil, Mansfield, Beula Smith.

4, Sunday: Lunch with Carleton Lacy after his sermon at Com. Church—"Swords against Beauty." Brought home a large number of books. Iraq troops fighting the British and the pipe line blocked.

5, Monday: School day. Dinner & bridge with Phil Dunbar: Beulah Smith, Tommie, Wilbur, Mansfield, Lyman.

6, Tuesday: Took Mrs Baxter to the AWC where we had a flower show and executive board gave a play — *It was a lovely meeting*. Signed 6 months lease on apartment.

7, Wednesday: Annual dinner at the Church. Fine music.

8, Thursday: Ruth Packard returned from U.S.A. Visited her in the evening.

9, Friday: A day at home reading. Went to bring Betty home from dancing and see about her tights.

10, Saturday: A rainy day at home reading, playing games, listening to music. Out to dine with Mary and Dwight and enjoy her beautiful flower arrangements. Also, Mansfield, Lyman, Brownie, Geo. Greene.

11, Sunday: Stayed after church to the Mother's Day Dinner for marines.

12, Monday: Permanent Wave at Andre's. Betty busy with dancing rehearsals.

13, Tuesday: Lunch and afternoon at Nita's. AWC where Jolin Huang spoke on "Modern Chinese Drama." Then to the Lyceum for Betty.

14, Wednesday: Good sun for winter clothes. Spent most of the afternoon expounding democracy to Louise Theune. Read *H.M. Pulham, Esq.* by John P. Marquand.

15, Thursday: Joint Committee Club Institute held at Community Church, with tea at Mrs Yang's.

16, Friday: Graded papers all the afternoon. Something to remember: Betty's face when she came in with the red rose. Dinner at Sun Ya with Bobby, Rosie, Phil and Sid.

17, Saturday: Made divinity. Took Betty for a permanent wave. Had guests to dinner and bridge: Ruth Packard, Phil, Maynard, Floyd, Einar Edwards, Eddie.

18, Sunday: Lunch with Nita and a visit in her nice sunny garden. Betty went to Elizabeth's birthday party, tired as she was from rehearsing and playing in the garden.

19, Monday: YW International Branch Committee. Ruth Packard taking over. May Yang and I worked in the Primary Dep't at Church. On to Marguerite Hsia's to plan for Sino-Foreign tea.

20, Tuesday: Knitting in the morning. AWC annual meeting. To the Lyceum to get Betty after a dress rehearsal of *Cock Robin*. Saw *Susan & God*.

21, Wednesday: M. Hoenigsfeld came with woes. I can do so little to help her. Bridge at Vanda Roper's with Alice Giovannin and Mrs Turnbull.

22, Thursday: Boys' concert at Medhurst. Then to the Lyceum with Betty for final rehearsal of *Who Killed Cock Robin?* The comfort of having hair done at home. The kindness of Mrs Charters to take us back & forth.

23, Friday: Painters arrived to refurbish walls and ceilings. Dinner at Mrs. Hsueh's for Ruth and Mildred: Mrs Tang, Miss Chen, Jeanne, Van, Lydia.

24, Saturday: Betty's dance recital at 3. John and Nita went and Nita came to supper. I wished I had gone, too, instead of saving $5.

25, Sunday: Betty's dance performance—very good. The painters struck and left us their buckets & ladders. Dinner with Geo. Carver, Archie McFadyen, Steve Goddard, Frank Ferguson, Muriel Tu, Dr. & Mrs CC Chen.

26, Monday: Spent at home with a sore toe. A.E. returned from Amoy. Lydia and Ruth came round with magazines. Read *Maria Chapdelaine* by Hémon.

27, Tuesday: Bridge at AWC with Mary Edwards, Lorene Parsons, Alice Giovannini, Sunday School meeting after dinner at the Stanley Smiths.

28, Wednesday: Stine and Mrs Suenson came to tea. We went to Nellie's to dinner and played bridge with her and Mac. Read "The American Presidency" by Harold Laski.

29, Thursday: Miss Li came bringing tsung-tzus for the Dragon Boat Festival. Tea at Mrs McLaren's with Jolin Huang, Shelly Sun, Eva Dunlap, Nita.

30, Friday: Lunch at the Mayflower with the Children's Aid Committee. Spent the afternoon with Nell. David Paton came to supper, also Carleton, Harry Silcock. Carleton brought Dick a tent.

31, Saturday: Went to the Hoenigsfeld—Schniermacher wedding ceremony. M.C.L. Bazaar. 1250 cones not enough! Ice cream in demand. Dinner at LCH with B. Read, Paterson, Gladys, Marion, Ethel.

JUNE 1941

1, Sunday: Guests to lunch: McGavins, Van Hengels, Onley. To the Suensons' to tea.

2, Monday: Whit Monday holiday for children. They put up the tent in Christine's garden. Callers — Mary Louise Allman, McGavins et al. Y.C. Tu very sick. Read *The Good Shepherd* Gunnar Gunnarsson.

3, Tuesday: Painters returned after being on strike a week. Went shopping for Myrna's blouse and a white purse. Ordered shoes at Kiangnan for Betty. J went to Missionary As. at St. John's and to see *Rebecca*.

4, Wednesday: Painters still busy, and house upset. US Gov. has taken over about 6 President ships. When will we get mail?! We hear on all sides how the Germans here are getting rich sending products via Siberia to Germany.

5, Thursday: Joint Commencement of Universities at Grand. Carleton spoke admirably on "Creative Imagination," Took Dick & Betty to see *Iolanthe* at Cathedral Girls' School.

6, Friday: Big mail in on the Coolidge. Busy with moving furniture for the painters.

7, Saturday: AWC Garden Party with Gladys Parker and Marion Harrop as guests. Guests here to dinner and bridge in spite of the painters: Ruth P, Carleton, George G., George Carver, Mansfield Freeman, Bernard Read. No. 11 moved away.

8, Sunday: A.E. preached at Community Church. Guests to lunch: Ethel Taylor, A.E. Chen, & Mr & Mrs Chen Pi-yao of Medhurst. Rosie came to tea and we had almond ring. Afterwards, songs.

9, Monday: Nat'l Executive YWCA at Mrs Loh's. Cora Deng

spoke. Nita came for a visit at supper time.

10, Tuesday: Executive Board Tiffin at AWC. Painters finished their work. Guests to dinner — Hsiao, Oliver, Hudspeth, Cora Deng, Paterson.

11, Wednesday: Letters for the Cleveland.

12, Thursday: First meeting of Industrial & Social Affairs Committee, SMC. Nell's IRP brochure approved. Mr Sakamoto came to supper.

13, Friday: Tea at the Morleys'. Children went to see *Iolanthe* again.

14, Saturday: Morning spent at the Church on SS material. Afternoon: deck tennis on the spacious lawn at the Lester Institute with Bernard Read. Phil & Maynard came to have dinner and play bridge.

15, Sunday: Joe Hardie & Heins Meyer came to lunch. Stine came for the day with Betty. Chinese guests to tea.

16, Monday: Y.W.C.A. International Branch meeting at noon. They've decided to buy the Chengtu Road property. Bridge here with Mrs Kucej, Vanda Roper, Lorene Parsons. Ruth Packard took children to see Disney films.

17, Tuesday: Knitting in the morning on the neckband of the first air force sweater. Dinner with Ruth Packard and Navy Y. contingent. Japanese shot on our street.

18, Wednesday: Went shopping for Betty's tunic material. Nita and I went to the Joint Committee open meeting on the Van Hengel terrace. Miss Margolis of the Refugee Committee in NY spoke.

19, Thursday: Lunch and afternoon with Nita. I took her some knitting needles. Lydia and Mildred returned from the Philippines bringing mangoes and coconut.

20, Friday: Finished *Random Harvest* by Hilton. A welcome day at home with household chores. Sorted the Lacy postcards.

21, Saturday: Had Betty's skates repaired, & took her to Stine's for the day. Tiffin at the school to farewell Mr Chen.

22, Sunday: Guests to lunch — Beynons, Sid, Hart. Guests to tea, teachers at Medhurst: Mr & Mrs Chen, Mr & Mrs Zau. Germany invaded Russia.

23, Monday: Went to look at the Chengtu Road property for YWCA. Mr. Bacharach came at 5.

24, Tuesday: Knitting by (?) morning. Called meeting AWC to raise dues from $36 to $60. Dinner with the Harmons and Ellisons.

25, Wednesday: Gave exam at Medhurst & wrote to Brenda. Margaret Schniermacher came to lunch, Dorothy Clawson to tea. Medhurst seniors after dinner. June floods and steady pelting rain.

26, Thursday: Kept in all day by floods. Schools closed. No prizegiving, though she'd get a third prize. Nita's drama tea party canceled.

27, Friday: Still inside because of floods. Made doll clothes for Betty and graded a few exam papers. The floods seem to grow worse each year.

28, Saturday: Braved the floods by rickshaw to go to tea at the Park Hotel with Mr Ling and his family in honour of Ling Tsutzung's graduation from Hong Kong U.

29, Sunday: A very hot, steamy day spent at church and at home.

30, Monday: Took Betty to school for books and reports. On to town to shop in the heat. Nita asked me to teach a course at the U. of Shanghai. Ironed dolly clothes and wrote to Elise about her problem. Letters in from America & Eng.

JULY 1941

1, Tuesday: Commencement at Medhurst held in SMC School, Singapore Road, Chuan Lu Po & Tsai Hsi-nien tops. Dick's party in Nita's garden for 6 boys, a very enjoyable affair. Very hot weather.

2, Wednesday: Met with Margaret Frame, AAUW Relief Com. Bridge at Columbia Club with Lorene Parsons. John has decided to see Consul-General George about service with the army. It behooves me to bear up.

3, Thursday: Read *King Hall Letters* while the hairdresser worked. YWCA meeting at Ethel's to talk about building funds. Betty went swimming with the Charters.

4, Friday: We four went to see the Marine Parade at the Race Course. Maynard Guss came to lunch. He took me to the patrons stand for the baseball game with the Shanghai Amateurs who won from the Marines 12 – 9. Air mail from Brenda.

5, Saturday: Went to the Industrial Division graduation program for technicians. Excellent – March of Time films. In the afternoon to the Hudspeths to play Deck Tennis – with Scotts, Burkes, Carters, McGavins, Harrop, et al. They drink 5 cups of hot tea.

6, Sunday: Roasting hot day. Old boys came to tea. Still worrying and losing sleep over the war question.

7, Monday: Visited with Nita. John saw the recruiting officer. Only possibility: administration work in R.A.F. subject to medical exam. Letters in from Barbara.

8, Tuesday: A quiet wedding anniversary. Nell & Nita came to dinner. I went to the knitting bee for wool. John saw *High Command*, Elizabeth Price came to spend the day with Betty.

Very hot.

8, Wednesday: A relaxing day at home. Elizabeth Price came again to play with Betty. Children went to have tea with Ethel. Read *Outline of History*.

10, Thursday: Took the children and Roland and Christine down the River on the Kaochiao Ferry. Saw the Asama, Taiyo, Pierce, Joffre, Conte Verde, a Russian ship & all the Mollers. Very hot.

11, Friday: A cloudy, leisurely day at home. Phil and Maynard came after dinner to play bridge. R.Y. Loh has been kidnapped by Wu & is held at "76." Air mail from Ernest on the 43rd floor of Rockefeller Centre.

12 Sat Typhoony weather. All day at home. At night saw *Hudson's Bay* at the Grand.

13, Sunday: Nita came in the afternoon and stayed to supper. We played Beethoven's Sixth Symphony (borrowed from Boynton.)

14, Monday: Wore sweater and shivered. 76° max — Took Betty to town and accomplished various errands re eyes & teeth. John had a physical exam. Finished *Our Future in Asia* by Smith.

15, Tuesday: Pancakes with lemon ($2.10 per) at Ruth Clarke's knitting bee. Afternoon spent with Nell.

16, Wednesday: Helped Nita grade entrance exam papers before & after lunch. She came to supper and we went to see the British Newsreels. Mrs McLorn came to talk over the letter about radio plays.

17, Thursday: Jeanne came for the morning with her knitting. Thermos, stationery, paper napkins on breakfast table. 3 packages in PO. Fruit from Ethel. Candy — Lydia & Milly. Dinner at King Hwa Milly & Nellie Murray. But Nita forgot. Japanese cabinet resigned.

18, Friday: YWCA Nat'l Com. met to delegate authority to Chengtu. Lunch with refugees at Miss Frame's. To the PO to get packages from Ruth, Ruth Petitt, Esther. Nita came and we graded entrance exams before & after supper.

19, Saturday: A day at home with sewing and letters — Betty & Dick both out.

20, Sunday: John gave the sermon in Community Church. Went to sit and play in Nita's garden in the afternoon.

21, Monday: The Morleys came to tea. J & I had dinner at the Olivers with the Smiths, the J.C. Hsias, & Mr Van Evera.

22. Tue Knitting bee for a month's wool. Wrote letters for YWCA Kung Pu-sheng & Cheng Shu-yi — to accept Talitha Gerlach's resignation. Dinner at Sun Ya with Inabelle Coleman, Dr. Rankin, Nita. Letters from home. They were going to NY.

23, Wednesday: AAUW Refugee Relief Com. in M. Frame's office. Listened in the afternoon to May Yang's woes. Betty went to the Brownie picnic at Hungjao. Weather still cool. German V's being distributed.

24, Thursday: *Moonlight Follies* postponed because of rain — floods. Braved the waters to go to Jeanne's to dinner to celebrate Lydia's birthday. Played games with D & B in the pm. Germans guarding their buildings for fear of Russian sabotage.

25, Friday: Went round to Jeanne's to met Mrs. Kamaladevi of India, who knows about prisons from first hand having served 4 years in one. Rest of the day in, & children, too, because of floods. They spent the afternoon cooking.

26, Saturday: Another typhoon day. Kept in by floods. *New Statesman* & books arrived from Clare. The recruiting officer reports J's medical rating too low for active service. But he's very acceptable to the family.

27, Sunday: Borrowed 8th Beethoven Symphony from Boynton. Cool enough for cover during afternoon nap. Went to Nita's before getting Betty from the Suensons'.

28, Monday: Cholera injection. Sent gramophone for repairs. Went with Mrs McLorn, Mrs Carter, Nita to visit refugee camps in

Hongkew. Tea afterward at Mrs. McLorn's. Japanese ships afraid to land in US. Jap. credits frozen. Things on the move.

29, Tuesday: To hear Mme Kamaladevi of Indian National Congress at Church. DC approved my teaching in University. Dinner at the Dunlaps' and on to see *Ch'ing Kung Yuan* (*Tragedy of Ch'ing Palace*) at Aloha with Mrs McLorn, Carter, Dunlap, Nita.

30, Wednesday: To South Gate—the four—where we cooked supper outside and 'twas good. Sent off letters on Nitta Maru.

31, Thursday: Read *For Whom the Bell Tolls*. Tea at Miss Frame's to meet Jewish refugees for AAUW.

AUGUST 1941

1, Friday: Went to Mrs Dunlap's to hear her read poems by Madame Lo Chong, daughter of K'ang Yu-wei. Giant lantern procession at night in honor of recognition of Nanking gov. by Axis powers.

2, Saturday: Dentist. Met Nita in town, bought her two dresses and had lunch. Supper with the Djao family and on to the Symphony Concert in Jessfield, taking D & B. New World Symphony — Largo.

3, Sunday: Sizzling hot. Edith Chun came for the afternoon. Her mother couldn't come because her father was very ill. He died that night. Yang Moi-nan, Butterfield & Swire compradore.

4, Monday: Stine and M. Schniermacher came for the day. Pecan pie, um yum.

5, Tuesday: Knitting party at Mrs Wilson's, with ice cream & chocolate cake. Tea for Mme Kamaladevi of Mangalore, India — Suzanne, Mrs. Stacey, Grace Yang, Nita. Dinner at Jeanne's and then the *Moonlight Follies*.

6, Wednesday: Went out to the U. of S. campus to spend a few days with Nita at the Kelhofers'. Tennis and bridge and a full moon shining on the lotus pond.

7, Thursday: More sleep and bridge and tennis on the U. campus.

8, Friday: A typhoon. Nita and I graded Hong Kong Entrance exams. The children are sick and the cook, so I came home at night in spite of the typhoon.

9, Saturday: A day at home with feverish children. Must get *Problem of India* & *Toward Freedom*. Nell & V. journeyed out to the campus.

10, Sunday: At home with Betty. Rosie, Mary, Bobby, Alice came calling. Mildred and Lydia came to supper. I.S. Brown, Phil Dunbar, Wilbur Judd, Bob O'Bolger all going on the Coolidge.

11, Monday: Went hunting birthday gifts for Ruth, Esther, Elise. Phil and Maynard came for dinner & bridge. Bought *Problem of India* & *Toward Freedom.*

12, Tuesday: Knitting at the Country Club. Tea at Mrs Loh's for Chang, Kung, Owen, Liang, Smith. Girls waiting anxiously for permits from Washington so they can sail on Coolidge.

13, Wednesday: Anniversary of Shanghai war (1937.) Some grenades were thrown and barriers went up. Wrote letters to go on Coolidge and made candy for Phil and Milly. Betty sneezing her head off.

14, Thursday: Saw Phil, Milly, Brownie et al off on the Coolidge. Winnie Galbraith arrived on Harrison. She told us much during lunch. Saw her at Jeanne's also. Mail in from USA. Story of the world minus British Isles at Okaboji (?.)

15, Friday: The family went round to sup at McTyeire. Badminton first.

16, Saturday: Dinner-bridge for Mansfield Freeman — Mabel & Ivor, Geo. Greene, J.C. Greiner, Harrison King.

17, Sunday: Nita and Inabelle Coleman came in the afternoon. Betty and I went to call on the Suensons' and got caught in floods. John ventured out to broadcast.

18, Monday: Floods again. Took Betty to Dunlap who opened one eardrum. Lunch with John at Sincere's. Games at home all afternoon with Dick, Betty, Roland.

19, Tuesday: Took D & B through the floods by rickshaw to swim at the Country Club. It poured rain — worst floods yet. We played Beethoven's First all afternoon.

20, Wednesday: Worse floods. Not out all day. Costume picnic dinner party with John as the Mufti of Jerusalem, if not more.

Played Brahms' First Symphony & Beethoven's First. Strained eye prevented

21, Thursday: By taxi to town to see Dr. Dunlap. Called on Nell to make synopsis of play. Purchased vegetables for marooned cook. Played card games with children. Another typhoon. Floods bad.

22 Fri Took Betty to Stine Suenson's for the weekend. I went to Nita's for the night. We saw a modern Chinese play about the use of reason vs force to control workers in mining village. Nell, V., Shelly, E. Hale.

23 Sat Buses after 5 days absence due to floods. M. Schniermacher came for the day. We went to Mrs McLorn's to tea and heard Ruth Heinrichsdorf relate her experiences in a Nazi political prison for 5 years. 100 bags of U.S. mail "frozen" by J. in the post office.

24, Sunday: Betty still at the Suensons'. Church. Sleep. Read Chapter II of Nell's book. Went to the concert in Jessfield Park. McMullen says 6 months from now these times will be called the good old days.

25, Monday: Bus strike. Morning at YW facing problems of staff & finance. Afternoon at Nita's with English majors — 17 — Furness, Smith, et al. Air mail from Harriet took 4 weeks. Contained check which can't be cashed? (Was cashed.)

26, Tuesday: Bus strike still on. Many rumors and Japanese with drawn pistols and new barbed wire. To see Tsang and do shopping. Tea with Marie Tandy at Columbia Club honoring Betty Rogers.

27, Wednesday: Nat'l YWCA meeting to consider staff needs of Int. Br. Eye exam shows infection somewhere. Tests recommended. John golfing at St. John's. All 4 to the Days' for Christopher's birthday dinner (12.)

28, Thursday: John off to U. of S. Dick to Roland's birthday celebration. Betty and I spent the day with the Morleys. Bridge with Chambers, Barton. Wrote letters to be mimeographed.

29, Friday: Off to town for blood sugar test at Lester. Nita came for afternoon & night. Went round to see Ruth Packard about Int. Br. job. Betty at the Charters'.

30, Saturday: Stine came for the day and night. Elizabeth Day, too, to play. Saw Virginia with Nita at the Uptown.

31, Sunday: J. back from U. of Shanghai. Tea at Eloise's with a big cake for the children. Dick dropped it on the way out. A.E. came in with letters from Barbara.

SEPTEMBER 1941

1, Monday: Children off to school. Negative report on blood sugar, thank goodness. Letters in from Eng. & America. Elise, and others. $10 check from Stacey.

2, Tuesday: Knitting bee at Mrs Metheral's on her birthday. Gambling equipment moved into flat above. Dr. Wang gave negative report on exam. Walked the streets trying to get a metronome repaired. Woodard of Japan came & told his interesting story.

3, Wednesday: A day at home writing letters. J golfing. Telegraphing to Chengtu about Int. Br. secretary. Vera Brittain wrote saying that she worked for peace because she thought a few ought to hold up the ideal even in war.

4, Thursday: A day for letters and study except for a shopping outing. Package of garments from Elise (Mildred's) very acceptable. Walked with John round to see the Y.C. Tus.

5, Friday: First class at U. of S. and student assembly. Tagawa and Sakamoto came to dinner—two gentlemen if ever were. They give one hope for the future. Tagawa was vice-mayor of Tokyo & vice minister of justice. Was imprisoned for using his pen to impeach a prince.

6, Saturday: Went to Jeanne's and tried to ride a bicycle. We celebrated with some of John's summer school money by going to King Hwa for a Chinese supper.

7, Sunday: A rest from Sunday school. Guests to tiffin: Frank Short, Dr. Rankin, Mr & Mrs Stanley Smith. Nina Troy to tea.

8, Monday: To the town to shop & teach. Worked on AWC calendar and Nell's brochure. To the McCrackens' for the YM-YW group.

P. Djao can't get control of himself — mental.

9, Tuesday: To see Lelia about AWC Calendar and on to Lucile's for the knitting bee. Hard study in the afternoon on Anglo-Saxon times. Birthday letters off to USA.

10, Wednesday: Teaching two classes in far places means tall hustling. M. Schniermacher came round with her patient. Went to the hospital to hear Busby & Short speak on their areas. T.L. on edge. Problems for John.

11, Thursday: To AWC to work on Calendar. John had to rescue Fee Gee-kang from the police. His family (aunt) had reported him as a communist.

12, Friday: To Dick's school for prize-giving. He got a book about Pets! Amah sick with fever. I did some tall cleaning. Gar (?) 9:15 Club *Man Hunt.*

13, Saturday: Amah off to hospital. Nita to lunch. 5 to see *The Reluctant Dragon* with sodas at the For. Y. Walked to Seymour Road with Nita.

14, Sunday: Dick to the Damsgaards'. Work on AWC Calendar. To wedding feast of Mao Pei-sing at Mohammedan restaurant. Crowds & red banners.

15, Monday: Purchased brown purse and red umbrella. Worked in U. of S. Library. Went to the Auxiliary Tea at Church. Frank Short and Maynard Guss came to dine & play bridge.

16, Tuesday: To Jeanne's for the knitting bee. Worked on AWC Calendar and studied Norman lit. Ivanov, head of White Russians, assassinated.

17, Wednesday: Had to taxi to town because of tram strike and bus difficulties. Lunch at Choc. Shop. Dick's swimming meet at YM. He got a 3rd place for back stroke.

18, Thursday: Off to find bangles for bags and a brown purse. Very pleasant bridge with Mrs Kucej, Kann, Grossman at French Club. Gasoline rationed.

19, Friday: An afternoon of relaxation reading Joy Homer's *Dawn Watch in China.*

20, Saturday: Nita's big tiffin party in the garden. School boys here to tea. Delicious dinner at the H.C. Hous' honouring Dr. Earle: the Dunlaps, B. Read, Dot Damsgaard.

21, Sunday: Breakfast — waffles & sausage — with Harrison King at St. John's. Nell & V. there. Afterward watched the creek traffic. Stayed home to keep Betty company. She's a cold. Amah came from hospital. Flood prevention launched. Eclipse of the sun.

22, Monday: After classes read proof on AWC Calendar. To YW to work on campaign. Took children from school to Mrs Dunlap's where we heard Saint Saens, Debussy, Mozart, Gilbert & Sullivan. And picked grapes off the vine.

23, Tuesday: Knitting Party here for the morning. Bridge at Vanda Roper's with Lorene Parsons & Mabel Hunter. Betty to be Fairy Godmother in *Cinderella* at School.

24, Wednesday: Spoke at the YWCA Finance Campaign Luncheon at Foreign Y. Tried hats at Eve's. Gasoline rationing is topic of great interest.

25, Thursday: Went to Ave. Joffre to try on suit. Nita came for lunch. Went to AAUW at AWC. About 40 there.

26, Friday: Took the "Canterbury Pilgrims" [a painting] to school and amah to hospital — none too soon! Tried bicycling at Jeanne's. Went to A.E.'s to dinner & played Hell with Anne, Marion, Joe, A.E.

27, Saturday: Took Betty to dentist and shopping for beret, etc. Went to try on new suit while D & B went to parties. To the Fredericks' farewell party for Suzanne Adlam. To see *Underground* at the 9:15 Club.

28, Sunday: Wrote letters for the Sep. 30 ship. J. went to Church retreat 4 — 9. I went to dinner with Lydia, Lucius Porter, Jeanne, Van, Ruth.

29, Monday: Came home from U. of S. in a car bringing the "Canterbury Pilgrims" and pink roses from Nita. Saw *Citizen Kane* (Orson Welles.)

30, Tuesday: Knitting bee at Ruth Clarke's. AWC for Exec. and opening tea. About 60 there. Good days these are, though too busy.

OCTOBER 1941

1, Wednesday: To YW for opening meeting of finance campaign. Phil Sullivan returned & Gertrude Bryan. Fellowship here. Herman spoke on Cooperatives. 91,000 in China. Industrial 2,500. 87% credit coops.

2, Thursday: Mrs Chambers, Ruth & Grace Darroch to lunch. The *New Statesman* is a treat. Took Betty to dancing. Tried new suit. Guests to dinner — Mr & Mrs Mei Pei Sing. sing (?) Morning office hours being debated.

3, Friday: To lunch at Mary Louise Allman's honoring Gertrude Bryan and Mabel Hunter. To Betty's school for sports. Dinner for van den Bergs at King Hwa.

4, Saturday: The four Charters came to lunch. They leave soon for Australia. To the Dunlaps' for a weenie roast. J was golfing with Maynard at St. John's.

5, Sunday: Mid-autumn Festival. The Wus (4) came to lunch bringing mooncakes. Amah came home from hospital. J broadcasting on "Hope of a New World."

6, Monday: After school home with Nita for lunch and afternoon. We saw *Chia*, Chinese movie.

7. Tue A gloriously peaceful, warm sunny day in Mrs Gomersall's garden with the knitting party. Out with Mrs Kindness at 11, back at 5:30. Nana's birthday.

8, Wednesday: A visit to Dr. Riddell for X-rays which showed nothing. To the Palace Hotel to help Mabel clear away. Hunters, V. Smith, van den Bergs leave on Coolidge. Dinner at Sun Ya for Phil — Bobby, Rosie, Sid.

9, Thursday: Last visit of hairdresser. To Mary Edwards where 15 of us had lunch to welcome Mrs Chuan. Spent the afternoon sorting Mabel's things (35 hats plus much.) John took 2 Chens to see *Chia*.

10, Friday: Double ten holiday. Got Betty off to the Suensons' for the weekend. Wrote letters in the afternoon. Nita came to dinner and we saw *The Mortal Storm* at the 9:15 Club. Margaret Sullavan very good.

11, Saturday: Went bicycling at Jeanne's while J golfed. Maynard came to lunch.

12, Sunday: Guests to lunch: Blacks, Osborn, Gordon. German prop. bureau using Chinese girls to send letters purporting to be from former Chinese students to professors in USA universities.

13, Monday: After school to the Church for Auxiliary tiffin and YW campaign meeting. To the Hsias to look at a stove. Betty back from Stine's. Joe came and we played Monopoly.

14, Tuesday: Knitting bee finished first sock. To AWC where Mourne spoke on Indo-China. Politics in Chinese schools are the limit: students discussing question of proctor dismissed for bad conduct (drinking.)

15, Wednesday: To lunch with Nell after checking sinus with Dunlap. Back to U. of S. Library to read on Renaissance. Bought stockings at 23.50.

16, Thursday: Went to Jeanne's to ride the bike. Had permanent. 5 yd cloth at Tai's with 18 napkins = $26.50. Landlord returned rent check, wanting black market rate. Discussing new lease.

17, Friday: P.M. To the meeting to discuss heat & costs, etc. LMS group. Jap. cabinet resigned. Military group goes in.

18, Saturday: Second try at a permanent! Rode bicycle in Jeanne's garden. Guests to dinner & bridge: Geo. Greene, Ruth Packard, Mary Edwards, Phil Sullivan, Harrison King, Einar Edwards.

19, Sunday: Guests to lunch: Dot Damsgaard, John, Lois Ely, Joe Hardie. Guests to tea: Mr & Mrs Sakamoto, Jeanne. Went to take flowers from Church to Nita who had a cold.

20, Monday: YWCA Int Branch — tiffin meeting. Got $1,000 from Marden. Nat'l YW meeting.

21, Tuesday: After school 10 — 5 made calls to collect for YW Finance campaign. Marden gave $1,000, Haqim $500, Gimson $1,000. LMS thinks our rent too high — $700.

22, Wednesday: Lunch with the Blacks in Embankment House. YWCA campaigning and the final rally where $182,454.15 was reported. Goal $180,000. Ruth Packard came round to talk over YW problems. Plumbing troubles.

23, Thursday: A day at home catching up on papers and lessons. Missed AAUW.

24, Friday: YW meeting to phrase recommendation re IB staff. Ind. & Soc. Committee approved publishing cost of living figures. To Nell's for tea. To the Beynons' for dinner & bridge. US ships won't call here.

25, Saturday: Nita came for the day & night. We went to see *Escape*. Maynard off to USA on Tuesday — while he can get.

26, Sunday: Went to call on Mr Gordon. Lydia came in the evening. Mrs Kucej sang beautifully at church. German reprisals in France = executions.

27, Monday: To tea at Mae Yang's — the father's house on Foch — and Mrs S.Y. Chen's. Grand Chinese high tea with revolving table. To Jeanne's for Hallowe'en weenie roast.

28, Tuesday: Knitting bee at Mrs Stacey's. Cut the AWC visit to Cotton Mill in order to study lessons — grade papers.

29, Wednesday: After morning classes to lunch with the Baxters. On to YWCA to consider I. Br. staff question. Back to Miss Frame's to meet Jewish refugees.

30, Thursday: Margaret Schniermacher came to lunch and told of her Italian case — hallucinations. Took Betty to dancing class. Dinner with Miss Ely & Mr Marx. Bought cord for electric stove

$98.00.

31, Friday: Final warning issued to Britons to leave Shanghai. Postage doubling.

NOVEMBER 1941

1, **Saturday:** Hallowe'en Tea Party for children. Neighbours moving from up and across. Coal $800 – $900 a ton.

2, **Sunday:** Go to Church Sunday – 224 there. Miss Tsai & Julia Chen came to lunch. Studied Shakespeare all afternoon. Saw *Ch'ou Ch'eng (Tragic City* – Shanghai) with Mr & Mrs J.H. Sun. Banker's Club amateur performance at Lyceum.

3, **Monday:** After school to Ave Joffre to have some tailoring done. Tailor's prices went up 80% on Nov. 1. Postage abroad doubled. Student came to confer about thesis on Keats. Busy studying Shakespeare.

4, **Tuesday:** Knitting bee. Bridge at the AWC with Mary Edwards, Dr. Thompson, Ruth Packard.

5, **Wednesday:** After the landlord for a lease and bathroom repairs. Holland sugar $25 for 10 lbs! Coffee $13. SMC trying to control prices. BB Wool $60 a lb.

6, **Thursday:** Servants went off to a wedding. I took Betty to dancing and went to try dresses. Anniversary of Shirley Small's death.

7, **Friday:** Home with Nita to lunch and for afternoon & night. We read *Philaster*, walked out for flowers. Nell came to supper. We saw *Arsenic & Old Lace* at the Lyceum.

8, **Saturday:** Went from Nita's to Dick's music lesson. Ruth Packard came to lunch and took pictures of the family. Went round to McTyeire to play badminton with Rosie.

9, **Sunday:** At home to write review of *Dawn Watch* and study lessons. Medhurst teachers came to tea. Betty went to Stine's. Marines may be withdrawn.

10, Monday: Wrote Christmas letters. Saw *Lady Hamilton* at new Majestic. SMC has got foreign exchange and got control of rice — depots for sales & prices.

11, Tuesday: Knitting bee. AWC for program of wood cuts. Saw *Night Train*, Br. film at 9:15 Club. More talk of Br. women departing.

12, Wednesday: Wrote Christmas letters on the holiday and went to tea at Church to welcome new members. Hardoon funeral.

13, Thursday: Had a bridge four: Mary Edwards, Vanda Roper, Sonia Kucej. Got forms and tax receipt so as to buy a bag of rice.

14, Friday: Y.W. World Fellowship Program & Annual Meeting. Letter in from Brenda (Sep 7) Marines ordered to leave China.

15, Saturday: To Mrs Dunlap's where she read Tagore's poems to the University Eng. Lit. Club. We had a dessert party and games: Hudspeths, Olivers, A..E, Eloise, Paterson, Gladys, Ethel Taylor, Margaret Frame, Mac for the night, B. Read.

16, Sunday: A quiet day at home after Bishop Ward's sermon. Nell's Division took over permit for purchasing rice, etc. Farquharson of the LMS joined army medical service.

17, Monday: YWCA Int. Br. Committee followed by visit to new quarters on Connaught. Ethel & S.C. Hylbert going home in Jan! The cook spent all day trying to get permit for a bag of rice.

18. Tue To Mrs Gomersall's garden where we basked in the sun while knitting. Powell spoke at AWC on "America & World War II." Nell appealed for help in enforcing Byelaw controlling prices.

19, Wednesday: To lunch with Nell. I'd like to help her but I am unwilling to assume such time-consuming, energy-consuming work. I'd rather have time at home. To the Flower Show which was excellent. Tea with Mrs. de Sowerby — gr! (?) as usual.

20, Thursday: Thanksgiving Service at Cathedral. McMullen spoke. Missed the choir. Took Betty to dancing and paid a pop call on Nita. Quiet evening of knitting & music.

21, Friday: Home from school with Nita for lunch, faculty meeting, afternoon, dinner.

22, Saturday: Shopping after getting rice from the SMC depot for cook. Took Dr. Ly to 9:15 Club to see *For Freedom* & *China Fights Back*.

23, Sunday: Guests to lunch—3 couples from 5 C's Club. Went to the Symphony Concert with Ruth Packard—Cesar Franck symphony well played.

24, Monday: A dull dark day spent grading test papers and studying lessons.

25, Tuesday: Last knitting party at Mrs Stacey's. Miss Walker, Betty's teacher, to lunch. AWC Executive—walking home with Jeanne. Dinner at the J.C. Hsias and to see *Blossoms in the Dust* (Greer Garson) at Roxy.

26, Wednesday: M. Schniermacher came to lunch. They have to go into the Camp, alas. Bridge at Vanda's with Mary E. & Sonia Kucej.

27, Thursday: Doris' gravitol prescription produced desired result, accompanied by much misery. Thanksgiving dinner: Jeanne, Van, Ruth, Lydia, Maurice Gordon, Irvine Dungan. Turkey (10 lbs) at $60.

28, Friday: Tea for the Farquharsons who leave for Australia early in Dec. Nana Black goes to Eng.

29, Saturday: Took D & B shopping for boots, shoes, etc. Ruth Packard came over with her thesis, "The Chinese Student Movement (1935-36)." Japanese removed Wu Ssepao and all his guards from our lane.

30, Sunday: Y.C. Tu spoke very well at the Church, John presiding. Afternoon studying round the fire. To spend the night with Nell. KGEI (?) failed to come through.

DECEMBER 1941

1, Monday: Nita came home with me from school. After lunch we chatted round the stove. More servant trouble at her house. Neighbors in flats above us moved out.

2, Tuesday: Knitting bee at Ruth Clarke's. More British women departing. Took Betty to Dunlap, but no ear trouble. Played Beethoven's Fifth & the Unfinished—and studied *Rape of the Lock*.

3, Wednesday: Saw Wendy Hiller in Shaw's *Major Barbara*. Gold being carried to Tientsin as covered buttons on overcoats. Woman kept gold nugget in handkerchief in her hand as she was being searched.

4, Thursday: Grading papers. German Consul (Tientsin) Widdeman arrives in Shanghai for Nazi conference. Embroidery women won't work & sell outside, making $5. Prefer to buy rice in settlement.

5, Friday: Ruth Packard's birthday celebrated by tea at Chocolate Shop, *Major Barbara*, dinner at Lucille Oliver's. No ships coming. PO announces packages mailed after Oct. 15 still piled in office.

6, Saturday: Took D & B to see *Pirates of Penzance*. Then Anson Wang's wedding & feast at Banker's Club.

7, Sunday: Luncheon guests—Inabelle Coleman, the Blacks, Sid Anderson (his birthday). Nellie Murray's ship was turned south after leaving Amoy, so she is sailing the seas.

8, Monday: Japan declared war on America & Britain Jeanne telephoned the news of Japan's declaration of war. City occupied by Japanese. Taught at Medhurst & then stayed at home. John couldn't get home, could get no pass. German neighbor read news from Russian newspaper and got German broadcasts.

9, Tuesday: Br. & Am. required to fill in forms for J. gendarmerie. Br. & American property occupied — Navy Y, etc. Jeanne, Lydia, Ruth came to visit & we went to McTyeire, J & I. John got in at Jessfield Rd. America & Br. declare war on Japan.

10, Wednesday: Got to town by showing passport, had photos made for registration. Taught 10 students at U. of Shanghai. Had sandwich with Nita at Choc. Shop. Visitors — Moli How, Eddie Pai, John Smith. Many telephone calls. Thought of cabling home — but no money for it.

11, Thursday: Went to register with the J. Sign in office reads "Polite & Kind." Mr Baxter gave us $1,400 and said, "That may be all you'll get." AMT Funds divided equally. Called on Helen Ling. Two British ships sunk. Dark days.

12, Friday: Walked to school. Full classes both places. Saw the J. occupying Hong Kong-Shanghai Bank houses. Long queues at banks. Played bridge with Mary Edwards (date of long standing.) Germany & Italy declare war on US.

13, Saturday: Stood 2 hours in queue in biting north wind at bank waiting to draw out money. Nita came to lunch — one dish meal. A.E. came in evening to talk about economies. He is very pessimistic. Thinks we face slow starvation. Will be begging food from Chinese friends in ? months.

14, Sunday: Went to church with Mo-li How. Just got out before barricades were closed. Mo-li couldn't get back in. Jap. soldier shot in Zau Ka Doo. Afternoon John tried to get out to apply for pass, but barricades were up tight.

15, Monday: J. seize Dutch Bank, I.C.I. Jardines, etc. Drew another $1,000 from bank and got J. pass, eating lunch as I stood on The Bund in line. YWCA Int. Br. meeting at Winling. We'll lie low for a while.

16, Tuesday: John stood 2½ hrs in line to get his J. pass.

17, Wednesday: Nat'l YW meeting to frame statement of purpose, program etc to have ready for visitors. Finance problem up, too. M. Schniermacher here — in desperate straits but smiling.

18, Thursday: Went round to Bei-Djen Fengs' and found them blockaded. Pass got me through. She gave me money to buy some food for the children. Took Betty to dancing — last time.

19, Friday: After school to the Fengs' to take food and milk. They are still blockaded. To the Christmas PM in hospital — the Beynons. On to spend the night with Nell who sits by the radio listening to outside world. Food bought for Hankow & change given!

20 Sat Went to Gendarmerie in Hamilton House to apply for permit to move. Round again to take food to the Fengs. Lunch with John at Wing On — the four of us. I spent the afternoon with Nita with Betty at Stine's.

21 Sun After Christmas service at church went to lunch with Ruth Packard. Next door German children came to decorate Christmas tree & had tea. Mac came in and we sang carols.

22, Monday: After school to the gendarmerie to apply for permit to move. Sent cable to Dallas. One word — greetings — cost $95.20! $5 U.S. brought only $80. Wrapped Christmas packages. Medhurst is to be closed. Supplementary school?

23, Tuesday: Went to visit Christine & Mrs. Nash after school. M. Schniermacher came to lunch & brought silver ash trays. Dot D came to see about employing servants. Lei C. Ping reported that the J. kept M.P.S. a week, suspecting C.P., in New A. Hotel.

24, Wednesday: Lunch with Nita at the Indian Curry Shop. Excellent. Various callers in pm. Jeanne, Lydia, Ruth, Mo-li, Gimson, Nita. Nell came for the night. Many thoughts sent abroad. John made principal of "supplementary" school.

25, Thursday: The children were surprised to find quite a few gifts — food etc. One pkg of books from U.S.A. Went round to

Jeanne's & McTyeire. Guests to tea. Nita for the night. After dinner discussion of educational problems. Nita realises she's a prisoner on parole.

26, Friday: Taught in two schools as usual. Nita says no money to pay teachers next term so my U. class will be taken by another – a volunteer. Got permits to move and began preparations. Hong Kong reported surrendered. Nita says Am. Red Cross may be able to feed Am. missionaries here.

27, Saturday: Eddie Pai brought Formosan who says he will buy our furniture for $20,000 & take over flat. Hurried consultations with Baxter, Jeanne & Van, Nell. We need cash and this is a good offer, though I hate to lose the rugs.

28, Sunday: Busy with packing. Coolies from Medhurst made 4 trips carrying things by hand, in duffle bags, swung on one of D's stilts. Visits from Miss Lu, E. Pai, K. Zhoh (?). Chen girls to lunch. They say no history or geog. in SMC Chinese schools.

29, Monday: After classes, packing with Nita et al to help. Many things carried by hand. Furniture sale on, then off. Goodbye that $20,000. Formosan not permitted by Jap. to buy enemy property.

30, Tuesday: Moving began in earnest. Handcart man contracted for $140, taking everything in small carts. Medhurst setting up new school. A.E. moving to Hospital so we can have his house.

31, Wednesday: The last of the moving – walking with carts, with Jeanne to help. After lunch with Jeanne, back to the house to pay servants etc. Ruth Packard came to help sort books. Evening devoted to straightening. We hear E. Wise was on Harrison & is now in Hongkew.

* * * * *

NOTEBOOK 1

Monday, Dec.8, 1941

Firing heard.

6:45   Glorious rainbow. Planes (not J.) overhead.

7 am   No newspaper.

8 "   Jeanne phoned that radio said Japan declared war, Manila bombed.

8:30   Went to Medhurst to teach grammar. Great excitement.

10 am   Tried to get bus to town. Bubbling Well Rd. filled with Japanese soldiers. Phoned University office. They said, "Don't come; go home."

10:15   Yu Yuen Road blockaded. Got through on pass used in former blockade.

10:30   Found cook out shopping.

10:45   Washed hair.

11:00   John telephoned to say J. have taken over SMC, Navy Y, U. of S,, Marine Barracks.

11:30   Children came home from school. Told to listen to radio to see whether to go tomorrow.

12:30   Cook returned via circuitous route.

12:45   German broadcast states Pearl Harbor, Manila, Hong Kong, Singapore bombed. All Shanghai in control of J. Shops, banks closed. Radio stations shut except German.

1:30   Gwen Beynon called about Vannie who is taking Cambridge exams at Boys' School.

Japanese have taken British and American Clubs, and church (Moore Memorial) and various properties. American Consulate sealed. J. ask SMC to carry on.

Read "Stories of Heroes" to children.

John unable to get home. Tried from 3 to 6 to get a pass, without result. Called Sakamoto, Foo. Spent night with A.E.

Played games with children.

Vannie got home after facing a Jap. gun at barrier.

Jumped for telephone calls all afternoon – answered children's questions. Dick fearful that S. will be bombed.

Talked to Jeanne, Nita, Dot Damsgaard et al.

Evening spent listening to German news reports – all Br. & American stations shut. German neighbor came over – and brought her radio. She had Russian newspapers, which she read and translated to me in English as we listened to French news.

Letter from Mother (Sep 29) – one lone piece mail – arrived.

Tuesday, Dec. 9, 1941

No papers. Only *Shanghai Times* (Jap.) published.

After asking at various places, John got application forms for passes. All foreigners must register within five days.

J got home via Jessfield Road at 1 pm.

Vannie Beynon ran the blockade and came on for Cambridge exam.

J registered with Jap. gendarmerie.

No passes required, but passports must be carried.

Evening Post appears. *Evening Post* news broadcast on radio.

Jeanne, Lydia, Ruth came round. Children went to the Days'. John & I went to McTyeire at night.

Stories of:

the drunken sailors who turned up at the Y not knowing their ship was sunk.

the Chinese friends who offer help – wearing clothes to safety, offering money, food, etc.

caretaker at Moore kicked downstairs & killed.

purchase of only 1 lb, 1 tin permitted each person.

Ruth Packard's passport in the Am. Consulate which is sealed.

Rumors -

Russia has declared war on Japan.

Chungking has declared war on Japan

Wednesday, Dec. 10, 1941

Took Betty to school—30 children there. Morning session only.

Proceeded to town on No. 1 bus, showing passport at barrier.

Purchased ginger snaps at Choc. Shop (3 lb limit.) Empty shelves.

Had photos made for registration blanks.

Taught 10 students (out of 22) at University of Shanghai. Addison & Steele's *Essays*.

Mobs of Chinese on streets. Crowds around various & numerous proclamations.

Long lines of Br. & Am. citizens running down Foochow Rd waiting to register in Hamilton House office.

Lunch with Nita in Choc. Shop. (A sandwich & cup of coffee $5.00)

Took blue shoe for repairs. Collected jade drop at Jade Shop, ready for zipper.

Left bus at St. George's and purchased peanut brittle.

Walked home via Jessfield Rd.

Visitors: Moli-How & others, Ruth Shen, Eddie Pai—Treasury Dep't employee who wants contact with Miss Jacobsen to see if she can pay his salary.

British consular & embassy people held in Cathay Hotel. Americans in Metropole. Mr Eggo and others in Br. Consulate were allowed out for 4 hours for shaves and clean clothes. Then had to return. He tried to signal to J. to telephone his wife. Mr Morley was kept two days, then released.

Sid says Moore Memorial is occupied by the Navy. The Jap. flag is flying there.

BWA activities suspended.

Telephoning still slow, but better than Monday.

Nell says J. have sealed rice stocks and negotiations (Council – Consulate – Military) are proceeding to release it. Rice shops are empty. Cook says Chinese are buying meal, because they can't get rice.

Gasoline also sealed. Flour, too.

Buses will not run after 8 pm to save fuel.

The J. queried Mrs Baxter as to her possessions, saying she must have $10,000 worth since she had on a coat costing $1,000!

Shanghai Times costs $.60 a copy.

North China Daily News suspended. J. has suspended the *Chinese Recorder*.

Speculation as to how long this war will last. Con Cater says 3 months. Ethel Taylor says 12 months. I say 3 years.

Every bit of food and material substance assumes a new importance in the light of the times – no ships to bring more, no money to buy more.

Banks opened a few hours. Can draw up to $500.00

The J. occupation has not been so cruel as it might have been. The J. have been polite to their diplomatic prisoners.

I am fortunate – so far – compared to Mary Louise Allman, Mary Edwards, Mrs. Sheriff, Mrs. Hepner and others.

Mrs. Hepner left Berlin to bring 3 small children to Kunming to join husband (children's specialist – Christian but of Jewish descent.) He went on to America. She supported the children there by taking German people into her home. Did all the work herself. Bombings came. She had to carry the small boy with leg in cast to the fields. Came to Shanghai. Lives on proceeds of sale of his medical equipment. He sends little money. Can't practice in U.S. but is male nurse. They have one dish a meal. Food for 4 for 1 month coast her $230. Ours costs $600 – $1,000. Sleep on trunks. Have birds and flowers. She does all the work. Small child had scarlet fever which settled in blood and now has bad ears. Has no contact with 3 brothers in German army, with her mother, or with her husband. Does not belong to any group here. Feels much alone.

Thursday, Dec. 11, 1941

News of sinking of 2 British battleships – Prince of Wales – Repulse.

8 am. set off to town to collect photos and register.

Met Nita at Hamilton House at 9.

Registration line very long. We got into registration office at 10.

Large sign behind the J. on the wall in written English:

Polite

and

Kind

(Office clock observes Tokyo Time)

Nita told of W.F.'s desire to get into free China & his need of a Chinese guide. A party left on Monday morning & hasn't returned. Nita may try to help.

F. says men from Wake are in Ward Road and he thinks all men of military age will be interned.

British Consulate burned secret papers on Sunday night so they knew what was coming.

Transport is controlled. No trucks except for essential commodities. SMC organizing coolies brigades for transport.

SMC asks for volunteers.

Tanks & trucks of soldiers and barricades moving west from Race Course to Hungjao area.

Outside Road area to be controlled by Nanking regime — Shanghai, Special Municipal Government to collect taxes.

Baxter called in LMS people. All missionaries in AMT given $1,400 out of AMT funds. Staff paid for December — rest divided among all missionaries. "It may be the last you'll get."

Went to the Metropole Hotel where U.S. consular people are quartered to inquire about Miss J. on behalf of Eddie Pai, Treasury employee who wants salary. Found she is staying in H.S. Bank Bldg.

P.M.

Took Betty to play with Christine in CIM Compound.

Sent Dick to swim at YM.

Mr E. is in Br. Consulate, sleeping on desk. His boss in solitary confinement. First day he got a cup of coffee & a biscuit. Afterward fed from some hotel. Mrs E. feels he may be sent to Japan. She was given a chance to go into Consulate with him but couldn't rough it.

Went to call on Helen Ling in hospital.

She told Myron's story of the Japanese General who demanded rooms. He gave them some at back. They demanded finest suites. He explained that the German ambassador has one, the German consul has another, Capt. Wiedeman, the third. He said, "If you can get these gentlemen out, we'll be glad to let you have the rooms." J. said, "Never mind."

Mr Wu unable to cash check at bank. Returned to me for endorsement on back, although it's a cash check. "Too many people."

J. take over Customs. Sir Frederick Maze resigns. 300 employees turned off.

Taxis have to suspend because of lack of gas. More men—the chauffeurs—unemployed.

John & I discuss ways to save: stop D's music, B's dancing, consider moving elsewhere to cut rent. Use candles instead of lights, etc.

[The following in pencil:]
Jap. newsreels b. movies.
2nd day—Morris missed only 1 or 2 performances.
Balloon over Race Course with (illegible) be calm.
Queues at every bank.
J. shops with Christmas sale signs.

Friday, Dec. 12
Walked to school to save the 15 ¢.
Full classes in Medhurst and U. of S.
Saw the J. occupying Hong Kong—Shanghai Bank residences.
Long queues in front of every bank. Truck with loud speaker parades the streets and J. scatter propaganda.
J. order games to continue on Race Course.
Went at 2 pm to keep bridge date of long standing with Mary Edwards. Children played at the Days'.
[In pencil] Mary Ed spent the day burning documents & books.
At the table Dick said,"If this is war, it isn't so bad for me. Is it bad for you, Daddy?"
Dad: "Well, I've had to suspend my magazine."

Saturday, Dec. 13, 1941
Rose with the dawn in order to get to the Hong Kong-Shanghai Bank before the queue was too long. Arrived there at 8 am and was in the first hundred in the line. Stood for two hours in the biting north wind—no sun—very thankful for a small blanket and

Russian neighbor's umbrella to keep off wind.

Read "Future of International Government" pamphlet by Carr & de Madariaga. Admitted to bank at 10. Shoved by Japanese naval man when asking about which line to stand in. Got $500 for John & $500 for me.

Nita came for lunch – a one dish meal – Chinese *mien*. 4 people $3.60. I walked with her to Ave. Joffre and we stopped in to see Helen Ling in the hospital.

U. of S. campus occupied on Thursday, but 5 men still living there and allowed to come to town.

Long talk with A.E. in the evening concerning economies. He expects the worst – slow starvation. Says he sees no chance of more money and thinks we'll be begging food from Chinese friends in 3 months. Nurses at the hospital already fearful of connections with foreigners. YWCA secretaries (all but Ch'iu) panicky and don't want Ruth Packard to come to YW at all.

A.E. thinks doubling up necessary and will take us in. Suggests also N.M.'s house as possibility. If we go to A.E.'s, we can take no furniture with us.

Hiding rolls of $500 in hat boxes and such places. This money may be worth nothing, so A.E. changed 500 into Wang Ching-wei notes, thinking they may be good later.

Sunday, December 14, 1941

Children and John went off to the church before 9.

Mo-li How had got 3 gallons of gas at $36.00 a gallon, so she and I went in her car. Just as we got to the Paramount, a J. in civilian clothes got out of a military car and had the guards close the barricades tight. He raced on to Bubbling Well Road and we dashed to Great Western and got through the barricade before he arrived. The Chinese chauffeur thought we shouldn't go but Mo-li ordered him on.

Very fine church service. Isaiah 40. O God Our Help in Ages Past. About 130 or more there. 6 people of 4 nationalities joined the church.

Firing heard during service.

Started home with Mo-li. At Great Western barricade no cars were allowed in. No Chinese were allowed in. We got out and walked thru barriers & on home. Mo-li must have gone on to stay with friends or relatives.

Bobby telephoned that Sid couldn't get thru. The servants say a J. soldier was killed or wounded this morning by some Chinese and that explains the restrictions.

Sakamoto telephoned that passes are being issued at 6 The Bund to all those with passports. John went out to get his and mine, if possible.

Baxter called a meeting at 2 to discuss economies, etc. John thought he oughtn't go out for fear of not getting back, but the pass business is urgent so he went for that.

...He has just returned – couldn't get through the barricades at all.

We feel it is urgent to move into the Settlement as soon as possible Jeanne & Van got out just after lunch to go for passes. Perhaps they can't get back.

Mr. Gordon of Chartered Bank advises us to draw as much cash as possible out of banks. His passport was in the Br. Consulate, so he has none. He moved quickly on Monday morning as soon as war was declared to the Fr. Concession – Brookside.

The cook says Dr. Birt's (German) 2 guards are Italians off a ship. They are afraid the J. will come to search so they've taken their possessions away!

Mr. Wilbur is financial sec. of the Church. He put last Sunday's collection in the Navy Y. safe and got a Navy Y. check for it. When the Navy Y. was taken over there was $700 in the safe. The J. in charge said he would keep it. All staff were turned off except 2 lift men who were kept to operate lifts. Several days later they were turned off and were given $5 each. When Wilbur went to ask about the $700 he was told it had been used to pay off staff.

The J. took over the Shanghai Club, entering at noon while people were eating lunch and saying, "Gentlemen, we give you 20 minutes." When it was explained that some residents were not even there, they agreed to give the residents till 4 pm.

Nita heard yesterday that her mission treasurer has no more money to give them.

Tonight we must make a list of absolutely necessary things to take to A.E.'s.

And I spend the afternoon studying romantic poetry of Thos. Gray!

A cable has been sent to London saying "All Well." We have no proof that it has arrived. We can't afford to send a personal cable. The $100 would feed us for a week or more.

Buses will run from 7:30-9; 12-1; 4-6 only. Gas is needed by the J.. in other places for other purposes. Trams still running.

A.E. says other people are more optimistic than he is. Banks may open without restrictions on Tuesday.

We have subscribed to the *Shanghai Times* for one month, but no paper came this morning. Perhaps they can't send to our area regularly.

The J. called a meeting last Wed. of Br. & Am. citizens to discuss difficulties & ask for suggestions. Powell, Walline, Hylbert, Braidwood & others went. Nobody knows who summoned them or how they were chosen. It looks as if the thing were staged for the benefit of the foreign press in order to record praise for the quiet courteous manner in which the J. took over. The J. military were very strict with Jap. nationals in Hongkew. None were allowed over the bridge. All were required to get new passes. This prevented run-ins (?) and rowdy elements from causing trouble. It could have been hell on earth.

Bacharachs were coming to call but telephoned they couldn't get through.

After romantic poetry, helped Betty make Christmas gifts (capes) for her friends.

Gordon says the J. are not wanting Chinese to come into Shanghai but are glad to help them leave. 15,000 have left in the last 3 days, going on boats up river to Yangtze ports.

It was easy to foresee a food shortage, in the days when we were expecting war, but it wasn't so easy to allow for the behavior of people faced with a food shortage.

Sam. Johnson said to Boswell, when Boswell felt he was putting too many little incidents into his diary, "There is nothing, sir, too little for so little a creature as man. It is by studying little things that we attain the great art of having as little misery, and as much happiness, as possible."

Monday, December 15, 1941

Walked along to Medhurst.

At 10 hurried to Hart and Avenue to catch tram, since buses do not run at that hour. Just reached the U. of S. in time for my class.

Hurried to get $1,000 from the bank. They allow $500 to be drawn from each account on each of 3 days. Limit $1,500. Different banks have different rules. I got $1,000 from each of our two accounts but have no chance to get the other allotment. Chinese banks are reported to be opening for business tomorrow but it is not known what foreign banks can do.

Took my stand in the line to wait for a J. pass at 6 The Bund. Ate my sandwiches and read the *Shanghai Times* as I waited. Sakamoto was there in charge. Got pass after 1½ hours. The J. men worked till one, though they were supposed to stop at 12. Very kind &

courteous. Very well organized as all their projects seem to be. On to a YWCA Int. Branch meeting at 10A Winling. Decided to lie low. Some secretaries don't want to associate with Br. & American people.

Some Chinese schools are closing. 2 Gov. universities have closed. Others (Chiao Tung et al) have become private institutions. Plans have been made in advance. Chinese families looking for tutors.

I witnessed the taking over of Jardine Engineering Co. on Yuen Ming Yuen. All Chinese employees were standing in the street with the Navy in front of their usual sign—so familiar—seen on so many doors.

Occupied
by I.J. Navy
Any persons.........

The Imperial Chemical Industries was occupied today.

All British & American employees of the Customs (200) have been turned out of jobs & out of houses.

About 9,000 Br. & Americans have registered. 1156 Americans — rest British. Many of there are Eurasians, to be sure, with Br. passports.

Walked home from Joffre & Say Zoong. No buses running till 4:30.

Mary Louise Allman came in. She had been to one of the Child Welfare Homes where the matron was frantic because she had no money for food. Child Welfare got only $500 out to feed 3 institutions. They came & the J. with them. After several visits the same day they said, "Mr. A. isn't in town so we'll just take this office." They moved the partners into one small room and let them carry on there as, or if, they can.

Mrs. Moo went to see Mary Louise. Their 2 sons were kidnapped two weeks ago.. The kidnappers are asking 15 million cash.

Ruth Packard came round. She hopes to get her pass tomorrow so she can move around and out of this area.

Dutch Banks were seized this morning. Dutch E. Indies sent some submarines to help in Malaya.

Christian schools debating whether to close at end of this term. Chinese do not want to bow in any way to the J. They do not want to carry on if they have to teach the idea that the J. are the saviors of China, etc. They prefer to close the formal schools and carry on in a supplementary fashion but are not quite clear as to how and where they could carry on. Presence of foreigners is a complication. J thinks it would be better to carry on the schools for sake of the students even if J. has to be taught. But he dares not say too much to them.

Tuesday, Dec. 16

John waited 2½ hrs in line to get J. pass.

Blessed be sunshine. I'll never again take for granted such blessings as hot water and bus service. And bread, It was not to be.

Wednesday, Dec. 17, 1941

A terrible time I had trying to get to my class downtown on a tram.

The rice queues are heart-rending. I saw poor fellows breaking branches off trees on Edinburgh Rd—for fuel.

Mrs Baxter called to say that provisions intended for Hankow are available—to be paid for after the war! I grabbed at oatmeal, prunes, cheese, margarine, chocolate.

Police stations do not give permits to move. Must go to J. Gendarmerie in Hamilton House.

Flour very scarce.

Friday, Dec. 19

Took the Christmas meeting for the Mission at the Lester Hospital.

Round again to take food to the Fengs.

The Mission has given us some dried fruit and oatmeal, etc. We eat now and pay after the war! Food was intended for Hankow but couldn't be sent.

Spent night with Nell who sits glued to the radio, wanting news of the world. She's having to deal with strikes. Taxi drivers and other workers realize that their jobs are permanently finished. They make heavy demands and will not believe that foreign firms can't get money to pay them.

Sat.. Dec. 20

Applied at gendarmerie for pass.

8:40 am Chocolate Shop had no bread. Line of people at the Uptown Branch.

Cantonese rice for lunch at Wing On's with John—the four of us, followed by limited Christmas shopping.

Spent afternoon with Nita. No one knows what the school situation will be. Some students are withdrawing from the University because they fear the J. will force them to do certain jobs for which the J. have not enough trained men. It is said that Hangchow and Soochow are being urged to go back to their cities.

Universities will divide next term into 3 parts, taking tuition for one at a time. Then if they are forced to close because they can't meet conditions, students don't lose so much money.

Middle schools will probably close and then reopen with different principal, different name. Thus the original school shows loyalty to Chungking. Students say to Americans,"You must stay here because you are prisoners, but we are slaves if we stay here. We ought to go to the Interior."

Chinese are loyal to Chungking but the J. consider them loyal to Nanking.

Sunday, Dec. 21

Very nice Christmas lunch with Ruth Packard after Christmas service at Community Church.

Moore Memorial Church is meeting in Community Church auditorium for services.

The next door German children and their mother came to help decorate the Christmas tree.

We had the hard task of telling the servants that they must go when we move. Where to?

Hong Kong is in a very serious situation. Surely they can't hold out long.

Monday, Dec. 22

Rather difficult it is to carry on with so many conflicting claims on time and thought:

Efforts to secure food — milk, bread, margarine

Efforts to concentrate on romantic poetry and the rise of the novel — classes still continue

Plans for moving

Worry over the servants and their plight

Attempts at celebrating Christmas, for the children's sake

Concern about Medhurst and the future there

The gendarmerie assures me that a permit can be issued this week for us to move. But it seemed otherwise this afternoon. There was a second and last meeting of J. and Br. & Americans to ask questions, etc. The spokesmen said no moving would be permitted now, perhaps not for another month. Not even the Customs people who have been ordered out are permitted to move to their temporary quarters in the Church House.

A man who handles refrigerator parts was asking a permit to move his parts so he could repair refrigerators for people to keep food.

Sent cable home. One word "Greetings" with address cost $95.20.

Of 1,100 Americans 700 are men, 400 are women.

Children started carrying toys & books to A.E.'s. Moving by hand.

No private cars allowed on the streets after today without special permits. Measure to save gasoline.

Tuesday, Dec. 23, 1941

$1 brought $10 Ch.

Mrs E. went to see husband kept in British Consulate. Was allowed to stay 2 hours. He has room of his own and can have companionship with 6 others.

Sawyer was allowed out for a few hours & went to see the Olivers. Jailers very courteous.

L.C.P. reports that M.P.S. was taken off at 3 am by J. to New Asia and kept a week—accused of connections with C.P.

M. Schniermacher also has many troubles. Went to get into a Camp, but there are 800 waiting & no beds.

It's terrible getting only J. news. We feel entirely cut off from outside world.

Wed., Dec. 24, 1941

Went round to Mrs Nash's at her summons to get Christmas pudding and candy. Lunch at Indian Curry Shop—four of us and Mary Lucile Saunders as guests of Nita. Various callers in pm. Christmas spirit doesn't come very easily. Nell came for the night.

LMS approved John's connection with school to replace Medhurst, of which he'll be principal.

Nell says that Council has decreed a a 2-month's moratorium on rents and by then landlord must adjust rents. Hurrah! That's substantial help for many.

Thurs., Dec. 25, 1941

Quite a few gifts were under the tree—food, and things dug up out of trunks. We used some of our precious little flour to send cookies to some neighbors.

Walked with Nell to Jeanne's and on to McTyeire.

Guests to tea in afternoon:

Bobby, Mary, Alice, Rosie, Eloise, Sid, Phil, Jeanne, Van Ruth, Lydia.

Fare: 1 cake, cookies, open sandwiches.

Nita, John & I after supper discussed the educational outlook. Universities will divide the term into 3 parts, students paying tuition & getting credit for each ⅓ as they go, in case the schools have to close. Many problems in middle schools. Some will close, some carry on.

Nita began to realize that we are prisoners on parole.

Stories:

Teruoko, deputy sec. of SMC called McMullen at 5:30 on Monday, saying, "Will you please get up and come to Council office? Your country and mine are at war."

Dr. Dunn was in Hongkew and fell into conversation with a J. who was guiding him somewhere. The man spoke perfect English and Dunn asked him about it. "Oh," said he, "I'm an American. I was just visiting in Japan last summer and the bastards caught me."

Got permits to move—one for J. & one for me.

68

Friday, Dec. 26

Taught in 2 schools as usual.

Eddie Pai proposed that he knows a Formosan who might buy over our furniture.

Sat., Dec. 27

Formosan and wife came and offered $20,000 for furniture. We feel that we'd better take cash and do with A.E.'s furniture. Most friends agree that it's a good offer

Terrible business of moving by hand. School coolies made + trips, John with them, carrying things, walking.

Sun — Wed, Dec. 31

J. would not permit the Formosan to buy enemy property.

We moved all our possessions on handcarts.

Stories

J. went to inspect St. John's Library. They took away Plato's *Republic* and the Nat'l Geographic magazine. At the YMCA Library they took *Victorious Living* by Stanley Jones and *Christian Revolution*.

When the J. went to the Red Swastika Mental Hospital the Chinese nurse in charge pretended to know no English. She made signs and wrote Chinese characters to answer questions. They asked, "What kind of hospital is this?" She answered, "Ma-ma-hu-hu-ti" and tapped her head. They moved back. They asked her if she were not afraid. She said no. They asked about the other building and she said "TB." When they didn't understand she coughed to show what disease. They went away quickly and asked no more questions.

Mr K. had cautioned Mrs K. about being too specific over the telephone. He called her one day and was talking about food.

Mr K—We have no meat.

Mrs K—Why don't you eat the chickens?

Mr K—They are laying and I hate to do without the eggs. But of course if I thought the J. were coming I'd kill them.

Rope ran down the middle of Jessfield Road. Right half barricaded because of the Sharrock shooting. Mrs Meyers wanted to get shoes which amah had embroidered for Ruth's birthday. They were in a shop on the blockaded side. Amah couldn't get in and neither could Mrs Meyers. They shouted to shop man to throw the shoes across to them when guard wasn't looking. He did & they left the money in a shop on blockaded side to be paid later.

Two J. officers went to Meyers' garden to shoot birds. Had been businessmen, now gendarmerie. Came for "sport." Never really shot but took aim and stayed to visit. One had been an Olympic champion in Berlin. Several days later one of them waved vigorously to Mrs Meyers on Jessfield Road, shouting and waving his revolver.

For. Y. has J. adviser. (Jan. 28, '42) J. asked Chinese representing Christian organizations to a luncheon. 6 J, 6 C. They asked questions. Ch'iu & Hsueh went.

Eddie Wise left San Francisco on Nov. 4. From Honolulu had escort & was blacked out. Heard war was declared on Dec. 8 early am. Captain tried to make for Vladivostok. Bomber came over. Dropped bombs, which missed but gave no directions. Captain proceeded but finally stopped. After hour Nagasaki Maru came up. Captain tried to dash for Shanghai. Couldn't make it. Ran ship aground on rocky island of Sha Wei Shan. Crew 166 & Eddie took to boats and finally landed in cove. 3 killed by propeller when boat was upset. Many in water, later picked up. Spent night in lighthouse, wet walls & floors, foghorn blowing. Had bedding rolls & provisions from ship. Japanese landing party came (about 12) very much afraid. Talked to captain, who then next morning ordered crew back to ship, which was listing badly, 11-12 feet of mud in holds. Every day at high tide, steamed up engines trying to get off mud. No use. After a week or so Japanese salvage crew came and worked for 3 or 4 weeks with pumps, etc., finally floating the ship. For 3 weeks the men in crew had no water for washing hands, even. Finally water was brought from Shanghai. Lived well on ship's provisions. Christmas Day had 32 items on menu — liquors, cigars, etc. Came up the Whangpoo to Hunt's wharf. E managed to send notes to town J. Embassy & Navy disagreed as to his release. Navy finally released him. Courteous treatment. J. guards on ship (about 10) left their guns in cabins & cabin doors open. Allowed to bring off all baggage. Films & projector kept overnight & then returned to him.

Mar., 1942

J. are taking trees & hedges out of U. of S. campus to transplant in a park somewhere.

They came to the RAS with 150 crates & took away all files of periodicals. Gave no receipt to librarian as they "deal with Navy people only."

All people from Harrison taken from ship. Officers interned. Others free.

* * * * *

1942

Worrying

JUST AS IN 1941, the entry in the diary for the first day of the year in 1942 gives an indication of what was to follow for the rest of the year. Socializing with friends is mentioned, scarcities of food are a preoccupation and world news. "J. 20 miles from Manila" is on my mother's mind. What was new was that we were "Settling into Small house."

This was not a matter of the size of the house, which was, in fact, larger than our flat on Yu Yuen Road. The inhabitant of the house was A.E. Small, an LMS colleague of my father's. His family had left for Australia in 1941 and, since he was living in this house within the International Settlement on his own, he kindly moved elsewhere so that the four of us could move in. (As it happened, both he and an LMS nurse, Ethel Taylor, began moving in on Nov. 29 when the Japanese took possession of the places where they were living. We lived together for a few weeks until we were all interned.) The house, in Lane 1522 on Nanjing Xi Lu, still exists in what is now an upmarket part of Shanghai near the Portman Ritz-Carlton Hotel.

The shortages of food and fuel were what concerned my mother most during 1942. Over and over again she writes about searching for margarine, flour and, especially, sugar to feed her family. On November 9 she writes: "Nita hurried away after lunch to buy sugar and was 269th in line." Matches, salt and candles were also in short supply. The Meyers family gave us some lettuce seedlings and Mother, for the first time in her life, I think, began to garden. She also collected supplementary rations of wheat for Americans from the Shanghai American School (which I would later attend after the war.)

The lack of coal meant that we could use our kitchen stove, which also heated the house and the water, only sparingly. Mother mentions the cold rooms in the winter and the joy of occasionally having a hot bath.

Lack of fuel for the residents meant also a lack of fuel for transportation. On January 11 Mother writes: "No buses running at all." During the year she seems to have walked a great deal – to Community Church on Ave. Petain, to fetch me from my friends' homes and to the Bund to see off her departing friends. June 29: "Up at 4:30 & walked in rain to the Bund to farewell repatriates on Conte Verde. 22 buses & 3 ambulances pulled up and discharged the 639." (As ever, Mother somehow knew the statistics!)

The gradual changeover from one kind of currency to another – *fa pi* to CRB – created more uncertainty. May 23: "Exchange differs every day" and May 26 "...frantic buying of CRB dollars." Some shops accepted one currency, some only the other.

More worrying than the physical difficulties, however, was the mental stress of the ever-increasing restrictions and the uncertainty of what lay in the future. On January 20 Mother writes: "Outside area blockaded because Shamrock of Police was shot. Children couldn't come from school." All during that year we could never be sure whether we could get home that afternoon or evening.

On January 5 Mother writes: "Am. & Br. members of SMCouncil resign at request of J. All committee members, too. Met Liddell at 11 and sent in letter." However, three days later she says, "Invited to serve again on SMC Social & Industrial Committee." This is a matter of which, as a child, I was totally ignorant.

Later in the year the struggle between the Japanese and the Allies became more obvious. May 30: "Beginning of Br.-Am. Annihilation Week. Posters everywhere & parades & meetings." To me, the following entry is somewhat amusing: (June 3) "Witnessed the 'great' Anti-allied parade & demonstration from the tram window." What was not at all amusing was the news coming from places like Manila and Singapore, both of which fell to the Japanese army much more quickly than anyone had imagined. In both those cities, enemy aliens were interned very rapidly.

In Shanghai, however, from October 1, 1942, red armbands with numbers and "A" for Americans and "B" for British had to be worn by all adult "enemies." On October 14, the significance of the armbands became clear: "...Announced that from 12 tonight enemy nationals cannot go to movies, restaurants, race course, etc."

In Shanghai, in 1942, there was still hope among the foreigners that they might be repatriated. Rumors abounded and the diary is full of such hopes being raised and then dashed. It seems that Mother had hoped to take Dick and me to the U.S.A. but that was not to be. By December 12 she writes: "Strong BRA rumor of total internment."

In the meantime, throughout the year, life carried on as 'normally' as possible. Educational institutions held classes, my father continued with his teaching at Medhurst College but Mother took on a student, May Yang, whom she coached in English and history. Always quick to make use of any opportunity, she also studied the Japanese language. In early February, she began a three month course at the YMCA. On February 4 she reports going to "...a Japanese lesson — 13 men + Anne MacKeith & me."

Dick and I were walking to our schools on Yu Yuen Road every day and we, too, were learning Japanese. (March 24: "Japanese to be taught in all SMC schools.") Sadly, about all I can remember, apart from simple counting, is,"Ohayo gozarimas, Iijima Sensei." (Good Morning, Teacher Iijima,) said with a deep bow.

At that time I was a child and I was never separated from my parents or my brother. We were together as a family. For Mother, one of the worst aspects of life under Japanese occupation was the lack of news from home. Throughout the war years we were severely restricted with regard to correspondence. On May 8, 1942, she writes for the first time: "Sent off letters of 25 words thru Int. Red Cross to Dallas and Drumloist." (See section on PEOPLE for the meaning of 'Drumloist'.) That was the only kind of letter she could write for the next three years. On Oct. 23 she writes: "...my first letter in 11 months."

The enemy aliens in Shanghai all knew about "the wretched conditions of Br. & A. prisoners in BH." (Bridge House, where the Japanese Gendarmerie tortured those whom they suspected of being spies} (March 1). How could those still left in the city not worry about their own future? Most of the time, Mother was optimistic. But on November 6 she writes: "After a sleepless night, a calm day."

JANUARY 1942

1, Thursday: New Year tiffin at McTyeire, extra special. The Baxters & Nell called. Settling into Small house. J. 20 miles from Manila. Margarine very scarce. Flour unobtainable. We operate the kitchen stove on certain days only.

2, Friday: Event of the day: found some flour at Wing On & got 5 lbs. No margarine available. Still settling in. Manila was occupied. Dark days. No news from abroad. Christian colleges may close.

3, Saturday: Nothing for sale in Chocolate Shop except "Army Biscuit" — thick crackers.

4, Sunday: Tea at Jeanne's because of her birthday. Transport problems — had to walk to the Suensons' to get Betty.

5, Monday: Am. & Br. members of SM Council resign at request of J. All committee members, too. Met Liddell at 11 and sent in letter. Went to schools to ask scholarships for children. Miss Yang came and I agreed to coach her in Eng & history. Margarine, 2 lbs flour and a pie from May Yang.

6, Tuesday: Exam at Medhurst in a very cold room. Found sugar at Little Choc Shop. We ate vegetable soup cooked on *feng lu*. Kitchen stove on 3 times a week. Water is very cold on other days.

7, Wednesday: Exam at U. of S. — 4 out of 22 absent. Guests: Eddie Pai, with apples; Mary Edwards, with marmalade. Cachita sent 5 lbs of flour from Portuguese Coop.

8, Thursday: Struggle at Wing On's to buy 5 lbs of flour. Jeanne, Nita and others doing the same. Invited to serve again on SMC Social & Industrial Committee.

9, Friday: First session coaching Mae Yang in Political & Social History of Modern Europe. Lunch & afternoon with Nita. She has a bicycle!

10, Saturday: Visited Tsang with a sore eye. Marshmallow roast round our grate in the evening — Jeanne, Van, Lydia, Ruth. J. say Kuala Lumpur about to fall.

11, Sunday: Semi-annual meeting at Church. 121 present. Each family brought own lunch. Soup & coffee sold. Snowy day. No buses running at all. Papers say enemies interned in Manila.

12, Monday: Stopped studying history to have 11 o'clock tea with Mrs Nash. Other eye very sore. J. take over foreign banks and will liquidate.

13, Tuesday: J. take over public utility companies — bus, tram, etc. Taught my pupil, walking to Petain. John has trouble keeping the J at Institute *pai-lou*. Wishes for Harriet to share the adventure.

14, Wednesday: Wing On area cordoned off because of a shooting. Shop people kept there. Nita and I spent the night with Nell. J. trying to induce thousands of unemployed to leave Shanghai. Nell's division will license sub-lessors.

15, Thursday: PO says letters to USA can go via Siberia! Studied history of France. 20,000 Jewish refugees starving. Telegrams to USA bring no money. Can't buy flour or margarine.

16, Friday: U. of S. is to close. Shops are very particular about worn paper money. Joe Hardie has 2 pupils. City Gov. offices moving into Dr. McCracken's refugee hospital.

17, Saturday: Went with Nita and Mary Lucile Saunders to the U. of S. where we lunched with Hart Westbrook and sniffed Vic's tobacco sweepings.

18, Sunday: Tiffin with the Stanley Smiths — then to make calls for church budget. Called on the Hepner family. They say Eddie Wise is either in Hongkew or on the Harrison which is being refloated.

19, Monday: Nell's birthday. Special cake, made with the last bit of margarine, for her tea. Nita & I invited Mrs McLorn, Grace Yang, Myra Olive, Jeane van Hengel, Dr. Lawney.

20. Tue Outside area blockaded because Sharrock of Police was shot. Children couldn't come from school. Barbara Adams came to lunch. I took beans to Dorothy Day who ate on corner as she waited.

21, Wednesday: Mrs Suenson and Stine came. Also M. Schniermacher & Ruth Packard. Went to Nell's where Nita and I spent the night. Proclamation as to goods J. will confiscate.

22, Thursday: Hastened home from Nell's because Betty had upset tummy. Drew last $30 out of bank. Harrison refloated. Eddie on it? Julia Chen has TB—living in small dark room in house with relative who has it.

23, Friday: After tutoring dropped in at the AWC. In the afternoon to the Meyers for a joint birthday—Jill & Ruth. J. in New Britain, Java, etc. nearing Singapore. It looks very bad.

24, Saturday: J.H. disappeared, thereby causing much trouble and disgust and anxiety. The family took a long walk to Hungjao stopping to visit Mary Louise Allman. Evening spent running down clues with no luck.

25, Sunday: No news of J.H. To Mary Edwards for a delicious tiffin. Also there—Geo. Osborn, Mary L. Allman & John, M. & E. Jansen. Bacharach came to tea & B. Read dropped in. J. had to spend most of the day on the J.H. case.

26, Monday: No news of J.H. 90% certain he's off to the west. Nita came for the day and we read *This Above All* and began *Toward Freedom*.

27, Tuesday: Visits to Meathrel & Morley. DC in pm. Called on Anderson of Am. As. to offer help of AWC for 1,200 interned Americans.

28, Wednesday: The Baxters came to look over possessions of J.H. Hefner family & Ruth Packard to tea. What a lot of talk about food! Plans announced by Japanese as to celebration here honoring fall of Singapore. Resign from positions held on Chinese boards, etc?

29, Thursday: Meyers family came to tea and also Eloise Bradshaw. Turned over to Hilda Haig books and outlines for U. of S. course which she will teach. Yenching teachers (Chinese) & students are in prison.

30, Friday: After teaching, a delicious luncheon with Mae Yang and Anne Mackeith. Investigating about lessons in Japanese. Mail in from Australia.

31, Saturday: Afternoon expedition — walking to West Gate — 7 or 8 miles — to see the Davises and Wests. Visited the Int. Inst. *pai lou* and the Pah Hsien Chiao Cemetery to show the children tomb of F. Moutrie, killed in 1879 by explosion during Grant's visit.

FEBRUARY 1942

1, Sun Royal spread at the Suensons' at tea time. Walked there and back. Eddie Wise was at church and how relieved we were to see him! American relief at SAS can house 1,000. Siege of Singapore begins.

2, Monday: Began lessons in Japanese, a 3 months' course at the Y.M.C.A. Eddie Wise and Nita here to dinner, Nita staying the night. Eddie told his amazing story of the "Harrison Maru". Nov. 4 (San Francisco) to January 27 (Shanghai). Sha Wei Shan, the chase, etc.

3, Tuesday: Church may be able to pay off debt on building by selling bonds to Chinese members. Jap. bank promises to return mortgage.

4, Wednesday: Lunch with Nita on Roi Albert and on to a Japanese lesson — 13 men + Anne MacKeith & me.

5, Thursday: Tea at Nell's where she had Shapiro (Polish), Lustig & Ehrlich (Czech), Mr & Mrs Yui. Nita & I spent the night. Social Dv. now investigating as to raw materials needed here so as to report to Planning Board in Tokyo in March. Harrop & Bojesen engaged.

6, Friday: Sent Eddie Pai off with a letter to apply to Nell for a job. New Year dish at Mae Yang's after a lesson. It is said that an international coupon can be got at Post Office for a letter to go via Int. Red Cr. Geneva. PO notified me to call for parcel mailed in October to Mother.

7, Saturday: A rainy afternoon at home. Bernard Read's 5th article on foods. Diets of children. Rice & flour both up in price. Bread 1.40 a lb.

8, Sunday: Guests to lunch: Yang & Hobbs. Betty home with a cold. Municipal Concert with Ruth Packard: Beethoven's 5th & Brandenburg Concerto.

9, Monday: Shopping for sugar & syrup. Japanese lesson. Papers say all Chinese must take a "new citizen" oath administered by Nanking regime.

10. Tue Jeanne came for the morning. Betty home with a cold. Jap. land on Singapore Island.

11, Wednesday: Made peanut brittle and cake for John. Betty home with cold. Jap. lessons continue interesting.

12, Thursday: Celebrated John's birthday at home with a chocolate cake. Went to PO to get package mailed last Oct. to Dallas. Was told to go home and wait for word from supervisor, since I am American. J. in Singapore. Medical exam.

13, Friday: Dot. Damsgaard taught me to mend stockings and stayed to lunch. Bobby & Mary came with gift for John. Van is letting us have 2 bags of flour.

14, Saturday: Snowy day—very cold. Delicious tiffin with May Yang. Nita came to spend the night and we had a valentine supper, as to decorations. Rice requisitioned by SMC. Accounts must be paid in Nanking money.

15, Sunday: Nita here for a breakfast celebration. Nell couldn't come because of ice and blockade. John preached at Church. We four lunched at Nita's. The church debt has been paid off & deeds are in our hands. Amazing Japanese!

16, Monday: Chinese N.Y. holiday. Visited McTyeire, Fengs, Van Hengels. Lunch at Mrs. Damsgaards. Numerous visitors in p.m. I called on Yang—Olive. Singapore captured.

17, Tuesday: Ruth Packard spent the morning & stayed to lunch. We talked of "Imperialism & World Politics." Bridge at Mary Edwards. Downtown still blockaded—Yuyaching to the Bund—because of 4 bombs Sat. night. Navy wants money from firms. Mac used her Jap. to get thru barrier.

18, Wednesday: LCH still blockaded, so Anne MacKeith came here for the night. First evening engagement since Dec. 8: dinner and bridge with Bernard Read & Dr. Earle.

19, Thursday: Read *Pillars of Society* & taught May Yang. Chiang & Mme in India seeing Gandhi and Nehru. Japan has returned Br. Concessions in Tientsin & Canton to Nanking gov. 2 day celebration of fall of Singapore, now Shonan.

20, Friday: Sent postcards to USA, Eng, Ger. All foods higher because yen & Nanking money are in demand, *fa pi* being pushed out.

21, Saturday: Nita came and we had lunch on the porch in the sun. Marion Harrop spent the weekend, newly engaged to Chris Bojesen. N & I read Nehru's *Toward Freedom*. Eddie Wise & Tommy Pond came for dinner & bridge.

22, Sunday: Marion & Chris & Miss Tsai Sui feng to lunch. Morley family to tea, using red, white & blue decorations. Story of how the Russians built hay fires 1 mile by 6 feet on road leading to Moscow & drove Germans back.

23, Monday: *Pai lous*, lights, parades, flags to celebrate fall of Singapore, 2 weeks' celebration. M. Schniermacher lunch. Jap. lessons very pleasant. Nita & I spent the night for the last time in Nell's 1001.

24, Tuesday: Nell thinks she will resign because she sees Shanghai industry will be used by Japanese war planners. Disagreeable waiting of 1½ hrs in line to change at par 50 for national money to Central Reserve (Nanking) money, now required by SMC. Soon by utilities.

25, Wednesday: YW had a meeting at Ethel's to hear about closing of hostel. Hospital is still blockaded so Mac came for the night. Farquharson has typhus. Eddie Pai got the SMC job. Broke my glasses, alas. $34 for a new lens.

26, Thurs Went at last to try on wool dress in Lily's since last Nov.
Decided that next winter I'd be glad I'd paid $100 for it now
Decided to see dentist also. B. Read says the stale flour won't
hurt us so we'll eat it, but ugh, the taste. Hospital blockade still
very fierce.

27, Friday: Nita brought her drama class to hear the *Mikado* records.
Two days ago we could change $1,000 into Central Res. notes,
but now only $300. All SMC accounts must be paid in those.

28, Saturday: Afternoon spent in Jessfield with Nita, M.L.
Saunders, Hilda Haig. Tea with Caroline Chen. Foreigners in
Union School have been asked to withdraw. John must answer
on Monday the demand that schools which closed must open
and carry on.

MARCH 1942

1, Sunday: Nell came to lunch. First day back in 504 for her. Large late evening with Wise & Kay, roast beef & Eddie's Alaska pictures. Talk turned to confiscation of motor cars, now underway, and the wretched condition of Br. & Am. prisoners in B.H. A. Damsgaard has returned having been thru the siege of Hong Kong.

2, Monday: Lunch with Nita at Roi Albert and then we read Nehru. Walked in the rain to Cafe Federal and then on to Jap. class. Blockade still on, more than 2 weeks, so Mac came again. Breakfast syrup jumped from $3.50 to $4.80 a jug, alas.

3, Tuesday: The Days and Mrs Nash came to tea. Now people are required to push their cars to the Ford Hire station to turn them over. Eve Curie reported to be in Chungking.

4, Wednesday: Farquharson died of typhus. M. Schniermacher came to lunch, looking thinner & paler than ever. Caviar is half the price of butter.

5, Thursday: Visit to the dentist. Left Miss Yang's early and just got home before the barriers were put up. John at six could not get through & went to the Blackstone for the night. Had to cancel tomorrow's bridge.

6, Friday: Blockade narrowed down & John got to school & home. Farquharson funeral at Bubbling Well. "Tea party" at Mrs Sun's. Marion Dudley interned in H.K. J. have taken 20 to 30 people here for questioning. J.B. Powell to have military trial.

7, Saturday: Blessed hot water for washing & baths. Rosie came to help children with first principles of composing. Walked in pm up to Jeanne's for mint, potatoes, etc. Actually found 2 lemons for the carrot marmalade.

8, Sunday: The 4 Hsias & Nell came to lunch. 1937 Medhurst Class to tea, then Bernard. They have a supervisor at the Lester office & expect also a technical supervisor.

9, Monday: To Auxiliary Tiffin (32 present) where Li Djoh-i spoke on work with delinquent boys. On to see Floryne Miller about Japanese books.

10, Tuesday: To Miss Knox's big tea (about 50) for Hobb's birthday. Demand for CRB notes increases. People stand in line for hours & can get none. Is this a flurry or not. Jap. have Java.

11, Wednesday: Bread must be paid for in CRB. Nita came to lunch. Walked with her to Joffre to try on dress & back along Haig to lay in more food. Japanese lesson & home, dead tired.

12, Thursday: School holiday spent trying trying to buy more food before *fa pi* is discounted. Salmon increased from 4.80 to 6.40 overnight.

13, Friday: 11−4 bridge. Mary Edwards, Vanda Roper, Sonia Kucej. SMC stops native rice coming in so price has soared to $50 for 17 lbs. Water bill must be paid in CRB.

14, Saturday: More panic over devalued money. Shops are beginning to require CRB. Matches, salt, candles now unprocurable, as sugar, soap, flour are. Cornish pasties with the Morleys, followed by bridge.

15, Sunday: Imported articles up 30% more. Rice $720 per gel (?). Stine came for the day and we received lettuce seedlings when we took her home. Medhurst '39 boys to tea (16.) Betty's ear sore again. 243 at Church, back in auditorium.

16, Monday: Planted lettuce seedlings donated by Suenson. Maud Beynon came with a coat. CRB notes required by milk, bread, water, etc. companies, but notes are unprocurable. People buying soap and thread in quantities. No soap in most shops.

17, Tuesday: The J. took 150 crates to the RAS and carted away all the files of periodicals. They are taking away 100 trees from the U. of S. campus – hedges also.

18, Wednesday: First trip to SAS for ration of wheat, farina, oatmeal. They give also directions for "clearing infested grains." Struggles to buy soap and macaroni. Jap. lesson & visit from Eddie Pai.

19, Thursday: Nell came and sat in the sun while I planted lettuces. She brought magnolia buds. To the dentist & Miss Yang's. Eddie & Tommie to supper & bridge. Hart Westbrook says J. are taking away trees & flowers from campus.

20 Fri Bridge day at Mary's, with Vanda & Mrs Kucej. On to Nita's for the Poetry Club where Cheng Lo-chi spoke on the Chinese *tsu* poems, set to music. I dream at night of going to a food shop and finding the shelves empty.

21, Saturday: Mrs. Baxter, Ethel Taylor came to plan Marion's wedding reception. Betty and I spent the afternoon at the Suensons'. Geo. Osborn came visiting in the evening.

22, Sunday: Li Djoh-i and Tsai Mo-li came to lunch. Nita and I walked up to Ave. Haig to have tea with Nell. Broadcasts from Chungking are picked up here. Cripps flying to India. McArthur in Australia.

23, Monday: Down town to get margarine, glad to be on the list for a pound a week from China Soap Co. 4C supper at Community Church with Nita's household to see Eddie Wise's pictures of Alaska. J. say there are enemies, neutral enemies, friendly enemies.

24, Tuesday: CRB rates fixed at $1.30 *fa pi* for 1. Some people make a million on exchange while others lose steadily. Japanese to be taught in all SMC schools. Jeanne came round to stitch.

25, Wednesday: Busy day at washing woolies – hot water on a sunny day. Jap. lesson Tale of sugar: Mar. 4, 10 lbs = $24.50; Mar. 21, $40.00; 22, $43.00; 23, $44.00; 24, $46.50; Mar. 27 $50.00

26, Thursday: Taught May Yang. Anna West's funeral at Bubbling Well. Saw *Man of Conquest* (Houston) with Nell at Cathay, first movie since the war began (Dec. 8)

27, Friday: Lunch at Sun Ya with Mrs Kucej & bridge at the YMCA Lounge with Mary & Vanda. Rumors of blockade. Wang Ching-wei, etc. Bought $300 CRB for $390. Must pay $18 CRB in advance for 10 breads.

28, Saturday: Ethel came for weekend. Lester Institute had visit from high official. Will their current expense check be cashed? Asia Dev. Board will take control of commodities, prices, etc. Bakerite taken over. 64 firms to be taken over.

29, Sunday: The Baxters came to lunch after preaching & organ recital at Community Church. Church deeds returned by Swiss Consulate, not accepting such papers now. Cook departed & new man arrived with daughter. Purchased $1,000 supplies ahead.

30, Monday: More trouble at post office trying to retrieve parcel sent to Mother. Require certificate from Swiss Consulate. Arranged with Hawkings re Bojesen honeymoon. Registered for repatriation at Am As.

31, Tuesday: Betty's play at school. She was the Fairy Godmother, a principal in *Cinderella*. Shanghai Com YW meeting to discuss cooperation, etc. Bought electric plate against possible coal shortage. Coal balls full of mud — no use. Scripps gives Br. plan to India.

APRIL 1942

1, Wednesday: Sat in Nita's garden after school to see the cherry blossoms against Chinese roof & blue sky. Planted more lettuce seedlings. Began intermediate Japanese class. More shops changed over to CRB currency.

2, Thursday: Rushed out to buy flour & sugar. Coffee too dear. S&W $40 a lb. Loose cheapest 16.00. Arranged for Marion's wedding at church. Went to Jeanne's for anniversary tea party, Sunday: & Pan guests to dinner before going interior — Siaowu.

3, Friday: Nita came and we talked war. We went to hear the Cantonese Church choir sing the Crucifixion. Nell says the Ger. consul general has protested to the SMC against employment of Jews. They go half around the world and still meet discrimination.

4, Saturday: Marion Harrop — Chris Bojesen wedding at Community Church & reception. Rain. Nita came for the night & we had supper with Grace Yang & Myra Olive. Olivers there. Talk of J. visit to her school & of parcel snatching.

5, Sunday: Easter. Nita entertained us & Nell at breakfast at our house. Nell brought white lilac and we later walked to church. Lunch and Beethoven's Ninth Symphony at McTyeire. Tea at Jeanne's & the Symphony with Ruth Packard.

6, Mon To St. John's for Jui Hong-jih's wedding & luncheon. Blockade in pm. J & Betty went to Nita's, Dick stayed at Tulloch's. J. got home at 10:30. Hefner family came here & prepared to spend the night but left at 10 when barriers were lifted. Cripps still in India.

7, Tuesday: Marion Morley came for the day and Mary Edwards to help me "landscape" the garden. British embassy folk have had word that they will leave at end of April.

8, **Wednesday:** Last of school holidays. Betty had Stine, Jill, Christine, Elizabeth to tea celebrating her birthday. Todman & Fuller on way to interior via India. Cripps mission to India apparently failing.

9, **Thursday:** Planted lettuces from Meyers. Taught Yang and went to Jap. class. Embassy departures delayed till end of May. J. want to evacuate by areas. America by condition of people. All interior foreigners in oc. areas being brought to Shanghai.

10, **Friday:** A day with the tailor letting down dresses. Children report that all Br police families are going to Australia. Ian Tulloch for the day.

11, **Saturday:** Ruth Packard came for the weekend. We went to Cachita's for *mien* & spring rolls with the Tiffin Club. Nell came to say that SMC people are No. 3 on list for repatriation. She has cabled V. to see IFC (?) and she hopes to get to Montreal.

12, **Sunday:** Symphonies in the morning as we sat on the veranda. Nita came in the afternoon – also Eddie Pai with many gifts and B. Read. Read *Europe in the Spring*.

13, **Monday:** Took children for physical exam. O.K. Missionaries from occupied China coming to Shanghai for repatriation. It looks as if everybody may go. First ships now scheduled for late May. Mission making list of those to go in order.

14, **Tuesday:** Finally got mother's Xmas parcel out of the PO after many complications. Saw Baxter with reference to repatriation. Thinks children & I should go to USA. Money for maintenance might be arranged.

15, **Wednesday:** Typhoid & cholera shots. Collected wheat ration at SAS. Phil Sullivan & Harrison King came at 5 to play bridge & have dinner. Bicycles now cost $1,700 and up to $5,000. Insurance companies taken over. Churches, schools, Y's filling out blanks. More students off to interior.

16, Thursday: Bread up again from $1.80 to 2.05 a lb. Repatriates arrived from Chefoo by ship. Housed & confined in hotels. J. pushing for total Am Br. evacuation. Nita's house filling up.

17, Friday: Hu Yih's wedding at Golden Garden Restaurant. White rented dresses. Too bad! Anti-Br-Am seals under glass table tops. Int. Br. Com. meeting & on to Poetry Club at Dr. Lawney's where she read *Free of Medusa* by Hermann Hagedorn. Walls are broken down by the courtesy of Jap. inspectors, etc.

18, Saturday: The Morleys 4 came for the day. After a good Chinese tiffin we played bridge. Mr. Baxter thinks I'll be put in a special category and will have little chance of taking the children to the U.S. I don't want to go elsewhere.

19, Sunday: Reported that Tokyo, Osaka, Nagoya have been bombed. Dick & J to Mac's birthday celebration. Betty & I in all day.

20, Monday: Spent the morning interviewing Swiss Consulate, Am. As. & Sakamoto about getting children into America. Cooking class at YW and on to J. lesson. Children home from school because of barriers. Reported that Wang Ching Wei is in town.

21, Tuesday: Nita came to lunch and Ruth Packard joined us to talk about war attitudes. J & I went to Mary Edwards' to play bridge & have dinner with Jansens, B. Read, E. Wise, & W. Leete. Nita at home in USA would tackle negro problem & Ruth would preach "no nationalism."

22, Wednesday: A busy day with hot water, the tailor & study. E. Wise says in Hongkew shops J. refuse to serve foreigners. Dwight telegraphed for Mary to come to Chungking. How could he! Barnett, Todman, Fuller, Gale reported in Chungking. Dick caught in blockade.

23, Thursday: Ship arrived from South bringing 110 repatriates.

Taught Yang & went to Jap. class. They say now that the first ship will go in June.

24, Friday: A day at home sunning things & reading. Many planes overhead. They are bombing nearby airdrome because of the bombing of J. cities. Think planes may have come from China.

25, Saturday: Exam at school 2nd 6 weeks finished. 23 students. Betty to Christine's and to Stine's party. John & I had tea with Nell at the Phillips. Hayim & Woodhead released. Called on van den Berg at Cathay Mansions, filling out forms and calling at liaison offices.

26, Sunday: Old Boys to tea. Took Betty to Jill's. The Meyers garden is beautiful.

27, Monday: Latest rumor: Americans will be repatriated via Vladivostok, not Lorenzo Marques. Sakamoto telephoned that I'll be able to take children to USA.

28, Tuesday: The Wallaces of Swatow came to lunch. They were 130 on a small ship coming up. Sleep in hold and were treated wretchedly before leaving & after.

29, Wednesday: Abe, just returned, sent for YW representative and announced that a rep. would come from Tokyo. Demanded that a telegram of welcome be sent today. Ruth came for the afternoon. Great doings in honour of the Emperor's birthday.

30, Thursday: Clipping on subject of Cultural Aggression. J. lessons proceed with interest. Shops have most things, but prices are sky high. Lettuce now ready to eat.

MAY 1942

1, Fri To the Clube Lusitano to help prepare for Ministering Children's Bazaar. Betty had tooth pulled by Dr. Wong. Now we hear that no civilians will be evacuated. Officials in Nov. SMC balances budget by taxation and economies.

2, Saturday: MCL Bazaar a great success. Stine came home with Betty for the night. Jeanne came to lunch. Roses & lettuce from our garden.

3, Sunday: George Osborn preached at C.C. He came back to lunch with us, as also Maurice Gordon, Hart Westbrook, Harold Snuggs. Betty to the King-Symphony-Ballet. Woolen singlet = $1,600. Bicycle $9,000 (some Eng. parts.)

4, Monday: Watched Marguerite Hsia make Chinese dishes at YW. Economy class. Then to Jap. lesson. Barricade for an hour, Sunned the smelly flour and collected 2 rations of cracked wheat from BRA. J. take Mandalay. Hitler & Mus have meet.

5, Tuesday: Hot water day. M. Schniermacher turned up. Gave her hot water for bath & hot tea. She wants to sell soap! Sid and A.E. came to dinner.

6, Wednesday: Lunch and the afternoon with Nita. Those sending food to JBP (?) have been asked to send it no more. W.F. caught. U. of S. will have summer school & will continue next year as far as is known.

7, Thursday: To see Margery Farquharson. Her small son Peter died of gastric flu last night. So much for her to bear. Latest rumour: Nanking bombed by guerrillas. USA has chartered Swedish Gripsholm for repatriation. To leave Sweden May 23 for NY.

8, Friday: Sent off letters of 25 words thru Int. Red Cross to Dallas and Drumloist. Latest rumor: 4 Jap. ships leaving early June to take repatriates to Lourenco Marques. E.C. Lin of Peking called.

9, Saturday: Trams placarded with colored announcements of Corregidor's fall. Big naval battle in Coral Sea. McTyeire folk (5) came to Chinese supper. Tea at Mrs McLorn's. Peter Farquharson's funeral.

10, Sunday: A warm-cool day in Jeanne's garden, having tea among the roses. Sid Anderson preaching at Church. 2 J. YWCA people due May 20. Pressure falls fast. John's exchanged shoes have rubber tire soles. Pressure on T sha (?) by asking to social.

11, Monday: Discussion of Household Economies at YWCA. J. lesson. Bacon $11.00 per lb.

12. Tue Nell had the first letter from V. dated Feb. 23. I went down to supper over it. Cook sick. Unsatisfactory substitute. Paid $65 for 5 lbs of ham.

13, Wednesday: A terrible day with a substitute cook who couldn't manage the stove. To SAS to get wheat ration. Geo. & Mrs. Wu to dinner & CC Lin.

14, Thursday: Taught Mae Yang & went to Jap. lesson. Hunted for mustard powder — not to be found. Germans pressing in Kerch (?) peninsula.

15, Friday: Very good concert by Andie Lee (Mrs Chow Ting Wei) at Jewish Club. YW meeting at Jeanne's. Went scouring for cherries, cocoa, etc. Fresh fruit too high, must hunt cheaper Chinese tins.

16, Saturday: Meeting of Children's Aid Committee at Chinese Medical Association where parents and adopted children also met. A great inspiration. Nell received cable from V. "Invitation arranged. Accept repatriation." Nita to supper. We wrote message for Waxahachie to go by Red Cross.

17, Sunday: Very fine semi-annual meeting at Church, showing progress, many people carrying responsibility. Stanley Smith serving another year. John as chairman for 2 years has done a good job. Harold & Vera Nash arrived from Nanking.

18, Monday: Wet cold day. Still struggling with substitute cook. Jap. lesson with a story.

19. Tue With Nell to Okazaki's Cocktail party at Cathay Hotel. Had to leave tram to be searched on way home. Cook Wong setting up vegetable shop came for help. Harold Nash sleeping in guest room. Nell had 2nd cable from V.

20, Wednesday: Bridge with Kucej, Mary at Vanda's 11 – 5. On to tea with Ruth Packard. Utilities increase costs by 2 & 3 times. Still sleeping under 3 blankets.

21, Thursday: A day for repairs – refrigerator $80.00, watch CRB25, etc. Visited the market, taught Yang, Jap. class. More troubles with substitute cook.

22, Friday: Waffle party with chicken à la king provided by Jeanne, Ruth, Lydia. Scrumptious. Others have arrived from the South. Nobody knows yet who goes on the ships, but everybody talks of repatriation.

23, Saturday: A day of mishaps trying to cook on the old coal stove. A beggar snatched the bread from Dick. The delivery man wouldn't leave the bacon because the cook hadn't right change. Exchange differs every day $100CRB=160 *fa pi*. To Suensons' for corn.

24, Sunday: Bottom falling out of the dollar. Prices soaring. Now 2 *fa pi* for $1CRB. Had lunch with Nell on Haig. The Sakamotos and Mrs. Fukuda came to tea. One YWCA person / Hikaru has arrived from Japan.

25, Monday: A hectic day of buying CRB notes and provisions. Crowds of sober people on streets. Exchange shops mobbed. Caught in two blockades. Nuisance they are. Jap. class. Whit Monday holiday for children.

26, Tuesday: To Ruth Clark's at tea time to hear Geo. Stacey read letter from Alice in camp in Manila. Crowded conditions. They know nothing of what happens here. More frantic buying of CRB dollars. Rates from 2.00 to 2.70.

27, Wednesday: Spring cleaning in the kitchen. Such dirt and smoke! Bought more CRB. Official rate now 2 for 1.

28, Thursday: Another day of buying tinned goods before prices climb higher. The same tomato juice is 3.30, 3.60, 2.75 CRB in different shops.

29, Friday: A busy day – the hot water on – washing everything. We must have the stove on only once in 2 weeks after this to save coal for winter.

30, Saturday: Beginning of Br. – Am. Annihilation Week. Posters everywhere & parades & meetings. Tea with Ruth Packard. Nita & Mr Sawyer there. Christine Eggo here for the day. Am. evacuation June 10 – 15. Br. a month later.

31, Sunday: Organ Concert by Dent at Church. To the Church of our Saviour to see E.S. Yu consecrated Bishop. Very significant, colorful. Tea with the Wallaces (of Swatow) in Beverley House. Still sleeping under 3 blankets & wearing coats.

JUNE 1942

1, Monday: More money difficulties. Farmers Bank notes not accepted. 2% tax on all purchases. *Fa pi* cannot be used after June 22. 10% tax in hotels, etc. Prices soaring! 1¼ yds ribbon $10.10. Nita came to lunch. We read *King Rich. III*. Jap. class. 20 Medhurst Seniors here to tea.

2, Tuesday: A day at home pressing and putting away Bathrobes. Ruth P. dropped in. Read *Richard III*. Wanting news from home.

3, Wednesday: Witnessed the "great" Anti-allied parade and demonstration from the tram window. Lunch with the Blacks. Myra Olive and Grace Yang to dinner and bridge. 6 foreigners sentenced for espionage.

4, Thursday: Called on Mr Lockhart at Cathay Mansions. He says he'll write Mother a note. Americans scheduled to leave June 15, Britons in August. Tram fares doubled and put into CRB which makes 4 times. Phone also -

5, Friday: Dick's school sports. 5th Performance of *Richard III* (ADC) not given because of Jap. instructions. What of Nita's party for Saturday! U. of S. Commencement at Majestic Theatre. Medhurst teachers decide to carry on school. If we four went 3rd class on tram to Hongkew Park — Cost $11.50.

6, Saturday: J. refused to let the ADC continue presenting *Richard III*. No answer till we went to Lyceum, then notice put up. No one knows why. J. take over Amer. Sch. putting out those living there & keeping whatever furniture they want. Grand tea at Nita's.

7, Sunday: Old Boys' tea at Yu Cheng-chung's home on Sayzoong. Many people getting several cholera inoculations in order to sell passes.

8, Monday: First day without school. Radio reports big battle near Midway. Went to demonstration of class work at Technical School for Machine Shop workers. SMC. Medhurst will open summer school. New committee.

9, Tuesday: Final exam at school. Tea in Nita's garden with Nell & Chu Yu-bao. Nell knows a man who has been told he's to go on the ship. Nell saw the letter. Conte Verde said to be in Japan getting ready.

10, Wednesday: Tea at Church for new members. First list released for the repatriation ship. Americans arrive from Hangchow, Hankow, Tsingtao. Housed at Columbia Club. Spring cleaning of 3rd floor.

11, Thursday: Busy day washing hair, clothes, etc. Hot water once in 2 weeks. Hot water coming out of a pipe seems almost a miracle. Repatriates' luggage to be ready Saturday. Not known when ship goes next week.

12, Friday: YW committee met here—10 present. Columbia Club is a sight—weeds outside, repatriates inside. All had various experiences with their particular J. branch.

13, Saturday: John & I walked, in spite of blockades, to Mary Louise Allman's to get some books. Wallace had heard that Churchill sent message: no British to evacuate. Nita spent the morning. A.E. and Graham to dinner & bridge.

14, Sunday: Church crowded with American repatriates. Blanche Groves & Nita came to lunch. Wallace of Swatow preached very appropriately. Bernard Read came round. Powell, Woodhead, Opper to be tried for espionage.

15, Monday: Went to Jeanne's to see Hazel Myers who came with repatriates. 300+ now at Columbia Club. Town full of rumors, Money situation very tense. To Jap. class and on to 4C's weenie supper at Church with musical program.

16, Tuesday: To the Church for Auxiliary sale and back in pm to Petain for tea honoring Miss Knox. CRB not being accepted in some shops. Making apricot jam and grapefruit marmalade. Ship to leave June 24 or 25.

17, Wednesday: Bridge here with Mary Edwards, Sonia Kucej, Vanda Roper. Ship to leave June 26 – 28. Letters from Chengtu reached Lydia – dated April 25 – from Maud who has TB.

18, Thursday: Busy cleaning house. Dragon Boat Festival. Beulah Chang sent *tsung tzus* and eggs. Press gangs are busy taking Chinese off streets, police under orders to assist.

19, Friday: Nita and I went in the rain to visit repatriates at the Columbia Club – crowded in like sardines – some without baggage. Li Djoh-i called.

20, Saturday: Ruth Packard arrived to spend her 2 weeks holiday with us. Reverses in Russia, in Lybia, in China, all around.

21, Sunday: 550+ at church – the farewell service for repatriates. Mary Louise Allman & the McCrackens are to go. Hazel Myers came to lunch and the Blacks to tea. The Conte Verde sails Wed. June 24 – 11 a.m.

22, Monday: Beulah Chang came to lunch. Had dinner at the Lester. Tobruk taken by Axis.

23, Tuesday: Repatriation ship postponed several days. We went round to get some of B. Read's books. The Lester Institute has been taken over and he will have to move.

24, Wednesday: Prize-giving at Betty's school. Nell came in the afternoon for a visit. Powell & Opper are to go on the repatriation ship. Barbara Adams, too, & husband. 4 Br & 1 Danish husband going.

25, Thurs Jap. lesson. Churchill in Washington. Axis forces in Egypt. Repatriation ship to leave June 29. Abe back from Japan, apparently having won out.

26, Friday: Margaret McFarlane, Angus, Fiona returned from

Manila concentration camp on a ship with officials. Wonders never cease. Still very cool. Blankets at night Took letter to Blanche Groves & saw Tsang.

27, Saturday: Went to the Roxy to Nell's showing of *Blossoms in the Dust*, in effort to stimulate the finding of homes for children. Went to see Nita, sick with chill & fever, and on to dinner at Eddie Wise's. W. Furnas is going on the C. Verde.

28, Sunday: The Angus family – Mrs & 3 children – came to lunch and rushed back for baggage inspection. Conte Verde leaving tomorrow. Kay & others say there will a second ship about September. J with tummy upset.

29, Monday: Up at 4:30 and walked in rain to the Bund to farewell repatriates on Conte Verde. 22 buses & 3 ambulances pulled up and discharged the 639.

30, Tuesday: Rosa May came and stayed on for supper and the night. We played bridge till 12. Germans in Egypt, 120 miles from Alexandria. Two registrations necessary: BRA for identification cards; police for *Pao Chia* records. 3 pictures of each member of the family.

JULY 1942

1, **Wednesday:** Dick's party for 8 boys and girls. Indoor games. Ruth had a letter from USA via Chengtu dated May 5. Many planes flying low these few days.

2, **Thursday:** Bridge four at Mary Edwards' with a bang up old time tea including iced coffee. Stowaway on Conte Verde was brought back. Busy at homely tasks in the morning with Ruth. First really hot day.

3, **Friday:** Nita came for the day. Ruth and I went to see *Maytime*. Nell developing staff & program to find homes for the many children being abandoned. Summoned to AMT for disbursement, due to imminent troubles. Churches, too, tis said.

4, **Saturday:** Ruth took the children and me to see *Prince & Pauper* at the Doumer. Eddie Wise came for dinner & bridge. Scorching hot day.

5, **Sunday:** A hot day spent at home. Christian organizations warned that something's ahead. Black dispersing his fund. For. churches on the list. Many people sick due to diet deficiencies.

6, **Monday:** Ruth P. returned home after 2 weeks with us. Took Dick to Dunlap, who suggests some food allergy. Betty spending the day with the Meyers. Feeling rotten myself — indigestion. J.H. and E.R. Hughes both in interior.

7, **Tuesday:** Delayed by a blockade, we were late to Mr Baxter's 60th birthday tea at the Harmon flat. Special Municipality having summer school for principals — 3 weeks at McTyeire. Nellie Murray sent cabled news of Black-Baxter families.

8, **Wednesday:** Tenth wedding anniversary. Nita came to dinner & we saw *Cheers for Miss Bishop* at the Cathay. Thinking of a chafing dish by way of celebration. J. propaganda preceded *Miss Bishop*, excellent Allied propaganda. John went for wheat ration but found them not giving.

9, Thursday: John, Betty & I went to dinner at McTyeire where also were Van Hengels, Ruth, Lydia, Sid, Phil et al. There was a spectacular shooting star. Mrs U. has returned home leaving Miss H. here.

10, Friday: Stine here for the day & Mr & Mrs Suenson to supper. Reading Moon's *Imperialism & World Politics*. J. is following the pattern even to the language used.

11, Saturday: Nita's for the day. Nell, Ruth, Inabelle came to tea. Still bothered by indigestion.

12, Sunday: A day at home recovering from ills — Bernard Read came.

13, Monday: Mrs Tang & Mrs Hsueh came to tea — and Ruth. Dick still sick — tummy. *Pao Chia* census forms turned in. Betty & John went for 2nd cholera shot.

14, Tuesday: A busy day with hot water. Moon's *Imperialism* almost finished. Can we build on the Mandate System after this war?

15, Wednesday: On the second trip to the Health Office got 2nd cholera shot. Very pleasant tea with Mae Yang — Mrs Kwouk, Mrs Tang, Miss Pen.

16, Thursday: John and I had dinner with Nita & household, the Shens, and Suns. Finished Moon's *Imperialism & World Politics*. 74 Br. police officials dismissed and replaced by Japanese.

17, Friday: A very happy birthday. Breakfast with Nita. Calls from Jeanne, Ruth, Lydia, Rosie, Nell. Called on the McLorns and Rene Morley in the afternoon. J went to investigate what was happening at church. Fence must go up to prevent noise.

18, Saturday: Nell came for a visit in the afternoon. Wrote first letters in 6 months — to Maud et al and Nellie in Chengtu. Betty to Christine's. Entrance exams at school. Took in 75 of 112.

19, Sunday: A hot Sunday to sit in church. Lydia has had a cable from Sarah advising repatriation and saying subsistence to be discontinued shortly. Fence up around church garden.

20, Monday: Read *Seven for a Secret* (Mary Webb) and *Mein Kampf*. Went to have tea with the Morleys and fetch Betty. Nita & Mary Lucile came after supper to tell the tale of the cook's departure.

21, Tuesday: Forenoon in town seeing after chafing dish, etc. To the Suensons' where 3 children (Ger., Danish, Br.) gave performance. Bunton and Nina Troy to supper.

22, Wednesday: To Yangtzepoo with Vanda & Mary to play bridge with Mrs Kucej. Typhoon winds terrific, but no rain.

23, Thursday: Rosa May Butler came for the night. Bernard Read to supper and bridge. He's moving to the Jessfield Rd. compound. 2,500 – 3,000 in 5 Jewish refugee camps. 1,800 people get 12 oz bread per day. Applying to SMC for camp maintenance.

24, Friday: Nell goes on the first ship. D, B and I went to Jeanne's to a tea celebration of Lydia's birthday. J. went to NCC meeting discussing repatriation, future work, cooperation, etc. Nell asked to vacate Hamilton.

25, Saturday: The Wallace family of 4 came for the day. Repatriates must depart without any idea of where they go after Africa. It looks as if we may stay on in this house for 6 mo. but no longer.

26, Sunday: J in bed with pain in back. Blanks from Suzuki filled in by church. Great hunt for recipes. How sick I get of the same old foods we have!

27, Monday: Baked bread and cinnamon rolls for a welcome change. Griffiths family to supper. BRA has objected to so few Shanghai people getting on ship, so changes. YW busy throwing away after *pao chia* warning.

28, Tuesday: Marion and Elizabeth Morley for the day. Rene & Mr to tea and bridge. Nell still has no definite word as to departure. John still with pain in back.

29, Wednesday: Nita came to lunch and we read Nehru. Went to the Swiss Consulate to inquire about repatriation and on to Nell's for tea and cranberry sauce! Dr. Tagawa and Mr. Sohn came to dinner.

30, Thursday: Jeanne, Lydia, Ruth came to call on John. Mrs. Griffiths came to stitch. Terribly hot. Civil air defense proclamation.

31, Friday: Went with Nita to call on Mrs Sheriff at St. John's. The Blacks looking frantically for a place to live, seeing A B's are to be ousted. M. Schniermacher called. They get a little bread each day.

AUGUST 1942

1, Saturday: Christine here for the day with Betty. To Nita's to dinner—also Nell & Vic Hanson—so cool in the garden. They have our former servants. Police families must vacate in 2 weeks.

2, Sunday: Wrote to Brenda, hoping to send it by the Griffiths who leave tomorrow. To tea with Ruth Packard to meet the Wong-Quincys. J.H. Suns also there.

3, Monday: Dorothy Day came with clothes for Dick. Betty at Stine's making a play. Went for bread ration cards. Read *Mein Kampf*—vicious stuff. The Jap. who announced a changed number at Orch. Concert wore kimono & spoke in Jap. only.

4, Tuesday: First Br. repatriation ship—Tatuta—left at 1 p.m. carrying 800, including 115 Indians "for personal reasons." Saw Haefeli of Swiss Consulate who says I come along with marine wives in classification. Short visit from Mrs Hsueh regarding YW agenda.

5, Wednesday: Sizzling hot. YW meeting at Mrs. Zau's. Our advisers think we should seem to be doing some work. Both have returned to J. Long promised ice cream party on Keissling & Bader roof: Jeanne, Van, Lydia, Ruth, Nita, Jackie & we 4.

6, Thursday: Miserable days—perishingly hot, continuous digestive troubles.

7, Friday: Nita came for the day and we read Nehru and dripped. Dinner at J.H, Sunday:'s with Nell, Mrs Hsueh, Mrs Tang, Ruth, Lydia.

8, Saturday: Wash day for hair, clothes, chair covers. Joan Read came to supper. Bread was a failure. Heat continues unabated.

Sleeping in the garden is the one salvation. Prickly heat terrible.

9, Sunday: Had Nita and household to supper. Gave for them the program of pieces and music.

10, Monday: Nell has final word & is leaving. We gave the program of poems and music after dinner, serving dessert to 14−4 from "98," 7 from McTyeire, Nell, Sid, Nina. Still steaming hot. Saw Ward. He says Cat. 1?

11, Tuesday: Went to Jeanne's, taking Betty and Chrissy to a splash party and tea. Nana Black and Margery Farquharson are to repatriate on Aug. 16. Went round to say farewell to the Eggos.

12, Wednesday: Dinner with the MacFarlanes. A.E. has letter from Barbara dated Apr. 4. Had Con in to deal with stressing continence. Disgusting. Wrote letters to Mother & Brenda to go on Kamakura with repatriates.

13, Thursday: A miserably hot day to lie abed. Chrissy spending the day with Betty, who had an infected toe. Dick with "swimmer's ear" which Dunlap had to open. Too many ailments.

14, Friday: Many people from North China have arrived but will not be repatriated on this Kamakura. Nana takes 6 children. Cook family all divided − mother on one ship, father on another, children on this. Morleys brought Chummy so we have a dog.

15, Saturday: Another day in bed. Nita came after lunch. Dick very sick with earache. Very bad news from Russia & Japs report great victory in Solomon Islands.

16, Sunday: Still recumbent. Rosa May came bringing pineapple juice for the invalids. All repatriates took baggage to Club for inspection & received their tickets. Nita off to South Gate for a holiday.

17, Monday: Eloise brought peaches; old cook, pears. Up at 5 and to the Jetty to wave Nell off. Saw also the Ellis Hayims and Mardens. Nana Black and Margery Farquharson left. At noon to St. George's to see off the Morleys & the Eggos. Kamakura sails at 6 pm.

18 Tues John went to visit the dozens out at the Columbia Club. Their plight seems sad, with no definite prospect of departure. Dick back to Dunlap for his ear.

19, Wednesday: Jeanne came with tomato juice; Inabelle Coleman with almond cakes. Still lying flat and not liking it. Read *Shadows on the Rock*.

20, Thursday: Still abed.

21, Friday: Off to Lester Hospital. Blood test. Unsuccessful lumbar puncture.

22, Saturday: In hospital. Lumbar puncture.

23, Sunday: In hospital. Visits from John, Betty, Nita.

24, Monday: In hospital. Gastro analysis. Off to Nita's after lunch. J. announce two American repatriation ships to leave Sept. 7. What upheavals!

25, Tuesday: Shopping for Betty's hat ($15.00) and shoes ($117.30.) Still on holiday with Nita. All Americans wondering who'll be chosen to go. Air raid blackout 7:30 – 11:30 with scout planes inspecting & dropping flares. Full moon & clouds in Nita's Chinese garden – something to remember.

26, Wednesday: Home from Nita's wondering as to repatriation.

27, Thursday: Ruth Packard spent the morning. Took two cotton dresses to Mode to be made.

28, Friday: Summoned to American Association to sign statement accepting repatriation, "if offered." Purchased two new cases. Went with John to the meeting at the Lester.

29, Saturday: Packed a trunk of linen, bedding, silver. Later heard rumor that those three cannot be taken. Rumor: big trunks of other repatriates still here. Dinner with Grace Yang & Myra Olive – 4 doctors, 4 teachers there.

30, Sunday: House tailor and wash man busily engaged. Sorting and packing all the day. Callers: Andrew Wu, Mrs Sun, Mrs

Nash.

31, Monday: Am. As. asks for photos and birth certificates of children. Latest report: only hand luggage can be taken. Callers: J. C. & John Hsia, Bernard Read, Li Djoh-i, Mrs Kyte, Mrs Suenson, Stine. Nita took Betty to Dr. Tsang.

SEPTEMBER 1942

1, Tuesday: Children & John off to school. Industrial & Social Division Committee approved Employment Service. Ship postponed indefinitely. Question: operation? Con says I must take hydrochloric acid.

2, Wednesday: Ship may go about Sep. 20. YW tea at Mrs Loh's with speeches and gifts of jade. Rumors: Ship's delayed because

3, Thursday: Town to collect passport & certificates at Swiss Consulate. Great crowds around stores with prices "controlled." Delightful tea at Mrs Sun's and dinner at T.Z. Koo's with flute music afterward.

4, Friday: To Nita's for a visit and on to the Suensons' for butter cake at tea. Hart W. & Harold S. came visiting.

5, Saturday: Beynon family to lunch. YWCA Int. Br. meeting at Jeanne's, elected her chairman. Dick sold train for $150 with $40 going to middlemen. Preparing AWC to take 100 men from North.

6, Sunday: After church May Yang & Li Djoh-i came to tiffin. Nita came in. Also Grace Yang looking for a house. Dance music censored. Paper has article on re-planning Shanghai. Stalingrad fall reported.

7, Monday: Trip to town to get money and do errands. M. Schniermacher came to tell of their new position. Dinner with the Baxters, all 4. Hospitals & various firms taken over. Foreigners being ousted from houses.

8, Tuesday: To Riddell to have tooth filled and to see Frau Hepner. How can she stand it! With the Chens to see *Ch'un (Spring.)* Newest Chinese movie at Majestic. Began taking hydrochloric.

9, **Wednesday:** Conte Verde arrived in the river with white crosses painted out. Rumor: no repatriation this year. Lester to have J. superintendent on Friday. Busy day washing & ironing. Betty to the Caters.

10, **Thursday:** Dinner at Sun Ya with Jeanne, Van, Lydia, Ruth and back to sit on their terrace. No news as to ship. Betty's dolls are now ready to go.

11, **Friday:** To the dentist to the tune of $65. Visit with Mourne Hudspeth, looking onto her green garden. She gave me blouses two. Wang arrived, so blockades. Stine staying with Betty. Wickings family to supper.

12, **Saturday:** Sent Betty & Stine off in a pedicab. Tiffin with Li Djoh-i—Cantonese *mien* and date soup. Tea with Nita—all 4 of us, on her veranda, with pink tablecloth. Reading *Mandoa, Mandoa*.

13, **Sunday:** Bishop Ward at church preaching that justice and love should go into the making of the peace. Drake and Adam Black to lunch.

14, **Monday:** Off to see furniture removed from Lester & to Moore's to inquire likely prices. It hurts a bit to part with things, part of a happy life, but one looks ahead & relinquishes. Bridge at Vanda's. Betty to Suse Wenzel's. Threatened barricades due to Wang.

15, **Tuesday:** Elizabeth Day to visit Betty. "Captain of the Wangle Maru" & story of the box of drinks labeled not wanted.

16, **Wednesday:** To McTyeire for a red & white dinner to celebrate Rosie's birthday. J. teachers appear in foreign schools. Frau Hepner's problem weighs on my mind. Mentioned it to Bishop W.

17, **Thursday:** Off early to see Mrs. Hepner. She has applied for divorce, appealed to German community & been told to accept no help from enemy nationals. To see Glathe who said he'd try to help her. To see Fukuda re new staff. Craig to dinner.

18, Friday: Visits from Ruth and Jeanne. Nita to lunch and an afternoon visit. Cool. Rumoured that compradores have been told to provision the ships.

19, Saturday: W.F. & Margaret Rowlands to lunch. Betty took Chummy to a Pets Party at Stine's and Dick went happily off to see *Hudson Bay*. We saw the Japanese prize film *Warm Current*. Fairly good but English rotten. "Make a study of me" – "I am going to spill it" – "Marry me."

20, Sunday: Tiffin with May Yang – also there Mr & Mrs Kwouk (Freda & Herbie.) Visited Con with another minor ailment. Heard Tchaikovsky concert over XMHA.

21, Monday: To the YW to go over finance lists for Chinese campaign ($300,000) with Jeanne & Ethel. Visit from Nita, with burned fingers, & M. Schniermacher & Ling Sze-tsin. Red arm bands to be worn Oct. 1. Nita wants 6!

22, Tuesday: Ruth and Rosie came to play bridge and dine. A.E. thinks he should sell piano, etc. as he may not be able to later. Alice Stacey arrived last night from Manila.

23, Wednesday: Busy day laundering – clothes, hair, dog, etc. Trying to make blackout curtains out of green drapes.

24, Thurs Bridge here with Mary, Vanda, Sonia Kucej. Rumored that letters taken on last ship were all destroyed. Marion Harrop taking over some of A.E.'s things. Russians still holding Stalingrad.

25, Friday: Tea at Cachita's with Jeanne, Ruth, Lily Awad et al. Grace Darroch very sick.

26, Saturday: Went to Nita's for afternoon & night. Dinner at Mrs Chou's – a Chinese foreign meal. Nita has two fingers burned – blackout accident. 90% street lights off. Streets very dark.

27, Sunday: John spoke on "Poetry" at Community Church. LMS annual service at Union Church, A.E. leading. Did Brooklyn

Museum scrap Japanese art objects? Were two negro soldiers shot in Va. for riding in white coach? 2nd anniversary of Tripartite Axis Pact. Supplement to *Times*.

28, Monday: Called at American Association for red armband to be worn Oct. 1 & after. J. have declared this Confucius (b. 551 BC) 2,493rd birthday, so school holiday. Called on Dr. Nance in his penthouse. Took Chens to see *Autumn* (*Ch'iu*.) Tea with Nash. Piano and refrigerator sold by A.E.

29, Tuesday: Blackout dinner at the Lester. Ethel recounted all the uses the Red Cross wheat bags have been put to—string to tie cords of babies! Bought black cloth and made curtains all morning.

30, Wednesday: To Ruth Clarke's to see Alice Stacey, back from internment in Santo Thomas. 3,333 people—queues. Traveled back on horse ship. Tea with Marion & Chris Bojesen. More ado with blackout curtains. Church & private houses sealed. Inventories required in 2 days.

OCTOBER 1942

1, Thursday: Grace Darroch's funeral. What a loss to the young! Red armbands worn from today by all "enemies." Blackout from today. Completely black. More houses sealed.

2, Friday: The Gendarmerie called and plastered the "protection" notice. Took silver to M.Y. who has moved to her youthful room on Foch. J busy at church with inventories & to McTyeire where offices are wanted.

3, Saturday: Futile efforts to see Tsang & buy tankage (?) for Chummy. Box family to lunch. Nita came to have supper & stay the night. She was asked not to go to the Chinese church. SMC employees wearing blue bands.

4, Sunday: Old boys' tea at Kan Lee-tung's. Plenty of red armbands evident at church. John went to Chaoufoong Rd. to arrange tea. 716 Jews there getting only bread to eat.

5, Monday: Medhurst teachers had a picnic on the Chaoufoong Rd. grounds. John, Betty & I rummaged among ruins finding bits of our china. Jews living in terribly crowded conditions. Sugar shortage. Can't buy.

6, Tuesday: Collected resident certificates at Police Station. Tried to buy sugar & flour but couldn't. Took Betty to Tsang for eye test. Raincoat lining will cost $80. *Pao chia* week. Big bill boards. Dunlap's bill for Dick $415.

7, Wednesday: A day of mending at home. Mrs. Sun sent *mien*. Eloise called. Still practice blackouts. Nita offered their piano for the children to practice Saturdays. Japanese emphasize study of languages of southern regions.

8, Thursday: Pleasant bridge at Mary Edwards' with Vanda &

Mrs Kucej. Rumored that Hong Kong & Malaya British will be evacuated before Shanghai people. J.B. Powell spoke over the radio from New York so he's not dead!

9, Friday: Laundry day with mending thrown in. No more blackout practice for the present.

10, Saturday: Scott family of 6 to lunch. Bojesens moved furniture. Ruth P. to tea. Mary Edwards & George Osborn to dinner & bridge, Mary staying the night.

11, Sunday: Lisbon reports an exchange of repatriates "the middle of the month." The Kwouk family came to tea and to discuss the world & the war.

12, Monday: Church Auxiliary tiffin. 56 there. Mr. Ching on "Soya bean." On to have tea & talk with Mourne & Wm. Hudspeth. Foreigners being stopped on streets to show certificates.

13, Tuesday: Betty's new glasses. Dr. Ly came to tea. Julia Chen to report on her health vs. interior. New lining for raincoat. I wish people would cease asking about the bloomin' ship all the time.

14, Wednesday: Out to Yangtzepoo to have lunch & play bridge with Mrs Kucej—Mary, Lucile & I. Announced that from 12 tonight enemy nationals cannot go to movies, restaurants, race course, etc.

15, Thursday: Lunch with Nita and then to Aurora to see Mother Thornton. Purchased cheese (6 oz $8.00) and enjoyed Nita's cottage cheese. Made chow chow. Mrs. Murray came to stay some days. Rumor: no repatriation.

16, Friday: A day at home re-knitting Nita's sweater. Mr. B. taken for questioning. Probably no more blackouts. Sentries shot & guerrillas got in. Gripsholm reported on way out with gifts for prisoners.

17, Saturday: Murray family to lunch. Nina & Grace Martin called. Eddie Wise & Tommie Pond to dinner & bridge. U. of S. foreigners given 2 weeks holiday. Story: Sikh police said to red-haired lady, "On with the British."

18, Sunday: Cantonese School choir gave a good concert. Decided to have Thanksgiving dinner at noon. Eddie Pai came to say his case still pending. Trying to stay off feet is a nuisance. Onley preached on covetousness.

19, Monday: Nita came to tell of the reorganisation of the universities and discuss repatriation. YW Int. Br. meeting at Portuguese Cub. Tea at Mabel Smith's with McLorn, Dunlap et al. Box supper Int. Fr. at Church.

20, Tuesday: More talk with Nita on repatriation, relaying John's opinion that she should stay. Dinner & bridge with Ruth & Rosie. Iran citizens trying to straighten citizenship. Australian Chinese (Yung) doing *pao chia*. Methodists in Sunkiang.

21, Wednesday: Joint Com. tea at Mrs Vajda's — very enjoyable. All enemies are being questioned as to income, resources, etc.

22, Thursday: Bridge at Vanda's with Mary and S. Kucej. Excellent marrow-ginger jam. Latest rumors: foreigners may have no servants; Tokyo bombed. Foreigners being questioned as to resources etc. Mrs Murray departed to the Club.

23, Friday: Took children's birth certificates to Am. As. as per request and purchased shirts, pyjamas, etc. Li Djoh-i came calling. Letter from Lil — my first letter in 11 months.

24, Saturday: Nita came to Chinese tiffin and Ruth stayed too. John, Nita & I went to Jessfield in spite of the cold wind. Children off to SS social.

25, Sunday: The usual — church, LMS PM at Union Church. Dick having castor oil.

26, Monday: Half-term holiday for D & B. Tsai Mo-li to lunch. Eddie Pai and family to tea. Mrs. Nash's 72nd birthday. Gave her marrow jam and ate her chutney. Began B's white socks on 3rd hand wool.

27, Tuesday: Permanent wave. ($40) To Nita's for the night, taking typewriter and her sweater, reknit—3rd effort.

28, Wednesday: Sat the sunny morning at Nita's making Betty's dolly sweater. Shopped for cheese and nuts. Still no sugar available. Letter from Maud Russell.

29, Thursday: Bridge four here—Mary, Vanda, Sonia Kucej. Solomons battle seems bad. Australia radio reports Nell in London. Mr. H. taken.

30, Friday: Masonic Hall taken. Geo. Osbor. came to deposit valuables a time. Lack of English speaking J. felt keenly. Questioners carry dictionaries. Nita's house had visitors. Her Hallowe'en Party postponed.

31, Saturday: Children's Hallowe'en Party, in spite of my lack of spirit for it. John busy answering questions about Com. Ch. Nita came to talk over her latest problems. Bobby cheered us with DD's confections & Greek Nougat.

NOVEMBER 1942

1, Sunday: Mourne came to lunch. She's had her share of trouble. J. at church the afternoon helping measure. Story of woman with dead husband & SMC harpist. They require date when each piece of furniture bought (bank.) Heard Toscanini.

2, Monday: Started new term of J. lessons. Went to Nita's musical tea. 40 teachers of J. have arrived and are assigned and will begin tomorrow — one in our school. 40 more due soon. John off to Hongkew pawn shop to try to recover Schniermacher winter clothes.

3. Tue Ruth came to sit and knit — and Inabelle Coleman to see J about SS class. John went to town to move the precious paper. Considering sending 6 Christmas cards.

4, Wednesday: PO says can send Christmas cards & letters, so I shall try 6. To Harmon for margarine. Sugar still unobtainable.

5, Thursday: Many men taken to internment camp. Christmas letters written yesterday destroyed today. Wanda had reason enough for us to cancel the bridge date.

6, Friday: After a sleepless night, a calm day. Tea with Evelyn Nash. Tea with Evelyn Nash. Ruth P, Djao, Wu, Chen called. 500 Br, 100 Am taken yesterday. All men packing bags. Good news from Egypt and Solomons.

7, Saturday: Deposited wherewithal at Suensons'. Bought duffle bag and enamel ware. Guests to lunch. Ethel Taylor for weekend. A.E. here gathering things. Men fed by Am. Rel.

8, Sunday: Moving service with Geo. Osborn preaching. Am troops land in North Africa. Story of Watari's torch & the Shantung sergeants.

9, Monday: Mrs Baxter came to stay a few days in order to be near him in hospital. Nita hurried away after lunch to buy sugar & was 269th in line. Got one lb aft 1½ hr. Americans active in N. Africa. Turn of tide?

10, Tuesday: Walked with John out to Columbia Club to see various folk and called on Baxter in hospital. Morley spoke in London, heard here. Am. troops crossing Tunis.

11, Wednesday: Cake and coffee in the Van Hengel garden with Ruth, Lydia, Jeanne. Tiffin and bridge at Mary Edwards. Hitler abrogated clause permitting Vichy gov. Lists of wants received by wives of internees.

12, Thursday: To Nita's for the morning and lunch, with Ruth there, too. On to the Buddhist garden for Medhurst teachers presentation of picture. Then noodles, *pa pao fan* at Sun Ya with Mae Yang.

13, Friday: More proclamations about property. Short wave sets must be surrendered by Dec. 1. Rainy wash day.

14, Saturday: Guests to tea: 4 from Club Milledge, James, Morris, Hanson, Black, Stephens et al. Went to see Mr Baxter in the hospital. Inspectors came, very polite, few questions. Mr Wu succeeded in getting 3 lbs of sugar for us.

15, Sunday: Chase for sugar in the am. Found a shop which promised some for tomorrow. Household tasks. Tchaikovsky concert. Betty home with a cold.

16, Monday: YW Com. meeting at Lucile's. Jap. class. Much red tape getting bread ration coupons. Got flour—5 lbs on Mr Wu's tickets. Burke, Sheretz returned.

17, Tuesday: Nita came for the day. We searched for lard, bought cranberry sauce instead. Lydia also to Chinese tiffin. Bei-tseng Feng to tea. Leaving 21st. J at church filling in more blanks. Marking all J's things.

18, Wednesday: M. Schniermacher came to collect coats. To J.C.

tea at K.D.S. Home on Hungjao. Story of Jap. & birthday cake. J busy about forms for Int. Inst. Heard Laski, Priestley et al on Future for Japan.

19, Thursday: Fall cleaning of the living room. Jap. class. More blockades lately. Lard available at $18.

20, Friday: Took J's class while he spoke at Cantonese School. On to see Mourne, who's had various minor troubles in addition. Lunch and bridge with Vanda, Mary, Kucej. Filled in red stripe blanks for J. marine office. J. came to tag furniture but we were out so they'll return.

21, Saturday: English Day at Mary Farnham. Girls gave plays and speeches. Beulah took Mac and me to lunch at Mayflower. Ruth and the Beynons here to tea. Betty visiting Stine and Dick to the SS party. J. at Nita's 4 days straight. Accepted our blanks.

22, Sunday: S. Smith at Church instead of Ward. Disquieting rumor denied. To Union Church for LMS PM. Committee of Central European Protestant Refugees meeting for first time. Heard Tchaikovsky concert. C.L.B. very sick in hospital. Shingles in eyes.

23, Monday: Gala (?) time getting $86 out of Specie Bank. Bought coal & stove at BRA. Jap. class. Julie Chen can't get off. Still has fever. Searched for jam and lard. 2 pounds for $45.

24, Tuesday: Two tons of coal purchased ($1,090.) Lunch at Nita's with Mrs Yen, H. Haig, Jeanne. Tea here with John Ahlers summing up. Allies on top late next fall. Reconstruction problems in China. Allies should give money without strings & privileges.

25, Wednesday: Heard Lelia's tale of AWC interviews & troubles. Took away some books. Ivy Greaves to lunch & weaving. Stalingrad defenders taking prisoners & gaining. Hair wave & preparations for Thanksgiving. Children brought notices of "structural alteration."

RUTH HILL BARR

26, Thursday: Thanksgiving Day. Brilliant & gay. Jeanne, Van, Lydia, Ruth arrived with poinsettias, candy, etc. Eddie & Sid also to dinner (noon.) Visitors in am to paste more notices. Nita came in.

27, Friday: Spent the morning trying to turn in Kodak. Too many people in line. Lunch at Sun Ya with Sonia Kucej and bridge here. Many rumors rife as to use of public schools. Barricades in West.

28, Saturday: Off in a pedicab at 8:15. Devoted the day to surrendering Kodak and projector. Wretched business. LCH foreigners given walking papers. A.E. & Ethel coming here. Betty at Janet's birthday party. Mrs. Dunlap called Dr. in hospital.

29, Sunday: Nita spent the afternoon beside our first fire. Coal delivered but no stove yet. Nita repatriating by order. A.E. & Ethel began moving in. John busy with tags at church.

30, Monday: Took inventory of provisions. Mrs Dunlap came to lunch. After Jap. class to McTyeire where bridge & dinner with Phil & Rosie. Last day for radios to be turned in. Good news in Russia & Africa.

119

DECEMBER 1942

1, **Tuesday:** A.E. arrived to take up residence. Morning devoted to clearing out room for two children in one room. Afternoon at the Suensons' warm flat with butter and lettuce for tea. SMC dept budget to go directly to Finance Com.

2, **Wednesday:** Store room converted successfully into a double room. Ruth came in the afternoon for sewing and tea. Living room stove set up. Children on holiday, asking questions a mile a minute.

3, **Thursday:** Tiffin with Nita and Mary at Mayflower. Spring rolls and almond soup. Japanese lesson. Futile efforts to light Wasca stove for first fire of the season.

4, **Friday:** Rushed to BRA to get 1½ lb margarine. They have to turn out again & were selling stocks. Chinese tiffin for Mary, Sonia, Vanda and then good bridge. Trouble at Club—old AC steward in, Mrs Chou out. Those 150 who came in Aug. must pay for themselves.

5, **Saturday:** Celebrated Ruth's birthday with a tea at our house: Mary, Ethel, Cachita, Jeanne, Lydia, Nita, Lucile, each bringing one dish. Bitterly cold. Stove working fine. Betty taking Thiazon for a cold.

6, **Sunday:** Celebrated Sid's birthday (7th) by going to lunch at McTyeire: chicken & ice cream. 52 people joined the church— inspiring service. Stove troubles. 8 nationalities—Ch. Br. A. R. Danish, Ger. Finnish Austr.

7, **Monday:** Foraging for jam, etc. Can't get sugar. Jap. lesson— then ironing—& so to bed exhausted.

8, **Tuesday:** Spent the day with Ruth at 98 Edinburgh. Radio celebration and parades and many flags. J. seem to be celebrating themselves without forcing others to.

9, Wednesday: Nita came to lunch, and Stine, and we spent the afternoon foraging & chatting. Blackout. Rumours of Am. planes. S. Gate schools taken over. Want plans of all LMS property 24 hrs notice.

10, Thursday: Jap lesson. Invited guests for Christmas tea. Honey now $33 for 3 lbs. Rice $1,000 for 170 lbs. Sugar $8 – $10 a lb.

11, Friday: Found Mourne on her sunny porch. W.H. 6 weeks away. Bridge after a waffle tiffin with Mary Edwards. Contract rummy, then stitching the small afghan.

12, Saturday: Guests to lunch: Martin Shepherd and Dr. Garnick. Quiet afternoon at home with dog and afghan – John and children to Club football. Strong BRA rumor of total internment.

13, Sunday: Bible Sunday with Hobbs preaching. Old boys tea at Medhurst. Latest rumor: Americans 75% leave in Jan. Others & Br. interned outside Shanghai.

14, Monday: Blackout for 10 days beginning today. Nanking bombed? Jap. lesson, Ruth walking kit.

15, Tuesday: Traffic control most of the morning but I got thru – walking – to Nita's to enjoy her stove & her company. Tea – reception at church for 61 new members. 46 new members, 65 in all there. Rommel retreating to Migurte.

16, Wednesday: Lunch and bridge with Vanda, Ruth substituting for Sonia. V. went to Haiphong Road and waved. YW cooperator has arrived. Mrs C.C. Chen is gen'l secretary.

17, Thursday: Busy making pencil cases for Betty to give at Christmas. Betty at Stine's. Japanese lesson. Didn't go to Teraoka's cocktail party. He goes to Rome. Air raid practices still on. Traffic blockades 3 times today.

18, Friday: Tiffin at Mayflower with Ethel & A.E. on his birthday. Christmas PM at Free Ch. Church, Mrs. Milledge. All short wave radios must be changed to long.

19, Saturday: Baked Christmas cookies. A.E. brought home Christmas tree and arranged Bern's lights and candles. Ethel in to tea after Hutton funeral. Betty at Stine's, Dick at Club football.

20, Sunday: Fine service at church, children taking part. 556 present, $3,100 contributed. Ruth came and we decorated the Christmas tree, A.E.'s gift. Wave reported going into Burma.

21, Monday: Trips to town are not to my liking. Vain efforts to find a calendar on 1 page. Jap. lesson. Beulah came to bring red eggs etc! Real butter from Sun! Chic. Santa Claus $40 – candy cane $4.00. It's no use to try to buy.

22, Tuesday: More rumors of repatriation. Am. As. telling folk their classification. Tea party at Nita's with Helen Ling & Kelhofers. Home in the blackout. *Mien* from Li Djoh-i. Evening spent reveling in V's paper & card. Tagawa here again. J saw him.

23, Wednesday: Pressure & threats to sisters in hospital. It's so hard to relax – always some upsetting angle turns up. Quiet day at home wrapping small gifts, playing radio, reading, singing.

24, Thursday: Callers: Ruth P., Jeanne, Mrs. Djao, Mr. Wu, B. Read, Caters, Mr. Sohu, Milledge, Wickings, Ethel, et al. Children out at parties. Quiet day at home for me. Dispensed cookies and enjoyed the tree and thought of many in U.S.A.

25, Friday: A beautifully decorated tree, with parcels underneath. Usual visit to McTyeire in the morning. Tea guests (about 20.) Nita and Ethel for the night. Darlan assassinated.

26, Saturday: Quiet day at home. Visits from Louise Feng, Mrs Hepner, Julie Chen. Children playing games. Dick taking castor oil. Betty at Stine's. Average church attendance for year 303 – 6 mos.

27, Sunday: After George Osborn's sermon to tiffin at the Stanley Smiths'. Delicious goose and all trimmings. J. (7) came into H's living room drunk. Betty to Christmas party at Suse Wenzel's. Toscanini & co. played Brahms Third Symphony.

28, Monday: McFarlane family to tiffin—Chinese. Jap. class and then to the Church where 95 gathered for Int. Fr. Chr. party. Carols by choir, be. (?) Still getting short wave news from friends. Fukuda now chief.

29, Tuesday: Lydia had a tea for dogs and children. We walked up with Chummy. Sorted Christmas papers & stickers. Betty's bursary to be continued. They go back Jan. 4 to same buildings after all.

30, Wednesday: Nita and Mary came to sit the morning. Afternoon to call on Dr. Dunlap, Gordon Day, Anne Herbert in hospital. Geo. Osborn to dinner and bridge. Betty & crowd at Stine's.

31, Thursday: Am. As. says we are in F7 which means no chance of repatriation now. More readjusting! Dick at the Parrs', Jill here with Betty. J & I spent a quiet evening over household accounts.

1943

"Going In" / Establishing a Community

IN THE DIARY, the year of 1943 revolves around a place called Lunghwa. The name will be familiar to readers of J.G. Ballard's novel "Empire of the Sun" and Stephen Spielberg's movie of the same name. A novel, a movie and a diary are, however, very different genres!

Mother writes about the preparations for "going in," the common expression used at that time, and then about the ways in which the internees, or "occupants" as they are called in the official notices in the camp, established a community within the barbed wire.

Lunghwa is actually the name of an ancient pagoda and temple which in the 1940s was to the southwest of the city proper of Shanghai. Today it lies within the greatly expanded city and is a popular place to go on New Year's Eve to strike the large bell for good luck. By extension, the district around the pagoda was, and still is, also called Lunghwa.

It happened that the best boarding school in the whole of China, Shanghai High School, founded in 1867, was situated in the countryside within sight of the pagoda. It had a large campus

Enamel plates used by Barr family in Lunghwa Camp

and, although a few of the buildings had been bombed earlier in the war, there were enough buildings left to house almost 2,000 people. The Japanese commandeered the school and it became known as Lunghwa Civil Assembly Center, the official term for the internment places where civilians were assembled. The short form, for foreigners, was "Lunghwa Camp." (See a sketch map at the beginning of the book.)

As at the end of 1942, there continued to be rumors about repatriation and internment but on January 24 Mother writes: "Full instructions given. All enemies to go sooner or later. Not easy, but we can take it." The following day she says, "...perhaps 3 months before families are interned" and on January 28, "Much to be done for preparation for going in."

The preparations included packing some household treasures into large trunks which would be left with a company called Scharpf Guenter which, however, offered "No guarantee." Kind Chinese friends offered to keep such things as precious china and books. The house was to be taken over by the Japanese. On February 26, "3 Japanese from Consulate came to question as to house." Furniture had to be left in the house and Japanese officials came to inspect. On March 8 "J came to "stick" A.E.'s furniture." I can remember seeing those white stickers which meant that we could not remove any piece of furniture.

Meanwhile, advice had come from those who had already "gone in" with regard to what to take into the camp. Rather than china, enamel ware was recommended for plates and bowls for food. On February 2 Mother went "to purchase green enamel ware" several pieces of which I still have here in Shanghai. Each internee was allowed four pieces of baggage but no mention was made of the size of each piece. I still remember the bedsteads and mattresses being laid on the floor on rattan mats and then being piled high with household goods of all kinds. Chinese packers then came to sew up four "pieces."

Life under the Japanese occupation was not easy for many reasons: (Jan. 5) "Ruth in with Nov. letters from U.S.A. They set me off." There was uncertainty about what might happen at any moment: (Jan. 7) "Round to see Margaret MacF whose husband was taken yesterday for interrogation."

There was also uncertainty as to which camp we might go to. Mother would have preferred to go to "Ta Hsia," a former private university, later known as Chapei Camp because it was in the district of that name. Most Americans were assigned to go there and most of Mother's friends were American. On February 25, she saw off Nita; 452 were going by bus, and Nita's bus, No. 12, departed at 1:30 pm. Two days later she writes: "Fine weather for Nita and Ruth. Bless 'em, how I miss 'em."

The British Residents' Association (BRA) had a difficult task, to say the least, in organizing the internment of thousands. Some friends were "summoned and then unsummoned all the same day." The same thing happened to us: "BRA called us and then uncalled after 10 minutes." Finally, on Apr. 1: "Summoned to BRA for orders. Have to go April 10, 8 a.m. Baggage on April 8. It's rather hard."

While our parents were preoccupied with all these matters, Dick and I were still going to school. The buildings on Yu Yuen Road were taken over by the Japanese and later used as an internment camp, mainly for SMC employees and families with small children. As a temporary measure, our schools moved to other accommodation (Jan. 18): "Betty's school goes to the Cathedral [Anglican on Hankow Road]. Dick to the Jewish School. [on Seymour Road]." But on February 22, Mother writes: "Schools closed for 'reorganization.' Teachers all going to camp."

On April 10 it was our turn to "go in." I remember well our sticking on the front door two long white pieces of paper in the form of a "St. Andrews" cross, with Chinese words declaring that this house was now under the control of the Japanese. We went by pedicab to the Columbia Country Club.

Below, you will read Mother's account of our bus ride to Lunghwa and even the conversations she heard on the bus. She then recounts the tale of our first few days.

The BRA had asked an Advance Party to go in first, in March, and had appointed a Camp Representative, Mr. Bates, who was to be our liaison with the Japanese Commandant, Mr. Hayashi. By the time we arrived, about one thousand people were already there and they turned out to welcome us. For Mother, "the most awful part was the first 10 minutes with no beloved faces among the host." Our group that day was called Assembly 22 and there were 360 of us. For the duration of the war my number was: 22/228.

Establishing a community under such circumstances was no easy task. The basics were shelter, food and water. Our accommodation was already assigned and we discovered that we were to be in a corner room facing north and west on the second

West Kitchen – 'A' team at work

floor of G Block, a former dormitory building in the school. The
area of the room was about 12' by 14' and it had formerly housed
two students. At least we had privacy as a family. Single people
living in bed-spaces or cubicles in former large classrooms were
not so fortunate.

As for food and water, Mother writes on April 14: "The J. dump
3 days' food supply and leave us to do the best we can. Drinking
water is hauled from Frenchtown and boiled here." That bald
statement is amplified over and over again as she describes in the
diary the struggles to provide enough food, even though we were
fortunate enough to receive food parcels from friends in Shanghai
and from the International Red Cross. The internees soon learned
how to construct small cooking stoves called "chatties" on which
they cooked "creatively."

Greg Leck, in his monumental tome, *Captives of Empire – The
Japanese Internment of Allied Civilians in China 1941-1945*, writes
that the organization of the camps was like "setting up miniature
cities." He says that once the daily routine was set up—work
rosters, meal times, measurement of rations—the internees then

set up committees: labor, medical affairs, public health, kitchen, bakery, education, billeting, discipline, entertainment, library, sports, canteen, maintenance, stores, gardens, women's affairs. This is precisely what happened in Lunghwa.

On April 13, "John went on duty in kitchen 2–8 daily." I presume that my father volunteered for this job and it is a matter of some pride that he later "rose" to be the Manager of the Kitchen. This was because he could be trusted (not to steal meat or vegetables.) It was, however, a family joke because he could not boil an egg.

Both my parents also volunteered to teach in the excellent school known as "Lunghwa Academy" (not just "School".) Someone was heard to say, "But how can Mrs. Barr teach you English when she's American?" Mother was teaching English to Senior 1 and Senior 4. On May 12 she writes: "The Senior 1 class will drive me to drink." Perhaps she was not accustomed to teaching Western teenagers!

Besides work, there was also play in the camp. By May 14 my parents were playing bridge with an LMS colleague and a Belgian banker; on May 16 they played with Carol and Eric Turner and on May 18 with John and Deirdre Fee.

Before long, squabbles arose among the internees. On June 3, "J's team on strike in the kitchen. Always up against pettiness of some people." On September 5, "Minds are restricted when bodies are." and on October 11, "How small our minds become!" As the war wore on, these problems inevitably became worse.

I had been waiting anxiously for my friend, Jill Meyers, to come in. Her father, Freddy, was very active in the BRA and was therefore needed in the city to help with the organization of the whole process of internment. Finally, on August 9, Mother writes: "Assembly 30–19 of them—arrived. The Meyers here at last. Betty very happy. Jill and Ruth spent the day with us." She had spent the previous morning cleaning their room—K 4—for them.

Unfortunately, it was on the other side of the camp, about as far away from G Block as it could be, but that did not matter.

For some reason unknown to me, Mother was very anti-mosquito nets. We were required to use them because of the prevalence of malaria, there being paddy fields, the preferred breeding ground for mosquitoes, all around us. Personally speaking, I quite liked the privacy under the net. Sure enough, my father and I both came down with malaria – at the same time. We had high fevers and shivered on alternate days. And it recurred, even after the war when I was in Dallas.

Mother herself had ailments but the member of our family who suffered the most, physically, was my brother, Dick. He was malnourished and had an infected fingernail which would not heal. A friend in California had an aunt in Lunghwa who remembered walking to the small hospital in the camp with Dick, both of them crying because they knew how painful the treatment was going to be.

To end on a more positive note, in November Mother was asked to take over the Labor Office with a friend, Mary Diack. It was "about the hardest woman's job in camp" (Nov.10,) but she rose to the challenge and was, I think, happy to have been asked. Before long, she heard via the grapevine that her good friend, Jeanne van Hengel, was doing the same job in the Chapei Camp. Their YWCA training was turning out to be useful in totally unexpected ways.

JANUARY 1943

1, Friday: Ruth came and we played the Emperor Concerto. Lunch at home with Ethel and A.E. An hour's visit with Mourne. Tea at McTyeire, with red & white table, well laden.

2, Saturday: Off to register as alien wife at BRA. Suse and Stine spending the day with Betty and Mrs. Suenson to tea. Spent the night with Nita. Mushroom soup at small tables round a glowing fire.

3, Sunday: From Nita's to church. Julie and Alice Chen to lunch. Tea at Vanda Roper's with Hawks, Proctor, Waterman. With reluctance undecorated the Christmas tree. A.E. received letter from Barbara Aug.

4, Monday: Tiffin with Ruth, Lydia on Jeanne's birthday. also Lucile, Ethel, Cachita. New book at J. class. Tagawa and Sohn to dinner. Children returned to school only to be told buildings not available. Temporary quarters on Great Western Rd.

5, Tuesday: Ethel and A.E. changing rooms on a very cold day. Ruth in with Nov. letters from USA. They set me off. Visits from Sakamoto, Vanda, Miss Webb, Mr. Price, etc. Children's schools still unsettled. News that Nell expected to fly to U.S.A. before X'mas.

6, Wednesday: At home, washing, ironing, mending. Dr. & Mrs. Milledge came in to tea.

7, Thursday: Busy day with hot water. J. lesson. Round to see Margaret MacF whose husband was taken yesterday for interrogation.

8, Friday: Cold sunny day for a trip to Glen Road. Delicious tiffin and bridge with Sonia. Addy came to dinner and read letter from Nana dated Oct. 15.

9, Saturday: Nita came for Chinese tiffin and afternoon — her first bridge. Wang declared war. Li Djoh-i came with professional problem. Fr. Concession starting Child Protection Scheme. Betty taking Thiazon & cough mixture.

10, Sunday: At home with semi-sick children till afternoon when we went round to the CIM for the Heralds program. Toscanini & co. played Beethoven's 8th.

11, Monday: Auxiliary tiffin at church. 71 there. On in the bitter wind to J. class. Coffee can be bought ¼ lb only.

12, Tuesday: Tea party with Muriel Garnick, Anne MacKeith & Ruth who brought cakes. We started our cotton jumper cardigans. Played bridge. It's good to be able to have friends and go about and keep warm. 19°. Very cold.

13, Wednesday: Collected church secretary's book from Maurice's room and proceeded to SAS for farina. To see Mrs Hsueh in Marg. Wmson. Hosp. Grand dinner and excellent bridge with Mary Edwards.

14, Thursday: Delicious Chinese tiffin with Beulah in private club. We still count our blessings. Wives allowed to visit internees. Burst pipes causing trouble.

15, Friday: Sonia, Mary, Vanda here for tiffin and bridge. D's school goes to Jewish School 1:40 — 5:30.

16, Saturday: To Nita's for the day. Dr. Lawney there also and *Siegfried* was read. Betty at Suse's. Dick at Club. J. seeing Tagawa. Found some egg powder.

17, Sunday: Annual meeting followed tiffin at church. 170 there. Soup and tea provided. More troubles with hot water tank. Toscanini concert.

18, Monday: YW Committee meeting here. Ethel telling of visit to Haiphong Rd. The rest went to hear Columbia C. Choir sing The Messiah but I went to Jap. lesson. Betty's school goes to the

Cathedral. Dick to the Jewish School.

19, Tuesday: Quiet day at home and visiting the sick: Gladys Parker, Myra, Grace, remembering Nell's birthday. Enjoyed shampoo. Worked on white cotton jumper.

20, Wednesday: Ruth came in and we knitted & talked. J.C. at Mme. Grossman's. 20 there. Soap shortage. Prices jump again.

21, Thursday: M. Schniermacher in to lunch. After J. to Sun Ya where we had a feast with Eddie Wise, Smiths, Olivers, Cuddeback, Dents. Then to the Dents' for bridge, fruit, etc. Dents' 13th anniversary.

22, Friday: Bridge and tiffin at Mary's. Vanda's account of her visit and the uniformed men throwing kisses to Lou. Betty to Cathedral School in pm.

23, Saturday: Lunch at Ethel's to celebrate Mary's birthday. Tea at Frame's for AAUW refugee women (10) 5 doctors, 1 librarian, 1 pharmacist, 2 teachers, 1 technician. Children to Nantao. BRA notified A.E. re internment on Jan. 31. Missions building closed.

24, Sunday: 600 men without dependents summoned to go to Segregation Centre on Jan. 31. Full instructions given. All enemies to go sooner or later. Not easy, but we can take it. 1st dose typhus vaccine.

25, Monday: A busy day with comers, goers, telephone calls. Purchased slippers & cotton yarn and went on to Jap. class. A bridge evening with the four of us. Music to Marjorie clothes to Smith. Perhaps 3 months before families are interned.

26, Tuesday: Nita came for the day. Ruth and Eddie Wise had dinner and played bridge. The Milledges came in at tea time to farewell A.E. Latest rumor: everyone in by March 15.

27, Wednesday: Waited at home all day for J. to come pass on A.E.'s things, missing lunch with Ruth. They never came. Helped Ethel make A.E.'s pocket. Djao Li-ling came with fruit for D & B.

28, Thursday: After sugar and then via Djao (china) to Ruth's for lunch. All SMC employees will be interned Feb. 8 in SMC Schools. Lester people got their passes. Much to be done in preparation for going in.

29, Friday: Stream of visitors. A.E.'s baggage collected. Nita & I bought slacks and sleeved underwear. To PM and back here for DC meeting.

30, Saturday: Shopping with Ruth to get Dick's underwear, toothbrushes, marking ink, etc. To the Djao's with more china and on to Vanda's to play bridge and drink tea. A.E. had many guests, filled his forms and seems ready to go.

31, Sunday: A.E.set off by pedicab for Pootung. Not so easy to say goodbye. McMullen's very good sermon on Jonah and Dent's excellent organ concert. Trock and Frame to lunch. Nash, Wu, Stanley Smith came in.

FEBRUARY 1943

1, Monday: Morning spent preparing Chummy for departure. Took him by pedicab to Bund where Mr Kucej met him in car. Visited Swiss Consulate and BRA for data re internment. Children allowed 2 trunks. Chum's pathetic face!

2, Tuesday: May Yang came visiting. Lunch with Nita and on to purchase green enamel ware. Not so bad. Reports say Pootung camp unprepared & pretty awful. Dr. Ly and Nan Smith in, she asking to stay with us.

3, Wednesday: Re-packed trunks in preparation for "Civilian Assembly Centre" (new name.) 2 camps for Br, 1 for Amer. due to open on March 15. Lei C Ping brought medicine for Betty. Tea with Miss Coxon who showed pictures of Kuling. Scurry for tinned fruit. Fresh too high.

4, Thursday: Another 800 summoned to go to camp. More talk of American repatriation. Committees planning for education and religion in camps. Gift from Mrs F. much appreciated. Nita came in with NY cake. Blockade on way to Jap. lesson. Mrs Dunlap came in. Dr. still in hospital.

5, Friday: Single & unattached men to report on Sunday. Went to Drake's class. "Lessons for today from Chinese Sages."

6, Saturday: Betty off to dancing. Packed another trunk. Scharf Guenther will store trunk—no guarantee. Hair wash 10.00. Tea with Eloise, Nina, etc. in 23. We must hurry things out of the house. May be summoned soon.

7, Sunday: Americans & Dutch (?) to go to Ta Hsia. Brit. with children over 9 in one camp. Others together. One Br. (?) to Soochow (?), Norris (over 80) exempted. Men with alien wives

will be interned — wives & children not. Fine service at church.
Tiffin with Kwouk. To see Dr. Dunlap in hospital.

8, Monday: Spent the day parceling things out to friends, books
to Freda and Herbie, etc. Saw piles of beds & trunks going to
schools where SMC people will stay. Can't get Betty's Thiazon
& she's taken the last.

9, Tuesday: Betty at home with cold. Nita here to lunch with
Cachita in afterward to talk over plans for camp connection.
McFarlanes to breakfast. Saw them off & Fernandez to camp.
Last minute things dropped on our doorstep.

10, Wednesday: Morning in town for thermos bottles. Red band
folk buying rope, enamel. etc. Smiths to lunch. M. Schniermacher
in. W. Nash collapsed and had to go to hospital. Wash day. One
Br. camp to Yangchow (!)

11, Thursday: The hardest day yet. BRA called to ask which camp
we prefer. J says Br. I didn't know it would be so hard. Said
farewell to Mrs. F. Went over the house selecting things to sell.
Trials in Haiphong Rd (?.)

12, Friday: Sausages and Crispy Coffee to celebrate John's birthday.
Bought shoes for children. AWC Executive wound up affairs.
Drake's class on pre-Confucian classics — personal God — man's
moral sense. Observed life in Munic. School.

13, Saturday: Americans summoned for Feb. 25. Reports say,
"Take food. Never mind clothes." Betty and I had a farewell
big tea at the Suensons' with Miss Walker. Went to see about
Thiazon for Betty. Some available at $6 per tablet.

14, Sunday: Geo. Osborn rose to the occasion with sermon
on Malachi. Tiffin at McTyeire with Sid & Phil — reunion
before separation. They go to Pootung tomorrow. Jeanne &
Van summoned and then unsummoned all the same day.
Yangchow — Lunghwa — Ta Hsia. Met Mydans at McTyeire.

15, Monday: Nita here to tea — coffee, doughnuts, K.B. cakes from

Ruth, also here. Nita saw the men off to Pootung. Hart had some trouble. Nita's evening with "London Front." Sakamoto delayed in coming to supper because of Anti-Allied parade. Rostov retaken by USSR.

16, Tuesday: Saw Fukuda for 1 hr. Gifts from them very touching. Children to Wong—$75 for 10 mins. Americans went for internment instructions. Visitors: Harmons, Mrs Sun, Mrs Tang, Li Djoh-i, with gifts. Harmon to be commander at Yangchow where conditions seem as bad as possible. Sid Anderson's wedding at Pootung. "Cold Water—Hot Springs" "Am. landed in Pootung."

17, Wednesday: So much happens in one day, I can't remember to record it all. Dutch and Belgians may not be interned. Americans with one child over 2 called (Vanda.) Bacharachs to tea. Eddie Pai to see about kitchen things. Black says we get $5,100 from BRA and then no more. We must buy food and more food. Still debating alcohol stove. How to heat?

18, Thursday: "Stateless refugees" to be segregated by May 18 in certain Hongkew area. Fiendish! Bern came to advise on food for camp. Children to Cater—o.k. Dju Yu-bao came but would not talk. Very disappointing!

19, Friday: Morning devoted to buying apple & prune jam, egg powder, chocolate, etc. Medical exam and then to Drake's class. Baxter and others summoned.

20, Saturday: Tea with Nita at Sun Ya—D & B too. What good *mien* and Chinese dates! Gim sent $10,000 out of camp for food. Yangchow group to go Mar. 4. Dr. Dunlap still in hospital.

21, Sunday: Fine service at church—Stanley's last. Organ concert by Miss Yuan. Fukudas to lunch, bringing more tins and suggestion that we try going to SMC camp. Suensons to tea bringing lettuce & shoes. Saw Arthur & Ev. They go tomorrow. 600 Yu Yuen Rd. 300 Great Western.

22, Monday: Ethel summoned to go to Yangchow March 4. Interviewed Okazaki about SMC camp. He says "if room." New permanent wave. Russians still doing well. We get very little other news. Schools closed for "reorganization." Teachers all going to camp.

23, Tuesday: Morning at Nita's painting name on trunks & seeing Chinese guests. Ruth in for afternoon—and Lydia to say goodbye. J & I went to McTyeire. What a send off they are having! Gave us some. Betty at Jill's. Ethel goes to Yangchow Mar 4. Also Mac.

24, Wednesday: France relinquishes extrality. Fr. Concession to be amalgamated with Settlement. Eric busy bundling up Ethel's bed. Mao family to tea. Marion & Chris in. Long wait for Nita who came at 11:30. (Got money from Swiss. Bought new shoes.) Repacking, instructions, etc, so to bed at 1:30. The cruelty of kind friends! A stream of visitors kept Nita from packing. Lei C Ping brought gifts from his class.

25, Thursday: Guests to see Nita before breakfast. Off at 9 by pedicab to CCC. Procession of thermos bottles, string bags, etc—ivy, rubber boots, 2 hats on head. 452 went by bus—Nita's (No. 12) left at 1:30. Ruth & L . in No. 10.

26, Friday: Bought a lower camp chair. Gifts from students & Dr. Yang. Blockade prevented my going to Scharf Guenther. Baxter announced at PM scheme for food parcels to be sent to camps. Harmons off to Miss Craig's in order to leave early tomorrow for Yangchow. 3 Japanese from Consulate came to question as to house. Jeanne & Van go to Great China Mar. 3.

27, Saturday: To Scharpf Guenter & Swiss Consulate re storage of trunks. To tea at the Hsiaos with Bojesens & Gladys. Geo. Osborn came to dinner & bridge. Advance party to Lunghwa on Mon. 57 Danish sailors joining church next Sun. Fine weather for Nita & Ruth. Bless 'em, how I miss 'em.

28, Sunday: Seemed strange at church with so many absent. Osborn took service. 250+ there. Farewell tea at Medhurst with 50 at one long table—flowers, cakes, candy, speeches in plenty. A very fine appreciation of John—gifts and money for scholarship. 3 boys reported trip to S. Middle School & Bates came to hear about it.

MARCH 1943

1, Monday: Afternoon spent at Medhurst with Senior III farewell party — very well planned. Gift of knapsack and thermos bottle. Morning spent with food committee discussing what should go into parcels. May Yang came to lunch with Shelltox & marmalade. To dinner with the Hsias — Hobbs & Van Hengels & Osborn there. How good to see a house intact!

2, Tuesday: A day at home with some sorting and packing. Wrote to Nita & Ruth — notes for Jeanne to take in. G.D. got much information from the dean about the school quarters for Smith.

3, Wednesday: Superb dinner at Mr. Trock's — silver candles, lavender sweet peas and pink cloth. His pictures, books, and lovely things. They do help to make a home. Saw Jeanne, Eddie, Lelia & Charlie, et al off to Ta Hsia. Tiffin honouring John with the principals of schools. More gifts from boys. Li Djoh-i came.

4, Thursday: Up at 5:30 to get Ethel off to Yangchow. Nan went over to stay with Gladys. How nice to have a quiet house. Visitors — many — Sonia, A. Wu, Hsiao An-ming with creams. Betty & J to see Dunlap, still in hospital.

5, Friday: BRA called us and then uncalled after 10 minutes. Food Committee met here at 3 to decide on contents of parcels to be sent to camp. Glass jars to carry peanut butter cost as much as the butter. Oxford sausages @ $60 we cut out. 6 parcels should do for 9 months. To the PM. Mac came for the night. She leaves next Thursday for Yangchow. Meyers called to say we could go to Yangchow if we liked but we declined.

6, Saturday: Called on Miss Loh after getting Betty ready for Suse's. J & D took a jaunt to Hongkew Park. Purchased more stockings and socks. Packed two parcels to be sent to ourselves. More food for camp!

7, Sunday: 40 Danish sailors joined church. John's 3 scouts came back to tiffin after exploring & getting helpful information. Addy here, too. On to the Suensons' to tea. They are buying beans for next winter. Bates and boys back in evening. J said try for SMC & Am. camp since 300 & 400 must go there. Hard for me to know that he would go now it's too late.

8, Monday: Dick and I went shopping for thermos flasks and gloves & knife. J got Buttella, butter substitute. J saw Meyers. Looks as if we go Mar. 29. Julie Chen came and Mr & Mrs Yoh with Nulacta. M. Schniermacher came to supper, reported on her deficient patient. J. came to stick A.E.'s furniture.

9, Tuesday: Betty & I went shopping for wool socks – $45 a pr. A beggar snatched the cakes we bought. Joan Read came to tea. At SMC camp they paid $200 each in order to have meat. 4 people in Gen. Hospital. John on holiday, giving children lessons.

10, Wednesday: Meyers telephoned to suggest seeing Kay. I went. He saw Banjo who approved our going to American camp. Can't be very joyful about it since John is not.

11, Thursday: Kay called summoning us to come Friday for instructions to go to American camp. I still think that will be best from several standpoints, but almost wish I'd never urged it. Pleasant visit with Helen Ling and dinner – the four of us. Her lacquer & ivory Kwanyin is something to remember.

12, Friday: John went and received instructions from Am. Ass'n. We go at 9:30 on March 22. Nos. 17/418-421. Meyers girls came for the day. They are such nice children. I wish Betty could continue to play with them. Last LMS PM. Eric Bojesen came to paint names on trunks. Cachita called too.

13, Saturday: Kay called to say, "I am instructed to inform you that the Assembly for March 23 has been temporarily canceled."

What next! Enough uncertainties. Oh to get it settled. Sonia Kucej and husband came to play bridge and have supper. Betty at Stine's.

14, Sunday: Stuart Craig spoke at Com. Church. Listened to Wagner program on radio. Supper and music at the Bojesens'. No one seems to know why 22nd Assembly is postponed. Probably too many there, so we won't have a chance. Saw the Days, off to Yangchow on Mar. 18. Betty at Suse's.

15, Monday: Reported waterfall in sealed house No. 44. Mourne came to tea—and Eric, who was painting names on baggage. Those with small children have first claim, so maybe we won't get to the Am. Camp after all. The J. who have helped Mourne! Children's overalls doubled in price. Dick paid $40 for a used Chinese tennis ball which broke in one afternoon.

16, Tuesday: Went to General Hospital to see Winnie Nash and Margaret Kyte. Conditions in Yu Yuen Road Camp not too good. They are really hungry. Roy has rheumatic fever from working in kitchen. Going to Country Hospital. T.Z. Koo & Mrs came to supper. Li Djoh-i working in Fr. Concession.

17, Wednesday: D, B and I spent the day at Sonia Kucej's, mostly in the garden. Betty saw Chummy. Tea out of doors in the warm sunshine. Music when Mr Kucej came and Sonia sang. Such days will be cherished memories. No word yet as to which camp. Very unsettling.

18, Thursday: Kay says almost no chance for the American camp. Ahlers (2) and Hsias (2) here to tea. He talked of reconstruction in China and how Br. & Am. interests must be willing to help, not obstruct. Evans going to Ta Hsia on Monday, so wrote to Jeanne & Nita.

19, Friday: Baxters came calling. They say $700 per person from Br. Gov. for people in camp. IRC has permission to send in parcels. Beulah Chang came to lunch. Suse came to play with Betty.

BRA called but we were out. Got Dick tennis shoes. They now require an old pair before selling a new.

20, Saturday: Got $3,800 clothing allowance from BRA and London Guarantee. No more summoning this week. Saw Tsang. He says local infection. Rainy afternoon & evening at home playing games. Betty at Stine's. Phone seldom rings. Very quiet.

21, Sunday: Geo. Osborn preaching at Com. Church. Adam B. to lunch. Up to the Evans to give a letter for Nita & Jeanne. Evans go in tomorrow. Andrew Wus came and brought *mien.* for supper. One school for foreign boys, one for girls.

22, Monday: Bought shoes for Betty and me. John in bed with cold. M. Schniermacher to supper. British went off to American camp. Still no call for us. The man with an A armband who shouted out, "An American. Hello!"

23, Tuesday: A quiet rainy day at home. Used first sugar rationing coupons and made some candy with a little of the sugar. Much ado over Japan's relinquishing extraterritorial rights. When all this area is one big Jap. concession!

24, Wednesday: International Friendship Chinese dinner at Com. Church. T.Z. Koo spoke on India. About 65 there. Went hunting soap, jam, etc. Shop shelves almost empty. J. find camp space not enough so internment slowed down.

25, Thursday: Visited Kathleen Meyers, sick with rash, and Dr. Dunlap. Beautiful daffodils & forsythia in their garden. Baxters to tea & bridge. Next groups to Lunghwa April 5, 10, 12. Small children to Col. Club.

26, Friday: Einar Edwards, as always in good spirits, came to lunch. Next door Parrs and Nashes called for internment. Read *Fame Is the Spur.* Gifts of linen from 3 old boys—Ling, Jin, Hu. Another one brought a cake.

27, Saturday: Eva Liliastrom & Mrs. Mydens to tea. Discussion of Sweden & Finland. Nashes exempted. Osborn & Black called.

28, Sunday: John preached at Church on "Launch out into the deep." 52 present. 53 Old boys at Medhurst in afternoon. More gifts of tinned goods. Betty at Suse's, Dick at Jessfield. A blessed quiet afternoon reading *Fame is the Spur*.

29, Monday: A quiet rainy day at home. Cold. Packed up tinned goods etc in bags and boxes to go in kit bags & beds. Finished *Fame Is the Spur*. Very fine. Would make excellent movie.

30, Tuesday: Pleasant time having shampoo & set at Richard's. Bridge and tea with Baxters. Dick's rubber soles wore out in a month. 4th set of soles on Wanamaker shoes. Met Fukuda and had coffee at Mars Cafe.

31, Wednesday: Shopping for underwear, shoes, etc. for John and children. Spent over $2,000 with little to show. Meyers says we are sure to go on April 10.

APRIL 1943

1, Thursday: Summoned to BRA for orders. Have to go April 10, 8 am. Baggage on April 8. It's rather hard. Helen Ling & Bernard Read came to dinner & bridge. Creamed chicken — 2 lb chicken $54. Letter from A.E.

2, Friday: Meyers children here for the day. Shiller (Hungarian) filled two teeth ($250.) J went to Church tea for committees and farewelling George, welcoming T.Z. Bakewell there. CCC to be used as hospital — latest rumor.

3, Saturday: Djao family to tea. Got permit to move baggage to camp. Milk prices increased to $11.10 per qt. Sugar ration for foreigners 2 catties per 2 weeks. Bread increased to $3.30 for 16 oz. Wrote to Nita hoping to send by someone on Apr. 7 — last chance.

4, Sunday: Geo. Osborn preaching at church. Tea at the Chris Bojesen's on their anniversary. Mrs Suenson and Mrs Kwouk and Freda called. Parrs to supper.

5, Monday: Visitors: Cachita, G.D., Mrs Liang, T.Z. Koo, Mrs Hsueh. Peter Bojesen spent 4 hours packing one bed. Latest business is buying & selling old things such as boots, globes, etc to those who want to present old in order to buy new. Up at 5:45 to get Parrs off.

6, Tuesday: Betty had her birthday party since Thursday will be busy with baggage. Visitors: Li Djoh-i, Mrs Suenson, who will make a cake, praise be. Got hold of packers for beds. Betty pleased with cake from Kiessling.

7, Wednesday: Bed packed by Peter too heavy. Chinese packers did up 3 for $400. Very satisfactory. A quiet day without many visitors because of steady rain. By 11 pm all trunks closed & so to bed under blankets of Grace Yang's. Children sleeping at Li Djoh-i's 3 nights. Vain search for Lacovomalt.

8, Thursday: Mr. Gavrille's men took 16 pieces to CCC for $200. It looked like a lot but no doubt we'll need it. Called at the Suensons' for cake, cookies, lettuce. Excellent tea at Trock's with Church executive. J.C. & Trock & are Nanking trustees.

9, Friday: C.C. & C.A. Lin of Peking came. Last hair shampoo & set. Many visitors:

Dinner at Li Djoh-i's, then packing finished. Last night at home.

* * * * *

NOTEBOOK 2

WE SEALED OUR HOUSE *at 7:30 a.m. on April 10, 1943, and set off in three pedicabs for the Columbia Country Club. After a few farewells outside we went in and found seats to wait for the buses to take us to camp. No Japanese in evidence at all until time of departure, then Banjo and some consular guards appeared. This Assembly 22 was the largest so far – 360 people. Two cars of Japanese and Swiss officials headed the procession of ten red buses (Frenchtown ones) while a truck of luggage and a repair car brought up the rear. Each bus was half full of luggage and some men had to stand during the hour's journey. Most buses had a Japanese guard but ours did not. We traveled out Columbia Road, down Avenue Joffre to Winling and on past the peach orchards in bloom and the Lunghwa Pagoda.*

There was not a person whom I knew on our bus. Next to me was a family of Jews from Iraq and Aden, who kept nibbling on green olives and eating peanuts.

Remarks overheard in the bus:
"I wish it would hurry up and go."

"See you soon, very soon."

"What time did you go to bed last night?"

"We went at a quarter to one and got up at 5."

"You look awfully sleepy."

"How many buses are there?"

"Mrs. ___ left a roast chicken at home. There's a chance for you."

"How did you come?"

"By pedicab. We paid $30 and they wanted more."

"Daddy, how much did we pay our pedicabs?"

"My amah lives in Lunghwa and she's going to fetch some eggs along."

"I wonder how long it takes. Half an hour, they say."

"It seems to me all the best people are going today."

"I left my monocle at home."

"Look! the Picardie!"

"There's Zikawei Cathedral."

'They are putting on a special dinner for us today – fine Irish stew."

"That's all very well, but I don't know where the plates are."

"I'm quite glad to be going in."

"The trip back wit be nicer probably."

"My gosh, we'll celebrate. I have a few bottles of champagne."

"Look, Mummy, a dead baby by the road."

"The little kids think they are going on a holiday."

"Goodbye! Goodbye!"

After an hour's ride we turned off the main road and passed through the gates of the Shanghai Middle School hereafter known as Lunghwa Camp. The thousand people already there were assembled to welcome us. There were a few familiar faces in the crowd, but the first ten minutes were the hardest, with no fast friends rushing up.

* * * * *

Ruth & John arrive at Lunghwa!

10, Saturday: Breakfasted with Mrs Nash and set off to the CCC at 7:30. Buses left at 10:20, arrived 11:30. Rather dismal effect of gray buildings, no trees. Big crowd to welcome us, but oh the most awful part was the first 10 minutes with no beloved faces among the host. Lunch in our room. Supper first meal provided. Got beds up and that's about all.

11, Sunday: Devoted to settling in, hanging curtains — with breaks only for meals. Blackout practice 8:30 — 9:30.

12, Monday: Saw Smith who still says we are to have a fifth put into our room. We could manage beautifully if only that did not have to be. Rations very short.

13, Tuesday: John went on duty in kitchen 2 — 8 daily. The J. dump 3 days' supply of food and the kitchen squad do the best they can. Blackout again — dark to dawn. But the J. guards don't darken their own windows on. Mrs. Dixon asked Betty to sing — songs in dark after dinner in F.

14, Wednesday: New dining room ready for families only, unattached in old dining room. Meeting of G Block 2nd floor ladies to choose monitor — Mrs. Douglas. The J. dump 3 days' food supply and leave us to do the best we can. Drinking water is hauled from Frenchtown and boiled here.

15, Thursday: Laundry may be sent to Shanghai — 6 pieces per person. The building sent a delegation to Bates to protest against having five people in a room. He said nothing could be done. We'll have 2,000 or 2,100 here and they must sleep somewhere.

16, Friday: Good day for washing and drying. But oh! how hard the water is! They cook with tap water and add no salt.

17, Saturday: Spent the morning moving our beds to try to make room for a fifth person in our 12 by 14 space. Then heard that Hayashi would come to inspect, so moved everything back in order to look crowded.

18, Sunday: 72 new inmates arrived from other camps — Ash Camp & Yu Yuen Rd. They are disgusted with conditions here. There they had space, hot water, better food. Rainy days are very mussy. John washing rice after supper.

19, Monday: 275 new people arrived at 12 o'clock including Bernard Read, George Osborn, the Hawkings, etc. We had Bernard and George to tea. No fifth in our room yet. New system of messes for meals.

20, Tuesday: Those coming in say more rumors of repatriation in May or June. Across the hall is a family of Belgians named Bodson, 5 of them and they have 6 cats. They have 10 big trunks and many parcels and cupboards & rugs, etc.

21, Wednesday: The Baxters find dormitory life trying. They can't sleep well. Washing water ration cut in half. Water only every second day. Kedgeree for supper. Welcome change.

* * * * *

Notebook 2

Weds., April 21

LAST NIGHT THE ELECTRICITY *was out of order and lights did not go on till 9:15. Hayashi was due to inspect this building at 7:45. While people waited for him they gathered in the downstairs hall and sang songs. When they were in the middle of "There'll Always Be an England," Hayashi appeared at the door. People stopped in the middle of a word and scattered very quickly to their rooms.*

Last Monday 275 people came, mostly British with a few odd Americans and some Belgians. A family of 5 named Bodson, Belgians, moved into the room across the hall from us. They have brought six cats and ten big trunks and huge beds containing cupboards, rugs, chairs, tables, etc. They are rather perplexed as to how to fit themselves into a 12 by 14 room.

* * * * *

22, Thursday: Discovered that Roy Watson is here. He had no choice in the matter and his family don't know he's here. Was given 24 hours' notice. Beautiful view of river and countryside from roof of F. Front gates are always open. Road on boundary may be used in daytime.

23, Friday: Good Friday. John up at 5 to light kitchen fire. Missed church by standing 1½ hours in queue to register for showers. Geo. Osborn came to supper bringing ham and chicken. Men elected representatives to attend monitors' meeting.

24, Saturday: Mrs. Dart tried to find out who put the fish roe in the sink! Sent letter to Cachita. Baxter came for tea and our first bridge game.

25, Sunday: Easter. 10:30 am. Church of England service in one half the West dining room. Catholic Mass in the other at the same time.

26, Monday: Wanted to have Peggy Carter to coffee, but John's kitchen schedule prevented. Asked her for Thursday. Busy washing and cleaning windows.

27, Tuesday: Meeting of teachers. John put $3,400 in the C.A.C. bank.

28, Wednesday: Broke off half of a big back tooth on a stone in the rice.

29, Thursday: Celebrated the Emperor's birthday by having a coffee party after tiffin with Peggy Carter and Mr. Bates as guests. Baxter came for bridge. Dick off the food for a day.

30, Friday: Big concert of Scotch and Welsh songs in the dining room. Took Betty for her first shower.

MAY 1943

* * * * *

(Notebook 2)
Saturday, May 1, 1943

THE EVENT OF THE WEEK *was the opening of the showers, 44 for men and 44 for women. We booked times earlier and are grouped A & B, so that A group goes one day and B the next – a shower every other day. It's a very long trek to the shower building but the hot bath is worth the effort. The first day it was a scream. I laughed so I could hardly wash. They don't trust us to use water ad lib. Everybody waits outside in his kimono or whatever he wears till the group before us comes out.*

On entering, one must deposit outdoor shoes in cubby holes provided and don clogs. The undressing process is done in one small room, everybody together, with more cubby holes for clothes. The parade of nakedness with towels wrapped around parts then begins. Everybody must wait till everybody else is ready. At a signal from the woman in charge, there is a dive for the shower cubicles.

"Are you ready?" shouts the one in control. "Right, turn <u>on</u>!"
Interval of 1 minute.
"Water off! Water off! Soap now!"
Interval of ½ minute.
"Ready? Water on!"
Interval of 1½ minutes.
"Off! Water off!"

Some dry in the cubicle, some out in the open room. Clothes go on again, the book must be signed, clogs changed for outdoor shoes, and away you go.

* * * * *

1, Saturday: Betty and I avoiding rice and fish. Spent the morning repacking. Inspection at night. Auntie Carol entertaining children. Football & hockey going.

2, Sunday: [Written in faint pencil] We had both tiffin & supper at home, supplementing the dining room food with beef, tomatoes, oranges.

3, Monday: [Written in faint pencil] School began. I'm teaching Senior 4, Senior 1 English. Got our first issue from the canteen—4 lbs peanut butter, 4 lbs biscuits. Elected Maitland as Block representative. Hawkings entertainment meeting.

4, Tuesday: Sad mishap. John broke the red thermos. Got 15 eggs and 4 apples at canteen by standing 1¼ hr. Mail!—a card from Eva Dunlap. Mrs. March asked Ann,"How can Mrs. B. teach you English when she's American?"

5, Wednesday: Dick sick again. Con says must stay off rice & veg. Huckster not keen on Jap. class for silly reasons. Gramophone Concert. Dentist—the only—arrives—American named Butler. Piano came, too, Uchese Bizerta has fallen. Next assembly May 15.

6, Thursday: Got more eggs. No more apples. Some people bought eggs for $2 & sold at $3. Some auctioned apples and got $15. Some people who went to Shanghai bought too much and the Japanese here confiscated it. Biscuits went to schoolchildren. Tiffin at home—Mrs Kwouk's sardines.

7, Friday: More steamed fish, so another tiffin at home. Eggs & beans. Managed to cook some dried fruit on stove. Very enjoyable fruity tea with Peggy Carter on her "terrace." She shared some of her comic conceptions.

8, Saturday: Teachers' meeting after dyeing hands blue with washing winter slacks. Scrambled egg for tiffin. Variety program with Newton in charge in evening.

9, Sunday: Tiffin at home again because there was only fish and cabbage. Had to borrow the Maitland's frying pan. Why didn't I bring one!

10, Monday: Went to the music section meeting where they elected a committee of several, W.F. Rowlands, chairman. Betty and Dick both put ahead one form.

11, Tuesday: Took first walk around the Boundary Road after dinner of boiled egg & bread pudding. Too weary to go to Players meeting so stayed at home to knit a little. Want to study French but can't do everything.

12, Wednesday: Rainy day, so we stayed at home and scrambled eggs for tiffin. Dick brought the fish, cabbage, sweet rice from the dining room. The Senior 1 class will drive me to drink.

13, Thursday: Pea season is on. Kindergarten suspended so that the millions of peas can be shelled in the dining room.

14, Friday: Bernard Read and Lampo came to play bridge after dinner in the upstairs hall. Good time.

15, Saturday: First shopping day at Canteen. Bought bacon, soap, catsup, thermos flasks, etc. Got Red Cross blanks for letters to go abroad. Delightful classical concert—gramophone records. Ordered frying pan and boiler suit for John.

16, Sunday: Bridge and tea with the Turners in their room.

17, Monday: French class.

18, Tuesday: Peggy Carter came to tea. We sat out by the cedar trees and read *Ben Jonson Entertains a Man from Stratford*. Saw the view from E roof before playing bridge with the Fees.

19, Wednesday: The Turners came to say there is a woman here who is going to the American Camp. We found her & she says she may go. Wrote a note in her book to Nita.

20, Thursday: Assembly 27 (60 people) arrived. Mourne Hudspeth came. Cachita sent parcel by her sister and Mother, Mrs.

'G' Block, Lunghwa Camp

Block 'D', 'F', Assembly Hall, Hut 'C' and ruins

Remedios: new boiler suit for John, tinned fruit, etc. French class and afterward choral practice with Eric Clarke in charge. War news is excellent, they say.

21, Friday: The policemen called us at 5:15 am instead of the Maitlands. Typhoid shot.

22, Saturday: Good variety program at Night. Bridge in afternoon — Lampo & George Osborn.

23, Sunday: Bernard Read came to tiffin—sausages and corn for a belated celebration of his birthday. Mourne came for a drink after supper. Lovely sunset from E roof we viewed.

24, Monday: Great excitement when Deirdre Beare fell out a second storey window. They took her to town for X-rays. Remedios two and Mrs Baxter to tea.

25, Tues Sent letter to Cachita signed by John. Also sent letters to Nita & Stine & Joan.

26, Wednesday: Carol & Eric Turner came for bridge in the evening, played in the upstairs corridor. Cold, rainy day. Opened salmon & tomatoes for supper at home. 6 & 7 trips a day on the cobble stones wear me out.

27, Thursday:

28, Friday: Cholera inoculatiion.

29, Saturday: Ernest Box's birthday tea party. An angel food cake was brought from town by friend Paling for the occasion.

30, Sunday: Sardines and eggs and peas at home for tiffin. Adam Black as guest. Mosquito nets were put up. Still sleeping under double blankets, wearing coats to dinner.

31, Monday: Tea with Mrs Remedios and Leah who had cake from home. About 35 turned up to register for Japanese lessons. Only 4 admitted knowing some.

JUNE 1943

1, Tuesday: Determined to make a mop out of rag and a stick. Those in the wash room are always threadbare.

2, Wednesday: Lucky day for us in the canteen: frying pan arrived — $165. Shoes came back half soled $95. J got 2 jars of milk powder for children.

3, Thursday: Terrible rain all day. Tea & bridge with Baxters. John's team on strike in the kitchen — necessary surgical operation but mussy business. Always up against pettiness of some people.

4, Friday: Struggle with mosquito nets and wires. Nets required because of malaria. Quite a few cases already appeared. Wires came down. John had to put up more. 4 nets fill the room. Ugh!

5, Saturday: Tea with Peggy Carter in the afternoon. Mrs. Gasper also there. Bridge in dining room C with Turners after dinner. Concert canceled because of ceremonies for Yamamoto.

6, Sunday: Roy Watson came to have beef and tomatoes for tiffin. I tried a custard pudding made with cake crumbs.

7, Monday: Had Mr & Mrs Bodson to coffee. Power breakdown somewhere outside camp. No water all day — terrible. No lights at night in certain buildings. We conversed in the dark in French class. Had the concert just the same.

8, Tuesday: Big day at the canteen: got pickles, sweet and mustard; dates, Chinese plums, brushes, 2 apples, etc. Musical concert in evening.

9, Wednesday: Excellent musical program at night — violin, piano, voice. 7 pupils, 3 teachers at Japanese class.

10, Thursday: Sent Red Cross letter to Mother.

11, Friday: Jap. supply 1,600 calories. B.R.A. supplement up to

Kitchen team at work, Lunghwa Camp

2,200. Canteen purchases bring total to 2,900. A person should have about 3,000. German workers in last war had only 2,000.

12, Saturday: Typhoon—Very wet. A quiet day at home knitting, grading papers, studying Japanese. Visited with Mourne.

13, Sunday: A visit with Peggy Carter in the morning. She related her interesting early history. P.M. Read *Straight and Crooked Thinking*. One Russian woman said, "The only place for a British passport is the toilet!"

14, Monday: Whit Monday—School holiday. Sports canceled because of mud. Indoor sports. Read Dorothy Sayers *The Zeal of Thy House* and passed it on to Peggy Carter.

15, Tuesday: John and Deirdre Fee came after dinner to play bridge in the upstairs corridor. Big day at Canteen, purchasing jam, biscuits, honey, etc, dates!

16, Wednesday: Jap. lesson and gramophone concert after. Dvorak's New World Symphony was too much for me. Homesick no end—first sleepless night. Coffee and fruit cake with Bodsons after tiffin.

17, Thursday: Downpour.

18, Friday: First big consignment of Red Cross parcels arrived with heavy baggage of As. 30. 3 trucks of them. We have 4. Meyers still indefinite.

19, Saturday: Biggest day yet. Assembly 30 numbering 80 came. B.I. Remedios brought a suitcase full of things from Cachita, G.D. Chen, May ? Yang, including an Easter card from Miss Lillian dated '43. Bridge with Lampo and Bernard in pm. With Turners in evening. Taylors brought sweets from Kucej. Cut B's hair.

20, Sunday: Had the iron tested, plugs ok thanks to Cachita. Cut rhubarb. Collected first Red Cross parcels 4 — and also another from Cachita containing Bon Ami & mustard.

21, Monday: Last week of school before exams. A tiring day of ironing Betty's collected dresses.

22, Tuesday: Having orange juice every morning now — a real treat.

23, Wednesday: Sent letters to Cachita & Trock, Ethel & A.E. Japanese class now has 4 pupils, 2 teachers. Small group arrived — Sanger, Sutcliffe, Gulston. Assembly 31?

24, Thursday: Typhoony weather. Very cool. Betty received candy and letter from Jill.

25, Friday: Spent the morning on Mr. Tulloch's stool washing. Tea with Peggy Carter — chocolate pudding with strawberries and fruit cake out of her parcel.

26, Saturday: Took children to clinic. Dick weighs the same — 74. Betty has gained one lb. Felt in no mood for music so didn't go to the concert.

27, Sunday: Got D and B on soft diet to try improving their ailments. Went to bed myself with fever 102 and a severe tummy upset. Young people's service at church with George Osborn preaching.

28, Monday: Made out exam questions. Then went to bed with a fever.

29, Tuesday: Still feverish and weak and wanting to go home.

30, Wednesday: Spent morning giving an exam and afternoon concocting Dick's birthday "cake:" stale margarine, cookie crumbs, raisins, soda, etc.

JULY 1943

1, Thursday: Dick had 4 boys to tea: Roger and Nigel Philips, Ian Tulloch, Peter Potts. Menu: sandwiches, cocoa, "cake." Then I went to bed with a fever.

2, Friday: Final exam and school assembly. Spent the day recovering from the exertion of Dick's party.

3, Saturday: Camp organization announced. Executive appointed till election can take place a month hence. Walked the border with Peggy Carter who has inherited a cat.

4, Sunday: Celebrated by having a picnic tiffin-tea with Carol and Eric Turner. Ruth Clarke organized an American supper on the roof of E. Terrible sunburn I got at noon. Delightfully cool on E roof. Sylvia Walker told Hayashi we were celebrating.

5, Monday: Sorted and counted tinned goods. Graded exam papers. Still sleeping under blanket.

6, Tuesday: Dale called re repatriation. He says I'd be in Category 2 in the new scheme. Seems doubtful. I saw Bates and he said he'd let me know his interpretation. Carol and Eric Turner came for bridge at 3. Variety program at night.

7, Wednesday: Breakfast: stewed apples, congee, egg, bread, cocoa. Spent the day making school reports and copying them into permanent record books. Still treating sunburn. Not a line from Nita all these months.

8, Thursday: No special celebration. Tiffin at home and we opened the box of chocolates given by Medhurst.

9, Friday:

10, Saturday: Peggy Carter has heard that there are 300 cases of ptomaine in the Chapei camp. I wonder who. Bad pork. Thank goodness, our butchers had enough sense to bury our bad pork. Contractor claimed he lost $40,000. Dug up some & took it away to sell for lard.

11, Sunday: A leisurely day for once—reading *Moral Man and Immoral Society* am and studying Japanese 4 pm after tiffin at home.

12, Monday: Summer school began. Taking 1B as form mistress and for English. Lampo and Carol Turner came to play bridge in afternoon. 2 absent from J. class because refusing to move from dormitory.

13, Tuesday: On with the cleaning. Two shelves done today after school. It poured so we had supper at home. Betty had a letter from Stine. Very hot.

14, Wednesday: Richards and Mourne latest malaria victims. More & more. Bridge with Carol and Eric Turner. Ran away quickly to get home ahead of the storm.

15, Thursday: Sanger came asking me to be one of the six brain trusters to take part in the first program. Comfort funds have at last arrived.

Dew Drop Inn

16, Friday: Whooping cough raging in camp. What a scourge it is. Insufficient quinine for malaria cases, also on increase.

17, Saturday: Entertained at 11 am, serving tomato juice (cold) and sausages, etc. Guests: Peggy Carter, Carol Turner, Mrs. Bodson, Mrs. Maitland, Miss Penfold, Peggy Box. Took part in the Brains Trust in evening program.

18, Sunday: Clergy can't settle dispute over united service, so committee of laymen called in. They put onus of division on Dean. What a business.

19, Monday: E. 203 finally capitulated under extreme pressure and moved out to make way for couples and single men, still expected from Pootung. Dale came saying Jap. Consulate wants list of those Americans not wanting to go.

20, Tuesday: Shortage of coal. No hot showers. Hours for drinking water curtailed. Big football dinner — 250 people — to wind up the season.

21, Wednesday: Carol & Eric Turner came to tea and bridge. Bodsons celebrated Belgian national day interrupted by inspection. Power off again all day. No water. Letters to Cachita, Bobby, Jill, Louise.

22, Thursday: Blackout, dusk to dawn, 2 days. Nuisance. Finished *Gaudy Night* but still don't care for detective fiction.

23, Friday: At work again on my white sweater. Met Mrs. Rowlands with others to discuss hours of work for women, etc. In favour of a women's council. Sent cable to mother. Probably cost $800.

24, Saturday: Dinner (salmon, peas, corn, eggs, pudding & fruit) with Peggy Carter and Mr. Way. Then on to the Quiz program. Bern was sick and couldn't play bridge. He brought us a cantaloupe.

25, Sunday: A quiet day with 3 meals in the room. Torrents of rain caught me in the hut. Reading *Building a Cottage* by Esther Meynell.

26, Monday: Letter from home via Geneva dated Nov. 18, '42, answering mine of May 8, 1942. Rumors that Germans have collapsed in Russia and Mussolini has handed over to King.

27, Tuesday: Cable from Louise, bless her: "Hinder here. following developments. quiet hearts knowing courage sufficient. Gates." Letter from Scotland, Oct. 24, '42. True — Mussolini has resigned. What will develop in Germany?

28, Wednesday: I think of the differences between a YW camp and one such as this: here we are neither like-minded, like-hearted nor like-spoken.

29, Thursday: Quiet day doing room chores and reading on the east balcony. George and Lampo came to play bridge in evening amid the clatter of clogs and the whoops.

30, Friday: New assembly of 18 arrived. Children to clinic. Both have lost weight. Alice Stacey says 600 Americans go Aug. 20-30. That will be a hard day for me, when they go. 470 of occupants have had malaria. 8 new occupants arrived sitting atop their luggage in 3 trucks. Parcel from Cachita — cake, fruit, etc.

31, Saturday: Amplified concert on F roof. Very fine. Moved Peggy to tears. Chopin — Polonaise. Brahms III Symphony, 3rd Movement.

AUGUST 1943

1, Sunday: Betty, Phyllis, Eleanor presented their program of 6 items at 7 pm—well planned and executed. Adults getting whooping cough. Settlement & Concession returned to China. Barriers down. Shanghai one Chinese area.

2, Monday: Bank and school holiday. Supervised washing of all dolls' clothes. At last some fruit syrup available in canteen—Jap. variety. Carol & Eric came. They think Br. repatriation near.

3, Tuesday: John's name went up as nominee for the Council. Reading *Letters from Women of Britain.*

4, Wednesday: Requested by Sanger and a number of women to stand for the Council. It's a great temptation. But John prefers that I don't run. Very good musical program (gramophone) in our matshed.

5, Thursday: Still wanting to run and being asked by numerous people to stand. It's hard to do what I know I should do. Dodson hears that the Gripsholm is in Shanghai to take Americans.

6, Friday: Belgians summoned to sign for evacuation. Oral evacuated. Allies in Italy, we hear. Decided not to run for the Council in spite of numerous requests and accusations of "letting the women down." All very flattering.

7, Saturday: Baxter withdrew his name from Council nominees because of complications. He asked a person going to hospital to take a message to Bryson. Message was taken by someone else, who dropped letters out of pocket. All writers called up before Hayashi. Next assembly due Aug. 9. Meyers included.

8, Sunday: Spent morning cleaning K 4 for the Meyers.

9, Monday: Assembly 30—19 of them—arrived. The Meyers here at last. Betty very happy. Jill and Ruth spent the day with us. Rumors of Am. repatriation this month, British two months later. Packages from Cachita—cups, bedspreads, cakes, etc.— and from Mrs Dunlap, bless her. Mrs Suenson sent a butter cake. Letter from Eva Dunlap.

10, Tuesday: Peggy and Mrs Gaspar to tea to enjoy my quarter of the Suenson cake. Plums, peaches, apples, tomatoes, corn brought in by Kathleen. Such a wealth of good things all at once. War news good. Sicily crumbling. G Block Concert in the evening. Lalo's Spanish Symphony.

11, Wednesday: Disastrous typhoon raged all day, tearing roofs off buildings and whipping all our comfortable matsheds to shreds. Two huts had to be evacuated, some people to Assembly Hall. We took Leah Remedios. Dining rooms roofless, so meals served in various blocks. No power, so no lights and no water. Grim. London hasn't much on us. More work for the men.

12, Thursday: Leah Remedios came to sleep with us, being homeless due to the typhoon. They say 2 million dollars damage.

13, Friday: A few workmen arrived with few tools and no materials to repair damages. Stayed one day and went away.

14, Saturday: Carol and Eric came (with apple butter) to play bridge after noon. Canteen selling comestibles only through entrance to dentist's office.

15, Sunday: Took Jill and Ruth for the day so as to give Kathleen Meyers a chance to rest and recover from the recurrence of her poison rash. Up at 4:30 am to see fine eclipse of the moon. Fine concert in front of F. Sat with Peggy & enjoyed Lalo's Spanish Symphony.

16, Monday: School Assembly to pull classes together after typhoon disruption. Eggs again available, 4 per person, $3 ea.

17, Tuesday: Spent the morning washing for Barrs and Meyers

Refuge in Assembly Hall – morning after Typhoon, Aug. 11, 1943

families. First day at serving meals, squad leader with 5 helpers. That awful feeling when the meat ran out! Coal at last arrived, just when the kitchen was thinking they could serve only one hot meal a day.

18, Wednesday: The haycart ran over Dick grazing his back. Popular selections concert in front of F. Betty with a cold. Stacey over for tomato juice in morning. R. Huckstep taken to hospital. Would not permit Bryson or Ranson to go. Came back at 10 pm for one parent.

19, Thursday: Election day. Interviewed Candidate Barry. English teachers' meeting. Made more pickle & some apple sauce. Saw Bates re birthplace figures & Paterson re Betty's eyes. He is arranging for her to go to Shanghai to see Tsang.

20, Friday:

21, Saturday: Carol & Eric came for tea and Bridge bringing an apple pie, baked on their chatty in a borrowed oven. Latest rumour: American planes have dropped leaflets over Shanghai. Meyers says repatriation will surely take place.

22, Sunday: August IRC parcels have arrived. Election results announced. John was not elected. Braidwood 840, Renard 390, Penfold 385, Mrs. Porter 202. Still think I would have been elected. It's hard to stand aside.

23, Monday: Last Assembly arrived. Only aged and sick still out. Chocolate and pickles from Bojesens. Armbands now bear Chinese characters.

24, Tuesday: More and more malaria and Hong Kong foot. At last got thermos refill and bucket ordered long ago. Peggy and Way came to hear Beethoven's Fifth and other music at G Block concert.

25, Wednesday: Two letters from Nita! After so long a wait. Feb. 25 to Aug. 25 — 6 months to the day. Betty brought them to me while I was having tea with Peggy Carter — K & B fruit cake, peaches, coffee. Bates asked me to help with publicity and notices. Volunteered for canteen 2 – 4. Had to open cigarette boxes so all wrappings can be returned. Shortage of paper in Shanghai.

26, Thursday: Bernard and Lampo came to have pancakes and play bridge. My turn to serve food again.

27, Friday: Another afternoon straightening cigarette papers in the canteen. Kathleen & Freddie Meyers, Jill and Ruth to dinner. Jill for the night. Dinner outside just finished when rain began. No more eggs after this week sold in canteen, so they say. Rumor: bank insolvent.

28, Saturday: Tea with Miss Dennis, Mrs. Crawford, Peggy Carter. Volunteered for peeling potatoes in the morning. Prefer boiled potatoes to the mashed ones produced. Latest story: butchers told not to weigh meat because then they'd know how much the guards (?) squeeze.

29, Sunday: Serving meals again, with ironing in between. Finished Kathleen's frill for the dressing table. We can send 25 word letters on repatriation ship, 2 per family.

30, Monday: Devoted the morning to scrubbing the floor with John to fetch buckets of water. Great improvement tho burned spots show all the more. Afternoon spent on cigarettes in canteen. Figs again, so made some jam.

31, Tuesday: Block concert under the shed in the evening. Beethoven's Kreutzer Sonata.

SEPTEMBER 1943

1, Wednesday: First auction. Things brought fabulous prices: 1 tin beef (corned) $220; chair $400; raincoat $1,200; spiced beef $80, etc.

2, Thursday: Policed the halls during quiet hour (2-3:30) carrying the QUIET sign from AWC. Effective! Worked in canteen till 5 packing cigarette packages. Argument with Ballard re rest hour in pm.

3, Friday: Mrs Porter asked me to serve on Women's Advisory Committee. Carol and Eric came for tea and bridge. LMS meeting at night when Ernest Box and I spoke. Voted to continue parcels.

4, Saturday: Spent the afternoon sitting in our summer house with the guards giving a noisy performance before us. Allies invaded Italy. No newspaper for us. Not impressed with Virginia Woolf's *The Years*.

5, Sunday: Rumor: martial law in Shanghai. Service and concert on E roof, including Tchaikovsky Concerto No. 1. Visit from Mrs Hill re milk distribution, showers. Minds are restricted when bodies are.

6, Monday: School staff meeting 10-12. First meeting of Women's Advisory Committee considering milk distribution, showers, vegetables, etc. Miss Penfold vice chairman; I secretary. Mrs Porter, chairman.

7, Tuesday: Betty went to Shanghai for Dr. Tsang to examine her eyes. Kathleen and Freddie Meyers came for the Block Concert (Beethoven's Emperor) and we sat on the balcony afterward.

8, Wednesday: Inspection and roll call, the first inspection in a

9226

610

The COMITE INTERNATIONAL DE LA CROIX-ROUGE,

GENEVE (Suisse)
Service Internés Civils
Service Civilian Internees
Civil-Gefangenen Dienst
Please transmit the following message:

DEMANDEUR—ANFRAGESTELLER—ENQUIRER

Nom-*Name* BARR Nationality BRITISH

Prénom-*Christian Name-Vorname* MARGARET ELIZABETH

Camp-*Gefangenlager* LUNGHWA CIVIL ASSEMBLY CENTRE

Matriculation No. 22\228

Localité-*Locality-Ortschaft* SHANGHAI

Province-*County-Provinz*

Pays-*Country-Land* CHINA

AMERICAN RED CROSS
JAN 3 1944
INQUIRY UNIT

Message à transmettre—Mitteilung—Message
(25 mots au maximum d'un caractère strictement personnel et familial)—
(nicht über 25 Worte, rein persönliche Familiennachrichten)—(not over 25 words,
family strictly personal character).

10806 IN BIG BRITISH CAMP NEAR RIVER
SINCE APRIL. CORNER ROOM. COOL
SUMMER. DADDY TEACHING. KITCHENING.
MOTHER TEACHING. HOUSEKEEPING.
CHILDREN STUDYING. PLAYING.
LONGING TO SEE YOU.

Date-*Datum* SEPTEMBER 3RD 1943

DESTINATAIRE—EMPFÄNGER—ADDRESSEE

Nom-*Name* HILL Nationality AMERICAN

Prénom-*Christian Name-Vorname* MRS. J. R.

Rue-*Street-Strasse* 824 NORTH MARSALIS AVENUE

Localité-*Locality-Ortschaft* DALLAS

Département-*County-Provinz* TEXAS

Pays-*Country-Land* U.S.A.

ANTWORT UMSEITIG. RÉPONSE AU VERSO. REPLY OVERLEAF.
Bitte sehr deutlich schreiben. Prière d'écrire très lisiblement. Please write very clearly.

International Red Cross letter form sent from Lunghwa Camp to Dallas, Texas, Sept. 3rd, 1943 month. To Mrs Baxter's to consider contents of parcels to be sent in. Office says they treat a sheet of paper like a bank note. Cost $125 each. None issued without written order from executive committee.

9, Thursday: Hard work making a brick floor for our hut. Marksmen here to shoot dogs. Rumor: American fleet in Genoa. Hitler has taken over Italian air force. Italy has capitulated. Took Betty to Goodwin for eye drops. She has gained 3 lbs since April, Dick the same. Peggy sick.

10, Friday: News of Italy's capitulation confirmed. Conte Verde and Lepanto scuttled in Whangpoo. Dramatic! Sudden blackout at night without warning. "Military Manoeuvers." Washing for Peggy, still sick. Finished the floor of the hut. Letter from Bobby received dated Aug. 9.

11, Saturday: Carol and Eric came to play bridge. We sat in the hut on the newly laid floor. Stayed on there to cook pancakes, potatoes, onions for supper. Variety concert in pm in Assembly Hall.

12, Sunday: Betty sick with fever. Dr. Burton came. Thinks malaria. Too much of it here!

13, Monday: Betty with fever 105. John came home from kitchen with fever 104. Burton says almost surely malaria. Kathleen & Freddie, Carol & Eric came to cheer me in the evening. Second meeting about parcels.

14, Tuesday: A wearying day with both John and Betty sick. Fever 102 & 104+. Blood test for malaria. Kind friends do help with water, ice, orange juice, ironing, toast, etc. Oh, to be at home! Peggy better, sitting in hut. Betty quinine.

15, Wednesday: School opened. John's fever 104; Betty's 106. Grim time. Worn out, Friends very helpful: Carol and Eric, Kathleen & Freddie, Bob Richard, Chris McClennan, Yvette and Mrs Bodson. Americans and Canadians given notice to leave on Sept. 19. 24 hours for trunks. 200 lbs 3 pieces sent ahead. 2 suitcases in hand. O to see Nita!

16, Thursday: Patients improved. Baggage of repatriates searched thoroughly twice by gendarmes & by customs. No printed matter permitted. Tins & soap removed. Mrs Pate was brought by Hayashi to stay the night. Miss Martin came to bathe patients. Dr. Garnick brought custard and washed pyjamas.

17. Friday Patients on hospital diet. First classes at school—8 hours of Eng. Visits of repatriates allowed. Some went to other camps, some to Shanghai. 23 going from here—16 Americans, 7 Canadians.

18, Saturday: John and Betty up on wobbly legs. Gave Nina Smith, Lily Pate, Alice Stacey messages for Nita, Ruth, Rosie. Various parties for repatriates. Musical quiz at night. My thoughts in Chapei all the day.

19, Sunday: It was difficult saying goodbye to the American repatriates at 8 am. There isn't even a place one can go to weep in this camp. Tea with Mourne. Red Cross parcels came—5 for us, including one from Cachita containing vanilla & spice.

20, Monday: Pathetic sight: truck containing body of Mrs Ackerman who died of heart failure in the morning, followed to the gate by her friends. The wicker basket in back of truck with other things. First death in camp, though two in Shanghai.

21, Tuesday: After classes, cooking ventures on the chatty: custard (with newly received nutmeg); pancakes, candy. Kathleen came to the Block Concert and we heard Beethoven's Fourth Symphony.

* * * * *

Notebook 2

Making a Chatty

The children were always wanting to cook, seeing many other people at it. The public stove near the dining room was always crowded. Many people had individual stoves made out of tin, bricks, etc.

I produced an empty biscuit tin. Nothing happened. I proposed to Ernest Box that he take our tin and do the work and we both use the chatty. It took him some days to examine other chatties and find out what needed to be done. Mr. Thompson's help was solicited and he cut the proper hole and put in the iron rods, fished from the ruins, to form the grate for fuel.

Ernest got some bricks and somehow got some lime to mix with the mud which was plastered round the bricks inside. When the mud had dried, the chatty was ready to use. The children could hardly wait. Pancakes, custard, eggs and toast were the favorites. We had to make a rule that they could cook only every other day, not every day. The chatty was very convenient at times, but I never enjoyed trying to concoct things in camp.

* * * * *

22, Wednesday: Carol and Eric came to play bridge in our hut, where we also had tea. My gray shoes came back after 2 months in Shanghai. Teaching *Henry V* & Lamb's *Essays* keeps me busy.

23, Thursday: Very good review in Assembly Hall. Hayashi surprised us with announcement that Yangchow Camps are being dissolved. . Camp may come here late October. On Monday 140 Pootung men arrive here to make room for couples there.

24, Friday: Children's concert. Japanese lesson with 3 new men pupils. Women's Advisory Committee 8-10 pm. Then a long chat with W. Penfold. John back on kitchen duty after malaria. What will become of the school if men are housed in dining rooms? Freddie Meyers down with malaria.

25, Saturday: Spent the day with Peggy—having a holiday in the hut. Very quiet and enjoyable. Pork and beans for tiffin. Teachers cleaned one of big old buildings for the school.

26, Sunday: Great excitement over the escape of Conder sometime yesterday. Bernard cannot make purchases of food at gate because CAC Bank hasn't the money. No eggs, alas, and I owe eggs to 4 neighbours!

27, Monday: 140 men from Pootung arrived in the rain. Lawrence Denham refused to come. Some negroes included among Harrison crew, split up so as not to cause so much trouble in one camp. Tea with Kathleen & Freddie Meyers.

28, Tuesday: Had Stanley Gregory to tea and heard news of Pootung and the departure of the Americans. Choral Society practice. Harrison crew asked McGreal if he represented American interests here! School moved into building in new area.

29, Wednesday: John came home from the kitchen with fever. Return of malaria. Wild war rumors about landing in France. 8:30 pm roll call will interfere with evening classes. Jap. cut to 40 minutes. Canteen reopened, but still no eggs.

30, Thursday: First day of more stringent rules. Roll call 8:30 am and pm taken by Jap. gendarme. Each block will have an interpreter to go with gendarme. Mrs Stebbeds here. Women's Advisory Council meeting 7-8.

OCTOBER 1943

1, Friday: Good bridge in the Turners' spacious room, vacated by Greenlands. Reading *These Hurrying Years* Gerald Heard. More troubles in kitchen—threatened strike, etc.

2, Saturday: Kathleen and Freddie came for bridge and tea—also Jill and Ruth. Evening roll call relaxed—7:30 pm monitors make rounds—also 10:30.

3, Sunday: Spent the morning reading *These Hurrying Years* sitting in the sun in the hut. Afternoon inside studying lessons for the week.

4, Monday: Roll call changed to 9 am. Beastly nuisance—makes everything start late. Went to see Dr. Curtis about minor ailment. Jill started in the French School. Betty put up to 1A. Vaccinated.

5, Tuesday: Whole afternoon devoted to washing, accumulation of one week.

At the whistle's blast – the morning rush for water

6, Wednesday: Wilson came after dinner to get some jars and we talked till 10 pm. He is a UP correspondent who came out at 18. Was with Lytton Commission, etc. Quite interesting conversation.

7, Thursday: A busy day with errands, canteen, haircut, library, washing, ironing, copying "Orpheus" and "The Swan" to use in concert. Women's Advisory Committee. Chat with W. Penfold afterward, as usual.

8, Friday: Spent the morning cooking — sponge cake, pudding, custard sauce. Carol & Eric came for tea and bridge. Pleasant evening of bridge with Kathleen and Freddie, plus iced chocolate sponge.

9, Saturday: Deirdre and John Fee came to tea. Spent the morning producing a fried sponge cake and 7 minute frosting, borrowing Kathleen's beater.

10, Sunday: Polson and Bradford came to tea, bringing news of A.E. Still no Chapei list of those who departed. O for news of Nita!

11, Monday: Water off all day and no lights at night. Lack of water is our greatest curse. Walked by moonlight to see Kathleen and Freddie re kitchen doings. J Block couples vs singles squabbled and demanded separate food service. How small our minds become!

12, Tuesday: Still no water. Shanghai streets renamed to erase foreign influence. Bernard Read and Lampo came for bridge in the hut, therefore I spent the morning on sponge cake. Lecture by Sanger on "Future of Civil Aviation."

13, Wednesday: Japanese lesson and choral society. Water and lights on again, thank heaven. Bojesen baby, Catherine Ruth, born Oct. 12.

14, Thursday: Bacon ½ lb per card in the canteen. Literary meeting to make plans for Shakespeare reading. Block stove being tried out.

15, Friday: Coffee with Carol Turner and Enid Phillips at 11 am. George Stacey conferring with John re very bad kitchen conditions.

16, Saturday: A busy day trying to recruit vegetable workers for the Labor Dep't. Remarkable how many women refuse to do 2 hrs per week. Bridge with Carol & Eric.

17, Sunday: Kitchen upheaval kept John busy. Peggy Carter came to sit in the hut all the sunny day. Bacon, eggs, coffee for tiffin.

18, Monday: A crowded day with grading essays, teaching, washing, reading *Two Gentlemen of Verona*, choral, Japanese lesson, etc.

19, Tuesday: Letters sent to Jeanne and Cachita. At last lists of those who left on the ship. Nita went. They are now in Goa. I wish I were, too. Choral Society rehearsing every night for concert. Nominated for floor monitor.

20, Wednesday:

21, Thursday: Polished windows. More upheavals in kitchen. Carol and Eric came to have tea and play bridge. Women's Advisory Council discussing labor problems. Russian woman's aristocratic stomach!

22, Friday: Party for Kathleen on her birthday in the Hut: sausages, pickles, and a fried sponge cake made before 7:30 am. Choral Society Concert at 8:15 pm. John very busy with kitchen meeting, kitchen duty, teaching, house meeting.

23, Saturday: Read an outlaw's part in *Two Gentlemen of Verona*. Great to-do at the dance which lasted till 12. Hayashi said, "No lights out." Japanese and a number of foreigners drunk as lords. Disgraceful performance. Hayashi's "secret joy."

24, Sunday: A quiet day to catch up on sleep and visit the sick — Christine MacLennan — in hospital. Malaria still rife. Still using mosquito nets.

25, Monday: First visiting day. Husbands, wives, mothers came calling — mostly Orientals. Occupants in their best clothes with bunches of flowers.

26, Tuesday: Received letter from Ruth Packard dated Sept. 18. Was homesick the rest of the day, thinking of all those on the ship en route to NY. How much I miss Nita! Tea with Meyers family after a fine hot shower.

27, Wednesday: Fine crop of rumors: old German flag flying in Shanghai, Hitler repudiated; Nazi finance section in Switzerland; Hess carrying peace overtures to Germany; Sassoon cabled internees use Cathay & other hotels. Chinese & Japanese can't agree on running Shanghai city government.

28, Thursday: Actually sat still in the hut and knitted for 1½ hours. Rest of afternoon devoted to making fritters with help of Dick, Lampo, Bodson, et al. Used lard. Advisory Council met.

29, Friday: Bridge with Carol and Eric Turner. LMS meeting in the men's shower dressing room, shod in slippers.

30, Saturday: Sports meet in afternoon. Mid-term reports for school. Washing, mending.

31, Sunday: Peeled potatoes and chopped carrots the morning. About half the vegetable workers turn up. Labor problems! Got into the men's discussion on the question at night.

NOVEMBER 1943

1, Monday: Properly initiated into the job of being floor monitor, by having two women slay me with words. Determined to consider the source and not be fazed by it. School half-term holiday. Talked Labor with Sanger. Labor officer and Labor chairman both resigning.

2, Tuesday: Adamson came to ask me to take over Labor Office with Mary Diack. Chicken pox epidemic on.

3, Wednesday: Spent the day interviewing various men and finally decided to do the Labor Office job. Had to cancel two bridge dates — Carol & Eric — Kathleen & Freddie — because John was sick. Meyers' anniversary.

4, Thursday: Women's Advisory Committee. Learned that Jeanne is running labor office at Chapei!

5, Friday: John down with malaria again. Dick getting infected blister dressed at clinic. Helping Christmas Committee with materials and machine. The Russian woman who wants to sing is circulating a petition. Quarrels taken to Bates. How silly. Saw Mrs Rodger who gave real news of Nita & Chapei.

6, Saturday: Coal ration cut from 180 tons to 120 tons per month. Drastic cuts in drinking water, showers, hot water, kitchen, etc. Strong protest made to J. Sale of children's clothes successful enough. Debate on nationalization of banks.

7, Sunday: Vegetables again. Great sport listening to the ideas and reactions of the squad members. Turned over classes to Skues and Winifred Penfold preparatory to taking over Labor Office. Mr. Mothersill, Mr. Bradford to tea.

8, Monday: Turned classes over to Miss Penfold in preparation for

Hard labour – Tai-pans' Corner!

taking on new work. Washed in cold rain water all the week's laundry. Wrote a Japanese composition. John's malaria better.

9, Tuesday: Took Dick to Ranson who ordered him to bed to rest his tummy.

10, Wednesday: With Mary Diack took over the Woman's Labor Office — about the hardest woman's job in camp.

11, Thursday: Church Social with Armistice Day service.

12, Friday: An afternoon of cooking sponge cake, salad dressing, orange custard, etc.

13, Saturday: Bridge with Carol & Eric. Kathleen and Freddie came after us and we had an evening's visit on the subject of comfort allowances and restrictions of spending. Hot showers again.

14, Sunday: Turned over monitor's duties to Mrs. Bodson. Pork and beans tasted good. Block stove on, once in the week.

15-17 No entries

18, Thursday: Bitterly cold. Drop of 30° in 2 days. 70, Tuesday, 63 Wed, 40 Thurs. maximums.

19, Friday: Afternoon devoted to chasing slackers and pasting window with Bodson's pink paper. Coffee with Ruth and Eric in their de luxe cubicle.

20, Saturday: Sensational development: Swiss have suspended payment of comfort allowance. Red Cross parcels in. We got lard and bacon for all LMS, also things from Cachita. John and George debating on "Education has not kept pace." Choral Society rehearsing "Hear My Prayer." Long vegetable session.

21, Sunday: Busy with accumulated home chores.

22, Monday: Week's holiday from Japanese lessons.

23, Tuesday: Worked on suggestions with Mary Diack and journeyed to the farm to check. Choral Club practice for Sunday's concert.

24, Wednesday: Chose one committee member for Labor, now for one more.

25, Thursday: Celebrated Thanksgiving with Carol and Eric Turner and Patricia. Dinner at 5:30 in our room with sausages, cauliflower, apple sauce. Mrs Thompson produced turkey place-cards after 3 pm. A few browny-red leaves. Otherwise washing and canteen as usual.

26, Friday: Women's Advisory Committee in Mrs Hill's room. Much time interviewing people about changes of work. Russian song program at night.

27, Saturday: Read "Gertrude" in *Hamlet*. Good fun. Choral rehearsal of "Hear My Prayer." Worked at 1,000+ lbs of vegetables 2 to 4 pm. O! for an inspiration on rotation of work. Coffee at 11 with Peggy.

28, Sunday: Dick still has two fingers bound up. Food deficiencies seem to prevent healing.

29, Monday: No Japanese lessons because teachers don't wish to come out at night.

30, Tuesday:

DECEMBER 1943

1, Wednesday: Dick's nail being removed bit by bit. Two very sore fingers he has, which won't heal. Taking yeast, B1, cod liver oil.

2, Thursday: Stoves installed, but little hope of any coal to put in them.

3 -5 No entries

6, Monday: Carol and Eric came to play bridge and have tea.

7, Tuesday: Five children, aged 9-15, arrived here from the Weihsien camp. They have been in Chefoo schools and have not seen their parents for 3 years. Credit due J. for reuniting the families.

8, Wednesday: No music allowed in camp so Happy Fanny's concert had to be postponed. Mrs Henry (Swedish) departed from camp after four months here. Cable from Sweden, they say.

9, Thursday: Betty in with a bad cold. Looks after herself pretty well when I'm out most of the day. 9:30-12 stood in line to buy last issue of sundries at canteen.

10, Friday: Evening visit with Kathleen and Freddie Meyers. Coal is due but hasn't arrived. Only enough for one day. (?) No hot showers.

11, Saturday: Gomersall lectured on "Planning an Industrial Enterprise." French comedy, well done. Vegetable volunteers again—we found 16. Betty still in bed with a cold.

12, Sunday:

13, Monday: We have been asked to pay back to the Swiss the comfort money that has been received all these months by

12 stateless people here. J. consider them British, but British government doesn't recognize them.

14, Tuesday: Bridge and tea, Bernard and Lampo here.

15, Wednesday:

16, Thursday: John was appointed kitchen manager. He'll do a good job of it—tough task though it is. Bridge with Carol Turner, Mrs. Maas, Mrs. Rodger.

17, Friday: Women's Advisory Committee meeting in our room. Thermometer at 65° very mild and comfortable.

18-20 No entries

21, Tuesday: Japanese Consulate has sent us a Christmas gift—so marked on the paper—bags of cracked wheat still in the American Red Cross sacks.

22, Wednesday:

23, Thursday: Peggy Carter came to tea. Children off to Christmas and birthday parties.

24, Friday: John busy in the kitchen standing over the pork for Christmas tiffin. Heard Dearn read *Christmas Carol*. Helped with children's party where toys, one orange, and a packet of life-savers were given.

25, Saturday: To Church in Dining Room D after a breakfast of bacon & eggs. Guests to tea: Bernard Read, Geo. Osborn, Adam Black, Mourne Hudspeth. Betty & Dick to tea at the Meyers. Block Xmas tree with lights.

26, Sunday:

27, Monday:. John took over kitchen management. Had monitors meeting to consider vegetable fatigue scheme.

28, Tuesday: A hectic day what with people falling sick, Labor Committee meeting, etc. Dinner with the Remedios family between their beds in B East.

29, Wednesday: Sent letter to woman who refuses to work. Reading *Small House at Allington*.

Schoolchildren, Lunghwa Camp

Schoolchildren lining up, Lunghwa Camp ('G' Block in background)

30, Thursday: Worked all day on the vegetable fatigue business.

31, Friday: Spent the day trying to get the vegetable fatigue scheme going. Grand dinner in the kitchen at 8:30—looked in at the dance and at 12 sang Auld Lang Syne with Kathleen & Freddie, Mary & Philip Diack, B.J. & Braidwood.

* * * * *

From Notebook 2
Regulations of the Civil Assembly Centre

Article I. The provisions prescribed hereunder shall be observed by those ordered to live in the Civil Assembly Centre.

Clause 1. The Civil Assembly Centre being the best home for those who live in it, must be loved and cherished by all of them. All persons shall take care of their health and live in harmony with one another. There shall be no disputing, quarreling, disturbing or any other improper demeanors.

Clause 2. In the daily routine enforced by the Civil Assembly Authorities the turn-out, the roll calls, and the lights out shall be especially observed with precision.

Clause 3. Food and other allowances being fixed by the Government, no alteration in them shall be allowed. Complaints or manifestations of discontent against the food provided or against its quantity, or any complaints against living conditions or equipments of the Civil Assembly Centre shall not be made.

Clause 4. The orders given by the Japanese officials and police guards shall be strictly obeyed and there shall be no act of defiance.

Clause 5. No going out of the Civil Assembly Centre is allowed except with permission granted by the Commandant of the Civil Assembly Centre. Such permission may be given only in the case of illness necessitating special treatment outside the Centre or in case of other unavoidable circumstances.

Clause 6. For the time being one letter a month, subject to censor by the Japanese officials, will be permitted for each person. Such letters must be typed or written in clear and legible handwriting: letters hard to read shall not be accepted.

Clause 7. Those living in the Civil Assembly Centre shall be divided into a number of sections, each composing of about twenty members which shall have its own chief responsible for the section members therein.

Clause 8. The sections shall be formed into groups each of which shall have its own Captain. Orders and notifications by the Commandant or officials in charge of the Civil Assembly Centre shall be given to Captains and they shall be transmitted through Captains to the chiefs of sections who in turn shall convey them to their respective members. The Captains and the Chiefs of Sections shall act as intermediaries in communicating the wishes of their members to the officials in charge.

Clause 9. In order to facilitate self-administration in the Centre, there shall be divisions in charge of general affairs, accounts, food supplying, health, equipments, education, and discipline. The personnel of these divisions shall be selected by those living in the CAC.

Clause 10. The instructions of the Captains, Chiefs of Sections and Divisions shall be obeyed and no act of defiance or complaint shall be made of them.

Clause 11. As all members of each section shall be held responsible and punished for run-away of its member, caution should be taken by each of them to prevent such an occurrence.

Clause 12. No argument shall be made nor any rumor shall be circulated concerning the world situation, nor any criticism against Japan shall be allowed.

Clause 13. A fire would result in the greatest misery for all who live in the Centre; caution must strictly be taken by all members for its prevention. The Chief of Section before going to bed shall go on the round of each chamber and inspect ash trays and others which might be the cause of a fire.

Clause 14. Cooking and dish-washing, cleaning of the lavatory, bath, dining room, kitchen, playground, and others shall be done by those living in the Centre by turn. Each person shall serve his or her own meal.

Clause 15. The room shall be cleaned and put to order, bed made, and laundries done by each person.

Clause 16. In case when the dining room cannot accommodate all the members, a meal may be served in 3 or 4 turns. In such a case each person shall take his or her meal in less than twenty minutes.

Clause 17. The lights-out of each chamber shall be done under the supervision of the Chiefs of Sections.

Clause 18. Members of a section shall take care of the sick in its section; when medical treatment is necessary, request shall be made for it to the Japanese officials in charge through the Captain.

Article II. Violation of the above shall be dealt with disciplinary measures of short allowance, detention, etc. and in certain cases with severe punishments.

Article III. These regulations shall be enforced from the day of assembly at the Centre.

Article IV. When necessary, orders other than stipulated above will be given by the Commandant.

* * * * *

1944

Enduring

THROUGHOUT 1944 WITH the war turning against both Japan and the Nazis, the main task of the internees was to endure hunger, thirst and cold. The importance of food can be judged by the frequency with which Mother mentions it. On Febuary 10 she writes: "... Children's kitchen refused to cook meat sent by Japanese. Whale? Horse? Spiced beef? Awful smell to the stew!"

She kept a careful record of the amount of food sent by the Japanese, which decreased as time went by (see statistics at end of 1944.) We did, however, continue to receive monthly food parcels from kind friends in Shanghai and in April we received parcels from the American Red Cross (see 'The Happiest Day' on April 9.) Later in the year more parcels arrived, this time from the International Red Cross (June 22.)

Water was brought in from the city but sometimes it did not come for days at a time and the shortage of coal to boil it for drinking water only made matters worse. Whereas in 1943 Mother had even mentioned sending sheets to a laundry in the city, now (June 4) she writes of "washing 11 sheets in rain water."

Frequently, the lack of coal caused power cuts and various measures were taken to save electricity. Only 40 watt globes were allowed (Febuary 25) and on Febuary 23 all irons had to be turned in. "No ironing allowed."

Our health began to suffer and Dick was the member of our family who suffered most. During 1944 he spent two long spells in the camp hospital, one time for seven weeks. At this point I must recount a story which Mother does not include in her diary because she did not know it. In the camp there was a small farm on which there was one cow, several goats and a number of pigs. The tiny amount of cow's milk was reserved for those in special need, including people like my brother in hospital. I was asked by Mother to take a mugful of milk every day to Dick. One day, not having tasted milk for a long time, I took a sip on the way. The guilt that I felt thereafter has remained with me to this day.

The camp still had to be run and Mother continued her job in the Labor Office until September 7. She writes: "My resignation from Labour Office accepted – 10 months is a long enough spell." In the meantime she had been elected on March 11 "with 904 votes out of total 1283" to the General Council, Lunghwa's "Parliament." In many entries for 1944 she writes about the issues discussed there.

One of the most important issues was escapes. There had, in fact, been one escape on September 26, 1943, but at that time there had not been much reaction from the Japanese. On New Year's Eve, December 31, 1943, three more men escaped and this time there were new restrictions on our movement and freedom. (January 2) "Lights out 9:30."

On May 23, five men escaped and this time the "New Territory," an area separated from the rest of the camp by barbed wire, was closed. That meant that the school had to be closed as that was where Lunghwa Academy had been operating. One childish memory of mine is that I could see, on the other side of the barbed wire, radishes which I had planted as part of a science project growing – but I could not harvest them.

The most serious event in the whole of our stay in Lunghwa

was the escape of three more men on August 20. This time the Japanese reaction was swift and severe: "Confined to rooms, turn in books, no canteen, no library, no newspapers, 2 meals a day – no breakfast, etc." The rest of the story can be read in the diary. Things got out of hand and this led to a demonstration by the internees, an event we children called "The Riot." It was at this time that I saw with my own eyes the only physical violence I witnessed during the whole period of internment: a neighbor being slapped by a Japanese guard because his children were not at the door in time for an extra roll call in the evening.

The miserable year of 1944 was made even worse by the fact that the winter of 1944-1945 was one of the coldest in living memory. It arrived early – on December 1 – is mentioned again on December 6 and by December 9 Mother writes: "Roll call at 7 pm so people can go to bed earlier." The internees had actually asked for an earlier roll call so that they could go to bed to keep warm.

One ray of hope emerged at the end of the year: American air raids. On Nov. 11 Mother writes, "During morning roll call, several American planes appeared overhead…dropped several bombs on near-by airfield & on Shanghai objectives. Much excitement." And on December 16, "Air raid all morning till 2 pm. Beautiful sight – those groups of 8 shining American planes...."

This may be the appropriate place to mention people who were important to us during our internment – our guards and our Japanese Commandant, Mr. Hayashi.

The guards lived in small houses not far from G Block and their chief duty, as far as I know, was to count us at roll call every morning and evening. It turned out that they were not, in fact, Japanese but North Koreans – because at that period of history Japan was in control of Korea.

Opposite us in G Block was a Belgian family in which there

were three beautiful teenaged daughters. On December 3 Mother writes: "...The guard stood at the Bodsons' door for 40 minutes or more waiting for the girls to finish baths so he could show his photo albums. He's 24." I believe this same guard came back to see them after the war was over.

At other times, as recounted above, the guards were not so friendly, especially after escapes. This may have been because they were held accountable.

Mr. Hayashi, our Commandant, lived in London for four years before the war with his wife and young son. The family was from the Hiroshima area in Japan. He was a senior diplomat at the Japanese Embassy (perhaps Second Secretary.) After December 8, 1941, he was interned at the Savoy for a brief period, apparently, before he and his family were sent to the main Axis civilian internment facility, located on the Isle of Wight. He was then repatriated to Japanese territory in one of the first internee exchanges in 1942.

His home at Lunghwa CAC was one of the five red brick former teachers' dormitories and it still stands outside the campus of Shanghai High School today. Greg Leck's book, *Captives of Empire*, notes that Hayashi was "universally viewed as humane and helpful," specifically citing his willingness to not only permit sick internees to visit the hospitals in Shanghai proper for treatment but also allocate his car and driver for their transport to the clinics. In addition to that, he personally lent them money for medicine and treatment.

Captain (he apparently was given this title and rank during his WWII service) Hayashi was actually brought up before an Allied post-war tribunal in Japan but was exonerated and released without charge. J.G. Ballard wrote that his father testified on Hayashi's behalf.

In 2013, David M. Buchan, a Senior Manager in the British

Washing at the trough

Columbia Ministry of Forests, Lands and Natural Resources Operations succeeded in having his Member of Parliament, Mr. Murray Rankin of Victoria, read a statement honoring Mr. Hayashi on the floor of the Canadian Parliament in Ottawa. Mr. Buchan's mother was interned at Lunghwa and while the statement mentions Hayashi's role in 'saving her life' it probably refers to his granting of access to the Shanghai hospitals, as described above.

Mr. Hayashi's son, Sadayuki Hayashi, is the former Vice Minister of Foreign Affairs for Japan. He flew to Canada especially to witness the reading of the statement about his father on June 9, 2013.

JANUARY 1944

1, Saturday: Had Kathleen & Freddie Meyers, Mary Philip Diack to coffee, pineapple cake, after tiffin. Carol & Eric came in. Mock trial at night—K. MacKenzie tried for slaughtering pig. I was witness for prosecution.

2, Sunday: New restrictions on movement & freedom. Lights out 9:30. Due to escape of 3 (Rose, Ozario, McDonald) on New Year's Eve. Hard on children if we have to give up school.

3, Monday: Vegetable fatigues working. Refusals and criticisms & trials & tribulations many. Repetition of mock trial.

4, Tuesday: Played bridge with Carol & Eric Turner. Had some of their Christmas cake. Betty had Jill, Phyllis, Carol Taylor, Julie Davison to tea.

5, Wednesday: Letter from Anne MacKeith.

6, Thursday: Already sending us extra bread because the food

Taking food to the blocks, Lunghwa Camp

truck will not come for 3 or 4 days—Jan. 25 and following—
because of Chinese N.Y.

7, Friday: Women's advisory Committee met here. Wrapped them
up in blankets.

8, Saturday: Bridge and high tea for Mothersill and Drummond.
Tiffin at 2:15 because the fires wouldn't burn the leavings of the
coal dumps. No coal came in so it was that or nothing.

9, Sunday: Worked 6 hours on Labor Office report for the bulletin
board, which is now up in response to our plea. Military came
to inspect. Hayashi appealed no stoves be lighted, lights turned
on late, etc.

10, Monday: Coal—100 tons—due. Consumption was 180 tons
per mo. Cut to 120, then to 100. Kitchen struggling to cook food
with residue in old dumps.

11, Tuesday: Camp Service cutting & sawing beams to make fires
to cook food in kitchen. Coal overdue, has not come. Carol &
Eric Turner to bridge & tea. Labor Office Information board
went up in F foyer.

12, Wednesday: Woman whose thermos broke still refusing to
work. Very awkward.

13, Thursday: Coal arrived at last, just in the nick of time.

14, Friday: Women's Advisory Committee. Dick and Betty
performing with F 309 Company for children's concert.

15, Saturday: Levy, Wilson, Lampo came for bridge & tea.
Received 3rd double issue of bread to be saved for 25, 26, 27,
Chinese New Year. Choral Society practicing Schubert's "Mass
in A Flat." Read—Osborn debating heredity & environment.

16-21 No entries—for six days

22, Saturday: More restrictions on light to save electricity. 6:45-8
am. 6:30-9:30 pm.

23, Sunday: Finished Trollope's *Small House at Allington*.

24, Monday: Hot plates had to be turned in to monitors. Our block did very well, producing 18.

25, Tuesday: Much ado over the wedding between two Russian Jews on our floor. She said to be going out in a day or two. "Night wi' Burns" was highly successful.

26, Wednesday: Guards searched all baggage for electrical appliances, money, etc. We had good luck again. He came at 2:25 and we were ready for bridge with the Meyers at 2:30. Mirams lectured on architecture.

27, Thursday: Rumors that Eurasians will be the next group to go out. About 100 due to leave Jan. 31 for Shanghai, Weihsien, Chapei, etc.

28, Friday: Carol and Eric Turner came to have tea and play bridge.

29, Saturday: Bridge and supper with Kathleen and Freddie Meyers.

30, Sunday: Morning devoted to helping with vegetables.

31, Monday: Meat ration 30% short for coming month. More vegetables have to be prepared — more work.

FEBRUARY 1944

1, Tuesday: Afternoon of hard interviews on top floor of D. Block. Choral Society rehearsing Schubert's "Mass in A Flat."

2, Wednesday: Gardeners volunteer for vegetables for one month!

3, Thursday: Dick's finger much worse so he went off to hospital, arm on splint. Bridge at night with John and Deirdre Fee.

4, Friday: Afternoon bridge with Bernard Read and Lampo. Evening bridge with Carol and Eric Turner.

5, Saturday: Choral Society—Schubert's "Mass in A Flat" will be beautiful.

6, Sunday: Domestic day with ironing, hair washing, cake making, etc.

7, Monday: Had Mary Diack and Kathleen Meyers to tea to celebrate Mary's birthday (Feb. 8.) An enjoyable leisurely afternoon.

8, Tuesday: Labor Committee discussed labor pool, compulsory labor, etc. Women's Advisory Committee discussed policing vegetables.

9, Wednesday: Another beastly blackout. Children's kitchen refused to cook meat sent by Japanese. Whale? Horse? Spiced beef? Awful smell to the stew!

10, Thursday: Received a letter from Lelia Hinkley answering the one I sent by courier—letter and answer since Jan. 29. IRC says dire need clothing now being purchased.

11, Friday: Bridge here with Carol and Eric. Mrs G. came to slap the liver paste at John. This comic drama! How people play their parts!

12, Saturday: Guests to tea to celebrate John'a birthday: Bob & Joy Richards, Mr & Mrs Bodson, Mr Lampo, Mr Black. Two plays at night: Milne's *A Marriage has been arranged*.

13, Sunday: A leisurely day begun with bacon and eggs for breakfast. Made butter from lard. Visited the Meyers, the usual Sunday afternoon stroll.

14, Monday: 7½ hrs of work — largely interviewing defaulters in the veg. fatigue.

15-17 No entries

18, Friday: Bridge with Carol & Eric at 6:30 in their room.

19, Saturday: Voted for children's kitchen to remain. Dick'a finger still far from well.

20, Sunday:

21, Monday: Leslie Chalmers lectured on "Rise of the Lyric in English Poetry." Voted for congee instead of stew on Wed & Sun evenings.

22, Tuesday: Letters sent to Nita, Kwouks, Beynons, Jeanne. Choral Society still working on Schubert's "Mass In A Flat."

23, Wednesday: All irons turned in. No ironing allowed. Electricity consumption has to be cut to 70% of highest month last year.

24, Thursday: Washing with chilblain-y fingers and hanging out clothes in icy wind, no joke! Bridge at night with Baxters. Extra choral practice.

25, Friday: Bridge with Carol & Eric here. D. Block children's concert at 7.

26, Saturday: Scheme A lost to the present constitution by 31 votes only. Diack's lecture on parliamentary procedure and debate to illustrate. Mrs. Russell departed for CCC.

27, Sunday: A busy day cooking.

28, Monday:

29, Tuesday: Last Women's Advisory Committee meeting before election of new Council. Main question: sanitary towels. Can IRC send some? Choral Society still working away on Schubert's "Mass in A Flat."

Women's Dormitory

Dining Room, Lunghwa Camp

MARCH 1944

1, Wednesday: Sat outside in the sun to have tea and knit on Nita's sweater. John says we are now far behind in 7 food items supposed to be provided by Japanese: e.g. 13,000 lbs of rice, nearly a ton of sugar, oil, meat, vegetables, bread....

2, Thursday: Bridge with Carol & Eric.

3, Friday: Mrs. Hill put forward my nomination for the Council. Indefinite period—blackout—what a nuisance.

4, Saturday: Winifred Penfold's lecture on modern poets, begun by candlelight.

5, Sunday: Chatties allowed, so bacon & prunes. John up early to help with second half of camp's stocks.

6, Monday:

7, Tuesday: Mr. Adamson came to tea so John could talk about the kitchen.

8, Wednesday: Winifred Penfold to tea to talk about candidates for CAC Representative.

9, Thursday: Choral rehearsal

10, Friday: Bridge here with Carol & Eric. A.A. Milne program at night.

11, Saturday: Elected to General Council with 904 votes out of total 1283. Should rules be changed so that votes for women not required?

12, Sunday: Coal was brought from the brick works nearby. Our supply didn't come. Rumored that all camps together will have only 100 lbs. Will the PWD make shades for boundary lights. Hayashi congratulated John on my election.

13, Monday:

14, Tuesday: Had a talk with W. Penfold about Council affairs and people.

15, Wednesday: Families and relatives went to visit Haiphong Road Camp—in trucks. Had 20 minutes to visit. More than a year since they'd seen each other.

16-28 [No entries for 13 days—the longest period of no entries in the whole diary She had just been elected to the General Council. See the reference to "personalities" in the entries for the next two days....]

29, Wednesday: Short rations of drinking water because much stolen due to no hot washing water. Frantic efforts to find scrutineers. Women's meeting to arrange block duties resulting in disgusting brawl of personalities. Bridge with Lampo and Mothersill here.

30, Thursday: Council meeting—too many personalities creeping in. Lights out extended to 10 pm. Candles allowed after that. Decided to give back to each person $116 from canteen overcharge.

31, Friday: Hot water every day at Bubbling Well again. Washed corduroys and the week's accumulation. Played bridge with Turners. Saw the Coordinators program. Not "sailing away" this time but "cheerfully carrying on."

APRIL 1944

1, Saturday: Tea with W. Penfold after choral. She told how men in Haiphong Road had organized their questions. H. moving to town with help from our workers. Reasons for using them not known.

2, Sunday: Up early to fetch Mrs. Appleton to help butchers decide whether legs of the carcases could be roasted. To hear records of Stainer's "Crucifixion" in preparation for concert.

3, Monday:

4, Tuesday: Busy trying to get the once a week vegetable scheme going to supplement instead of the fatigues.

* * * * *

Notebook 2

April 9, 1944
The Happiest Day
On Wednesday, April 5, Dick looked out the window at noon and exclaimed, "Look! The Red Cross trucks!" We looked and there they were — 3 unprepossessing trucks flying the Red Cross flag. Just then a neighbor came in to return soap she had borrowed. "Have you heard?" she asked. "There are parcels from America arriving just now!"

We realized that these must be the parcels sent by America on the repatriation ship which arrived in Japan in December. Since then we had heard no rumor of the parcels. Their arrival was a complete surprise.

Doors of the canteen where the 1840 parcels were stored were locked. Police on duty. Japanese gendarmes tore open nearly all the parcels —

spent the afternoon at it. Women working on vegetables asked me to find out what was in the packages. I asked a Councillor who emerged from the sanctum, and ran back to report to them, "Chocolate, coffee, sugar, prunes, spam and much else besides!"

Parcels were to be distributed the next day from 2 to 4. At 12:45 a long queue was already forming outside the canteen. At 5 when I returned from a Council meeting our four parcels were occupying the center of our floor. But before I could reach our room the neighbors stopped me as I came along the hall, blessing America and marveling at the contents of the parcels. We could hardly believe our eyes. Butter! which we hadn't eaten for about three years.

Chocolate – emergency ration. Corned beef – great luxury.
Prepared coffee – a treasure.
Crosse & Blackwell jam. Cheese! What richness!
Cigarettes – our medium of exchange.

Perhaps the guards missed the message on the Old Golds:

Freedom
Our heritage has always been freedom -
We cannot afford to relinquish it.
Our armed forces will safeguard that heritage,
if we, too, do our share to preserve it.

How proud was I to be an American! People were astonished, over-joyed, praising the variety, the packing, the quality, the planning. They sang "God Bless America" and declared Columbus's discovery was certainly justified.

* * * * *

Dining room queue – Lunghwa C.A.C.

5, Wednesday: American Red Cross parcels sent last summer arrived in this camp, 1840 of them. What sweet relief and pleasure. Final rehearsal of "Crucifixion," all music copied from one book into notebooks. Others had letters from Goa—none from Nita, alas.

6, Thursday: American parcels distributed. Such a wealth. What exclamations of joy on all sides. Butter! and cheese! and corned beef. 29 articles in each parcel. Council discussing food deficiencies, cubicling, etc. Made cake for Betty.

7, Friday: Bridge with Carol and Eric after a morning of washing. Cake and coffee at 11 with Peggy Carter. Choral Society gave "Crucifixion."

8, Saturday: Betty had 6 girls to tea to celebrate her birthday. They ate a tin of butter, a jar of jam, the chocolate cake. Betty was sick all night. Tillie the Tiger pleased her. Choral Society repeated "Crucifixion." Visited Mary afterward.

9, Sunday: Easter. At last a day of rest for me. Read *Changing Governments* and copied addresses on kerchiefs. Pork thief confessed.

10, Monday: LMS tea for Mrs Baxter's birthday in Dining Room C.

11, Tuesday: Lettuce from garden distributed.

12-15 No entries

16, Sunday: Meetings here all day concerning kitchen affairs after a busy week of tales & troubles about getting women cooks into the kitchen.

17, Monday: Butler returned to camp but too sick to practice. How we need another dentist. George Osborn entertained us to bridge, tea; bridge, nineses with Mrs Gaspar, Lillian Perry, Muriel Dennis as partners. Afternoon & evening of it.

18, Tuesday: 15 occupants—3 families including Gomersalls departed for Yu Yuen Rd. 19 arrived. Sent letters to ARC to thank for foods and to mother.

19, Wednesday: Monthly parcels arrived—no sugar, no milk, still bacon & prunes & sweets. Large wooden boxes of clothing & toilet articles, cases, donated by American Red Cross were unloaded into the canteen.

20, Thursday: ARC goods: 50 boxes of clothes (10 men 40 women); 10 cases drugs; 1 case shoe repair kit. 4 teams of women cooks now established in kitchen.

21, Friday: Executive called McGreal & Wakeland & me to advise concerning ARC supplies.

22, Saturday: Went to inspect boxes of ARC supplies—contents jumbled but not much missing. How good it is to see things from home. Polished windows.

23, Sunday: Betty sick with 102 fever. Malaria? American men took over & distributed all ARC clothes for men. Also blankets & towels.

24, Monday: Smith to tea—more kitchen affairs.

25, Tuesday: ex-Catholic nun arrived from Zikawei, having been 14 years in convent. Strange, unsuitable clothes made for her there by nuns.

26, Wednesday: American group of 5 disagreed on question of which women should get American supplies. 3 for larger list of 30. 2 for only the 9 with passports. Meyers family came to play bridge 4:30-9:00 – supper included. Dick banked chatty successfully.

27, Thursday: Council discussing food – should have 2,400-3,000 calories. J. give us 1,735. Garden rules – rewards for services? Harrison Americans came to demand more toilet articles and right to distribute. "In God we trust," they said.

28, Friday: Harrison Americans went to Executive with demands and got what they want. Ex. anxious to interpret liberally: "It is the wish of the donors (ARC) that Americans should have first consideration." Bridge here with Carol & Eric. Winnie Watson arrived after 15 months in hospital.

29, Saturday: First visit of the season in the Hut. Smith and Mothersill to tea talking kitchen affairs. Concert of English songs, drawing room setting. Freddie Meyers elected to General Council.

30, Sunday: Water off again! John and his sheets? Mosquito nets had to go up again. Have we 7 months of sleeping under nets ahead of us?

MAY 1944

1, **Monday:** Matthews' lecture on "Modern Chinese Writers."

2, **Tuesday:** American Red Cross clothing and toilet articles distributed to women. Difficulties over case of woman whose husband was American, is now stateless.

3, **Wednesday:** Attended anniversary tea of Lunghwa Academy in new territory with George Osborn and Huckster making speeches. John went to Bees lecture by Hawkings while I talked to Council members about court being subject to Council.

4, **Thursday:** Council meeting discussing kitchen labor (Compulsory?), water conservation problem. Those with relatives in America still besieging me—and those whose relatives are or were American. Visited McCarthys at night.

5, **Friday:** Letter from Nita arrived at long last. 8 months to come from Goa. Bridge with Carol and Eric. LMS meeting at night.

6, **Saturday:** Great preparations for J. minister (?): no chatties in evidence; no showers; short tiffin, children in school, etc. Then he didn't come. Spent afternoon weeding by hut. Con's lecture on Child Guidance Clinics.

7, **Sunday:** Miss Venn Brown made us a cake using last raisins & nuts & essence—egg flakes, lard.

8, **Monday:** Hut tea party entertaining the McCarthys to bridge.

9, **Tuesday:**

10, **Wednesday:** Will Rowlands' excellent lecture on the music of Fr. Leo Rowlands.

11, **Thursday:** Program of short plays, not very suitable for children.

12, **Friday:** Worn out with washing. Carol & Eric to bridge & tea.

13, Saturday: 4 letters from Brenda arrived dated Jan. Feb. May. June 1943. Also 2 from Bertie.

14, Sunday: A morning of cooking prunes, oatmeal, beans, bacon. An afternoon of rest and reading. Finished white sweater at last.

15, Monday: W. Penfold's lecture on "Modern Poetry." Sent off letters to Ruth Estes, Mother, Cachita, 2 replies to Brenda. John wrote Bertie, Burnet, Meg, A. Beth.

16, Tuesday:

17, Wednesday: Parcels arrived. Milk, meat from G.D.Chen. Cake from Stine. Milk, sugar again, thank heaven. 3 hrs in pm at trial, Rodda vs. Buck, canteen fraud involving 1 lb lard. Case dismissed.

18, Thursday: Council concerned with piggery & cubicling. Planted flowers around hut. Cooked beans, bacon, eggs, etc.

19, Friday: A ½ day abed instead of washing, bodily machinery evidently needing a rest. Bridge with Carol & Eric. Jam very short for everybody.

20, Saturday: Yano didn't come. Chatties extinguished and school in session all to no avail. Took 2 dresses up to Jill. Still feeling rotten.

21, Sunday: Washing finished before 10:30. Mary and I visited over coffee. Their wedding anniversary same as ours—Bombay 1940. Heard Stewart's memorandum from 4-5:30.

22, Monday: Fuller asked me to carry on getting data re American women with dual nationality.

23, Tuesday: Discovered in early am that 5 men had escaped. New territory closed, no school for the children.

24, Wednesday: Draw took place for American miscellaneous articles.

25, Thursday: Council having debate on Piggery and Garden, deciding on more space for the iron ration pigs.

26, Friday: Finished reading *Swann's Way* by Proust. Guide—

Scout display (intended for Empire Day.) Bridge with Carol & Eric. "Camp Pie," program of the Coordinators.

27, **Saturday:** Meeting of monitors & captains with Braidwood and executive. Curtis, interpreter, leaving today to be permanently exempt. Rumor says she will marry one of the guards.

28, **Sunday:** Household chores such as cracking prune seeds. Afternoon walk – kitchen and beyond thru garden.

29, **Monday:** Dick to hospital. Spent all afternoon making mosquito net out of American yardage.

30, **Tuesday:** Hayashi doing military duty for 2 weeks. No one in Jap. office. Representative has to deal with police chief thru interpreter. Disgraceful letting the camp wag on. Rice practically exhausted. Bridge here with Deirdre & John Fee. Afternoon in hut with Mary.

31, **Wednesday:** Gardeners tools must be locked up at 4:30, with key in Jap. hands – reason: those escaping cut wire. Court case – depositions taken in Rodda – Buck case. Disciplinary Court up for Council discussion.

JUNE 1944

1, **Thursday:** Big schemozle [sic] last night with guards shooting at fence, then taking roll call and removing knives and scissors from all men in all men's dormitories. Bridge with the McCarthys in their cubicle.

2, **Friday:** Usual washing and usual bridge with Carol & Eric. Turned in list of 6 women who can produce American in addition to British credentials.

3, **Saturday:** John waited all afternoon for the food truck. Held up 5 hrs in a blockade, meat & bread in sun, meat somewhat spoiled, bread sour. Contractor says food situation at market very tense.

4, **Sunday:** Too strenuous a day washing 11 sheets in rain water. Made a cake which Stormes baked. Washed Betty's hair.

5, **Monday:** Bridge party in afternoon for Mrs Dennis, Mary Diack, Lillian Perry. Kathleen Meyers not well, going to hospital.

6, **Tuesday:** Commandant's order: all knives, pliers, hammers, etc. have to be handed in. Burton says diet is Dick's trouble. Roast pork for dinner! Papers admit Rome has fallen.

7, **Wednesday:** Read the *Assembly Times* brought from Chapei Camp—March to Sep 14 when Americans repatriated. Homesickness for Nita and the others set in. Invasion of continent has begun say papers. Block prayer meeting for 5 minutes at 9 pm. Well worth while, Remembering those who fight.

8, **Thursday:** Council ordered E 307 to move, to make way for cubicles. They have refused to date. Discussion on question of status of ex-officio members of Council.

9, Friday: Still Friday is the once-a-week wash day. Bridge here with Carol and Eric. Children's concert canceled because of total blackout. Roll call 8:45, lights out 9 — awful. Nights still cool. One blanket.

10, Saturday: 7 months on the Labor office job without missing a day. Resolved to take a holiday 1st two weeks in July. Great to-do among the guards because of singing in various buildings after 9 pm — early lights out because of total blackout. They thought insurrection afoot. Telephoned Hayashi. Consulate says they may shoot if people disobey their orders.

11, Sunday: Jap. still supplying 1600 calories. No supplements. Recognized League of Nations minimum 2,400. No tools from this block handed in, Monitor feared search this am. Rumor went round.

12, Monday: Letters from Cachita & Stine, with news in the former of Nita and home. Cachita's dated April 24.

13, Tuesday: Raw cabbage, cucumber, kohlrabi and spinach, peas, etc. being delivered form gardens.

14, Wednesday: Another night roll call in various blocks. Malaria patients hauled up in H. J. spent the day searching baggage for cash, tools, etc. Ours very superficial. Mary & Philip Diack to bridge & supper in the hut.

15, Thursday: Tis said comfort allowances will return shortly. Some concerned because rate of exchange give J. such a huge rake off. New center being opened for old and infirm, some to go from here. Council decided to use force if necessary to make women in E 307 move.

16, Friday: Usual washing and usual bridge with Carol and Eric. Spending 1 hr. or more a day weeding lawn in front of hut. Dick still in hospital (3 weeks) with diet trouble.

17, Saturday: Watched the sports meet with Mary Diack. Some difference of opinion as to whether sports should be held due

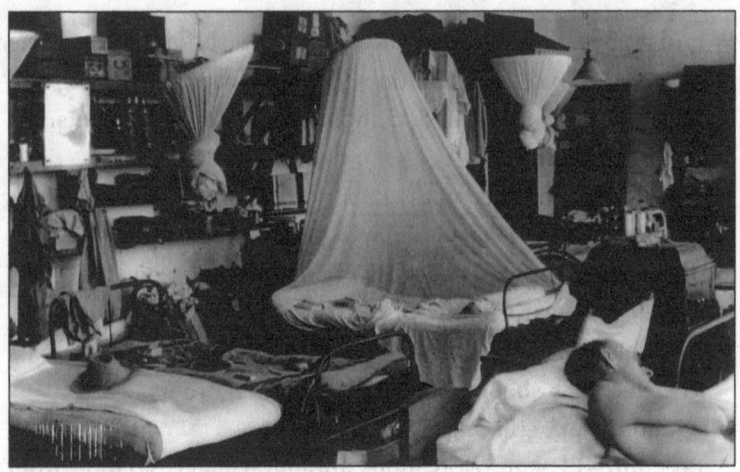

Dormitory for single people, Lunghwa Camp

to Jap. idea that if we can run we aren't hungry. Kathleen and Jill still sick.

18, Sunday: Industrious day of washing pockets, sunning beds, etc.

19, Monday: IRC letters sent off to Esther, Nell H., Elise, Nita and 2 replies to Brenda.

20, Tuesday: New center to be established in Bank of China residences on Lincoln Ave & Chungshan Rd. About 250 old people exempt so far to go in. All enemy nationals will go either to hospitals or to camp.

21, Wednesday:

22, Thursday: No Council meeting so Mary brought her sewing and we sat in the hut. IRC parcels arrived — excellent ones for us. Gave one parcel away to a family not receiving parcels.

23, Friday: 24 men & 13 women assembled ready to depart for Lincoln Avenue — advance party to prepare for old people's advent on June 28. Some of the crowd didn't get away till next day — trucks short. Played bridge at the Turners because Patricia was sick.

24, Saturday: Washing today instead of Friday because of water's being off.

25, Sunday: Church and Concert on E Roof after a strenuous day of cooking on the chatty. How I hate doing that in the heat.

26, Monday: Well apparently going dry. Flow decreased from 55 to 45 gal. per min (?) What to do? Afternoon with Dick in hospital. Better after a setback. Weaving blanket out of American cerise wool.

27, Tuesday: Two days' meat supply condemned and returned to contractor. Meat not well frozen on truck in heat from 9:30 am till 4 pm. Contractor says bread always delays him.

28, Wednesday: News arrived that Comfort Loans are again available at high rate of exchange. £1 = $94.00 CRB. $1 U.S. = $23.00 CRB. One view is that J. will profit considerably and therefore we should be loath to sign. Another view: have faith that governments know best and have made suitable arrangements.

29, Thursday: Council meeting discussed Comfort Loans & agreed to recommend that people draw only what they need. N.F.M. insisting all should draw & community fund function as before. Vegetable fatigue report finished & posted, thank heaven. Names of 16 non-cooperators posted.

30, Friday: Usual washing and usual bridge with Carol & Eric. Incident of Mothersill, the newspaper, the guard, the slaps and threats, Mrs. Whitfield's intervention.

JULY 1944

1, Saturday: Dick still in hospital, so no birthday celebration. Council met to decide as to debts and community fund in view of comfort allowance return. Hayashi absent since Tuesday — military training.

2, Sunday: Hot sticky weather. Rain makes weeds in garden shoot up over night.

3, Monday: During monitors' meeting, loud claps of firing. Air raid signals in Shanghai. Beginning of my 2 week holiday, sorely needed. Lillian Perry helping Mary.

4, Tuesday: Picnic tiffin with Carol and Eric & Patricia inside our block due to rain. Last Heinz pickles, sausages, tomato juice, eggs, etc. Tea also and bridge. Evening with John & Deirdre Fee who served starry sandwiches on striped paper.

5, Wednesday: Mitsubishi taking over the contract for canteen. Orders placed for 2 million dollars worth of spreads, etc. Hayashi came yesterday after a week's absence.

6, Thursday: Great excitement because occupants are sure they heard American planes overhead with sirens in Shanghai. Hayashi came to the Council meeting, answered some questions, but not a satisfactory interview. No warning so we could plan.

7, Friday: Yvette and others who went to town called to Hayashi because they bought ice cream & buns in the city. Bridge in the hut with Carol and Eric, Sat on E roof to cool off after supper.

8, Saturday: More rumors of American repatriation on Aug. 15. Man from Pootung says slips already signed there. Saw *Lovers' Leap* with Philip Diack, West, Lorna Lucas, Mrs. Horman-

Fisher. Couldn't rise to any celebration.

9, Sunday: Hayashi has 3rd 2 weeks period of military drill. Even the Consul General has to go. Vigorous cleaning of shelves, etc while John washed 10 sheets.

10, Monday: Mary and Philip came to sit in the hut after dinner. N.F.M. having difficulty with food distribution to kitchen workers. Now only one letter per month. No replies allowed. Morning devoted to scrubbing floor with brush.

11, Tuesday: Signed for one month's Comfort Loan (June only, not July.) Prices rising so fast that what we have may not be worth much in August. 12 more people left for Lincoln Ave. Center.

12, Wednesday: A quiet day of mending. Winifred Penfold came in the afternoon and we had tea in the hut. Dick still in hospital. Further restriction: must be in billets by 8:45 (by dark.)

13, Thursday: Council meeting to discuss air raid precautions, labor for gardens and hay making. Delightful concert on E roof.

14, Friday: Usual washing & bridge with Carol & Eric. LMS meeting at night.

15, Saturday: Mary came to hand over the reigns, as my two-week holiday ends on Monday.

16, Sunday: Heard story of the rescue of a pig by one guard and several occupants who left a big gap in barbed wire after pig driven through.

17, Monday: No celebration. On the other hand, back to work. Gifts from Kathleen, Mary, Boxes, family. Dick came home after 7 weeks in hospital.

18, Tuesday: Had to break down and wash clothes — must wash twice a week in this weather.

19, Wednesday: Great commotion because of incident in the clinic: chief of police felt insulted because sheet was turned

Carrying hot water from a hot water station, Lunghwa Camp

back when he went for anti-rabies injection. Threatened all sorts of restrictions.

20, Thursday: Council discussed garden policy, delay in canteen purchases, new commandant, shabby treatment of French players at hands of entertainment committee. Concert on F roof with colorful sky.

21, Friday: Washing, and bridge with Eric & Carol in the hut, with grass cut and flowers blooming.

22, Saturday: Red Cross parcels arrived. Most people who smoke entirely without cigarettes, paying any price. Mary off for her holiday. Tins taken by IRC after month's delay. Still rumors of American ship in August.

23, Sunday: Roof concert.

24, Monday: Rumors of internal troubles in Germany.

25, Tuesday: Russians very near Warsaw.

26, Wednesday: Cholera injections.

27, Thursday: Council considering ARP and how to distribute 250 lbs of peanut butter—to those with no parcels or draw.

N.F.M. brought up malpractices but could suggest no remedy. Moral standards in camp very low.

28, Friday: Smith resigned from executive because of attack by Freddie & Burton. Bridge with Carol & Eric, then LMS meeting. Garden around hut very flourishing, cosmos 5 feet tall. Red zinnias & morning glories.

29, Saturday: Special Council Meeting to deal with the case of Skinner striking Dumbarton in the dining room because he wanted seconds of potatoes and saw some on the side. Spent the afternoon dealing with juvenile workers.

30, Sunday: No canteen supplies for 4 weeks. Philip Diack agreed to defend Skinner in the violence case. Excellent roof Concert.

31, Monday: Sat with Mary who struggled through the trial. Philip did very well indeed, summing up especially well. Penalty $500, & keeping peace for 6 months. Council discussing Constitutional changes.

AUGUST 1944

1, Tuesday: Had Meyers family to supper, opening the one tin of black berries to follow the spaghetti.

2, Wednesday: Water schedule cut from 10 hrs to 5 hrs per day (24 hrs.) Great hardship in this hot weather. J. say 50% electricity cut must apply here.

3, Thursday: Struggled in Council to get Swiss donated supplies distributed on basis of need. Principle accepted but belied when sugar, flour, spreads, etc. were then voted to go all around. Excellent Concert on roof with full moon. Diacks and Meyers sitting alongside.

4, Friday: Usual Friday activities: washing all morning; playing bridge at 2:30 with Carol & Eric. Watched full moon rise from our grassy plot in front of hut.

5, Saturday: Lillian Perry finished her 2 weeks in the Labor Office. Mary to return Monday. Had Mothersill and Lampo play bridge in the hut after supper.

6, Sunday: Still no canteen supplies — 5 weeks. Smokers in terrible state without cigarettes.

7, Monday: Council met and decided we could have only 2 meals a day, as suggested by Commandant, in order to cut coal to 40 tons (former cuts 180 to 135 to 90.)

8, Tuesday: Occupants protested only 2 meals. Rowdy meeting at 11 am. Council met at 2 and at 7. Braidwood persuaded commandant to try for more coal.

9, Wednesday: Papers admit US planes flew over and dropped bombs in Whangpoo. Rumor says the Conte Verde, refloated, sank again. Total blackout 8:30 to 9:30. Electric switches pulled by Jap.

10, Thursday: Council discussing malpractices, right of police to search, etc. Occupants disapprove Council decision to keep Swiss donated rice for iron ration or working reserve.

11, Friday: Usual washing and bridge with Carol and Eric.

12, Saturday: A showery day on which we attempted to play bridge with Adamson and Lampo in the hut. Had to move in. Food truck late because of blockade.

13, Sunday: Many planes overhead on this anniversary of "Black Friday." Couldn't have gramophone concert on roof because

14, Monday:

15, Tuesday: Sent letters to Nita, Marion Witt, Cachita, Bojesen.

16-18 No entries

19, Saturday: IRC parcels and donations arrived. They can't buy peanut butter. Pleasant evening between showers on E roof with the Dennisons, drinking coffee. Americans beginning to circle round Paris.

20, Sunday: Three men escaped last night. What restrictions now! 10 drastic new ones posted on boards before noon to take effect at 2:30: confined to rooms, turn in books, no canteen, no library, no newspapers, 2 meals a day—no breakfast, etc. Russian man was beaten at 3. Mass demonstrations followed. High official came at 11 pm. 6 men taken to Shanghai for questioning re escape.

21, Monday: Only essential workers allowed out after 9 am. Meals and drinking water delivered to blocks. 6 men returned at 5 pm after being questioned at Consulate. E Block demonstrated. Newton taken to guard house for 3 hrs. Five incidents in our block during 50 minute roll call by J. guard. Beares slapped & kicked. Murrays attacked because children weren't out of bed for 2nd roll call.

22, Tuesday: Pass system put into operation for 300 essential people. Russian taken away to Shanghai and given one month in Ward Road Jail. Council meeting to consider Braidwood's report. Order to turn in books rescinded. Bread cut considerably due to escape. Meat also short. Watched the guards pull down and burn our four summer huts and destroy gardens there.

23, Wednesday: No rice for supper. Flour brought in as substitute. Inside all day. Children of all ages required to be fully dressed for roll call at 8:30 pm. All maps and gramophones & records had to be handed in. Can't get water for washing, can't hang clothes on line. Vegetables cut from 1,400 to 900 kilos (1,000 lbs) as punishment.

24, Thursday: All blocks free except E, F, G. First two because of collective responsibility for escapes. G because of infringements re chatties & lights. Working on brown sweater for diversion. Out on pass to Council Meeting. Banjo came and called for the 7 men he knows best. Asked why people escape from this camp only. In 2½ hrs the 7 told him much. Useful channel.

25, Friday: G Block released this morning so we can hang up clothes and circulate freely. All maps and gramophone records deposited in the library. Bridge with Carol & Eric. Bread so short that I was moved to attempt a cake (quite a success.)

26, Saturday: Jap. insist that they will apply collective responsibility for escapes whether we accept it or not. All will be punished, those closely associated with escapees will be punished more.

27, Sunday: E & F Blocks released after being kept in one week.

28, Monday: Willie Smith and Mothersill came to supper and bridge. Made coffee on candle heat.

29, Tuesday: IRC jam distributed. Soap and matches on sale at long last. Rations finally restored—bread, veg, meat, which were cut ⅓ after escape. Explosions and tracer bullets seen in air over Shanghai. Sirens sounded alarm.

30, Wednesday: 17 people arrived from Yu Yuen Road Camp and

14 of ours (pregnant women & families) departed. News that Hongkew and Kiangwan were bombed. Wharfs also.

31, **Thursday:** Council discussed escapes and issued a plea to all to suppress desire to escape and to promise to try to prevent others. J. might keep us in for all but one hr., puncture all parcel tins, permit military inquiry, etc., cut food so much that we'll be physically unable to escape. A whole week of terribly hot days. 93, 94, 95 on our thermometer.

SEPTEMBER 1944

1, Friday: Two more deaths, making about 10. House Monitors press Braidwood for measures to be taken to prevent escapes. Decided to ask each occupant to guarantee to group captain, to monitors, etc. G Block occupants take it seriously, some asking transfer. Turners came to tea. Eric too busy for bridge. No power, no light, no water, following rainstorm.

2, Saturday: Braidwood came for cake and cocoa after supper. Talked of Poland and China. About 11,000 internees in Far East, he says. About 6,000 in China. This is probably 3rd largest camp, after Manila & Hong Kong. Made a chocolate cake which cooked too quickly in the kitchen.

3, Sunday: Midnight roll call in E because 2 men were looking out windows when a third lit a cigarette with a lighter. Japanese guard thought a signal was being given.

4, Monday: Rumor: Germans in Shanghai told to keep calm and be ready for anything. Interrupted bridge with Carol & Eric. Under 7's excused from 8:30 pm roll call. Morning roll call returned to 9 am.

5, Tuesday: Still no newspaper but returning hospital patients report Brussels, Liege, Danzig, Posen in Allied hands. 12 pigs killed for a pork supper. Very tasty. Cooling showers.

6, Wednesday: Troubles with those who did not receive IRC donated goods because of labor records. Japanese tell us that whatever comes is our ration—should have 20 bags of rice—but don't always get it. Reading *English Saga* by Arthur Bryant.

7, Thursday: My resignation from Labor Office accepted—10 months is a long enough spell. "One of the outstanding successes," said Adamson. Braidwood not standing as candidate for CAC Representative. About 95% agreed not to escape, but quite a few wouldn't agree to try to influence others.

8, Friday: Bulletin contained: "The Council accepted with much regret and appreciation of...." Bridge with Carol & Eric interrupted again by John's supervision of the truck.

9, Saturday: Mary and I drank coffee after lunch, then wound up work in the Labor Office. Total blackout—great nuisance. Canteen supplies arrived, completing first 3 orders—jam, peanut butter, sugar, candy, cigarettes.

10, Sunday:

11, Monday: Still in the Labor Office, helping Lilian to start off. Canteen busily selling jam, peanut butter and cigarettes—sweets at $4.90 a lb. Mary started teaching Form 5, Dick's form.

12, Tuesday:

13, Wednesday: Visited Dentist Stewart Hill, keeping appointment made 6 weeks ago. He found 2 cavities, put temporary fillings. Next appointment Oct. 18.

14, Thursday: John resigned as Kitchen Manager. Council praised his work.

15, Friday: Bridge with Carol and Eric. A.J. Evans elected CAC Representative to take office when new Council goes in.

16, Saturday: Chatties today, after a long absence. Feverish cooking. 5 lbs per head of potatoes from canteen. Huckleberries, eggplant, peppers from garden. Lampo and Adamson to supper and bridge. Meat loaf & cake cooked in the kitchen.

17, Sunday: Had elevenses with Deirdre Fee and looked at her sketches. Read *English Saga*. Cooked mashed potatoes and custard. Still no newspaper. Really left Labor Office yesterday.

18, Monday: First session of Philip's economics class—3—4. Bids fair to be interesting.

19, Tuesday: First session of Matthews' Intermediate mandarin class — 6 — 7. John & I both going.

20, Wednesday:

21, Thursday: Last meeting of General Council. Discussed question of police.

22, Friday: Peggy Carter asked me to be hospital quartermaster. Declined. Very nice supper with Adamson and Meimei Ross: Campbell's soup, salad, beef.

23, Saturday: Elected again to serve on General Council for 6 months. A.J. Evans, chairman. Four women stood, 2 elected. Parcels arrived. Clothes, cookies from Suenson; many things from old boys.

24, Sunday: Cooking all the day on the chatty — potatoes,prunes, custard, etc. Elevenses with Deirdre Fee. Ordered some of her watercolors.

25, Monday: All day cleaning shelves — except for economics at 3. Making brown sweater shorter. Reading *The Windsor Tapestry*.

26, Tuesday: Lobbying for Philip to be Executive Chairman.

27, Wednesday: First meeting of new Council. Hopkins, Meyers, Diack elected to executive. Asked me to be Welfare Officer, but I declined.

28, Thursday: Council meeting to consider what questions should be discussed with the Swiss.

29, Friday: Swiss Consul made a visit. More than a year since his last. Very satisfactory discussion of all various points with CAC Representative: bulk supplies of food; school; visits, repatriation, etc.

30, Saturday: Council met to make appointments and hear of Fontanel's visit. Produced potato salad with corned beef, prunes, cake for supper honoring Mothersill's birthday. Jock Drummond, my bridge partner. Lights on at 7:15.

OCTOBER 1944

1-2 No entries

3, Tuesday: Enjoying Matthews's Mandarin class.

4, Wednesday: John really on holiday, reading, sitting, helping at home.

5, Thursday: Canteen selling onions, potatoes, eggs.

6, Friday: Adamson and Lampo came for tea and bridge. John and I were 13 up.

7, Saturday: Pork Issue Raw. Chatties. Cooked all day. What a deuced business! Lunch with W. Penfold & S. Purchas (also the Fees) in their rendezvous among the ruins. Special Council meeting at 6 pm to consider Commandant's order to billet all unattached men 16-60 in one place. Murray's lecture on words.

8, Sunday: Yamashita agreed to return newspaper, permit children to use school building, etc. Cooked all morning, pork, potatoes, onions, etc.

9, Monday: Newspaper really appeared. George's lecture on Marco Polo.

10, Tuesday: Letter from Mother dated March 13, '44 in reply to Betty's of Sept. 1943. Council met and decided to concentrate all of unattached men in E Block. Pandemonium there. Bridge with Carol & Eric. Canteen issued soap, t. paper.

11, Wednesday: Letter from Jeanne dated Sept. 30. E Block monitors and captains protested use of their block concentrating men. Coal arrived in nick of time. Had enough coal for tiffin by cooking millet for today's breakfast yesterday afternoon.

12, Thursday: Council reaffirmed E Block decision. Light situation very acute. If we have light the next 8 nights, J. will have to pay fine for 10% over. Will they? All coal to be locked up. Chatties Tues, Thurs, Sun. 9-5.

13, Friday: Churchill in Moscow. Reading on US Constitution ready for Nov. 6.

14, Saturday: Cleaned windows. Had Mr & Mr Denison to tea and bridge. Missed first Choral Society practice.

15, Sunday: Another cooking spree—potato cakes and scones. Took two to Peggy Carter, who is sick with a strange malady. Morgenthau's "Germanophobe" in the press.

16, Monday: New Territory open at last for school, after 5 months holiday.

17, Tuesday: Washing for Peggy and family in spite of downpour. Letters to Ruth Packard, Esther, Christine, Bertie, Cachita, Stine, Jeanne, Trock. Bridge with Carol and Eric over here.

18, Wednesday:

19, Thursday: Council concerned with Billeting Policy occasioned by concentration of men. Three-in-a-room families warned to be ready to vacate. A, H, for cubicle families.

20, Friday: 23 Belgians arrived from Tientsin, having been interned in their houses for 15 months. Back to the wall discussion after lights out with the three-in-a-family people. Bridge here with the McCarthy's.

21, Saturday: Parcels again, after their waiting overnight in the dining rooms. Cake from Beulah Chang. Tinned goods from School. 28 eggs from Stine. Making and icing Kathleen's cake took most of the day.

22, Sunday: Party for Kathleen on her birthday: varied sandwiches on the Bodson's platter and iced devil's food cake. Same guests as last year plus Mary, Dora Mellor, Betty Bland, Carol Turner. To the Meyers at 5:30 to sup with them and the Diacks—8 of us. Very nice.

23-24 No entries

25, Wednesday: Air raid in Shanghai. Paper says 2 planes, no damage. Heard signal at 9:30 am. Rumpus in school over pre-med students and their quarters.

26, Thursday: Council curtailing light—1¼ hrs per night to keep us within 100 units a day. What for children's Christmas?

27, Friday: Adamson & Lampo to bridge and supper. First stage of removals from E Block—Mary & Philip to H. Lillian Perry to J. etc. Americans have 3 divisions in the Philippines.

28, Saturday: Choral Society preparing for Christmas. Belgians' luggage arrived—terrific amount. They have food for three years, 'tis said.

29, Sunday: Lights continue off at night except for 1¼ hrs. 7:15—7:45 and 8:15 to 9. It's a game thinking of things to do in the dark.

30, Monday: Called meeting of Children's Christmas Committee, left in my hands by Council. Plan Boxing Day Tiffin and entertainment.

31, Tuesday: List posted of 31 women (Russians, aged, divorced, etc.) to be exempted. Great excitement. Carol & Eric came for bridge. Agreed to help on McMichael's Xmas Bazaar Committee. Why, I don't know!

NOVEMBER 1944

1, Wednesday: Roof of J Hut collapsed in one section making it necessary to evacuate 12 women who had just moved in. Great discussion as to whether to billet all 55 elsewhere, move offices there if permitted, etc.

2, Thursday: 31 women and children departed. Int. Red Cross came to get them—under protection of Swiss—allowance will be paid. Baggage inspected am. Many feared conditions outside. Two listed didn't go. Mme Backaert went.

3, Friday: Finished speech on "U.S. Constitution." Council still on billeting, women cooks, children's food, lighting, sign-up on Swiss for eggs (to cost $1,000 per month). Total allowance only $2,000. Swiss trying to send bulk supplies. J. don't want to increase allowance.

4, Saturday:

5, Sunday: John spoke at the evening church service on the first two commandments.

6-9 No entries

10, Friday: Bodson family greatly excited because M. Annette, mgr of French Club, managed to come to the gate in J. car, bringing them baskets of excellent food supplies. We had pate and white bread with them at 8:30 pm. Guards took some but not too much. Bates and Adamson to bridge and supper.

11, Saturday: During morning roll call, several American planes appeared overhead. J. used anti-aircraft guns. Planes dropped several bombs on nearby airfield & on Shanghai objectives. Much excitement. Kept in buildings till 2 pm. J. guards at doors. Bridge with McCarthy's 3-7. Yvette's birthday.

Softball game, Lunghwa C.A.C.

12, Sunday: Hayashi and 3 Swiss rode in and walked around on an unofficial visit. Paid $840 for week's supply of 28 eggs. Air gun advertised for $50,000. 2 *mow* + plus house.

13, Monday:

14, Tuesday: Tiffin with the Bodson's—a really home-like feast—roast lamb, potatoes, tomatoes—coffee and sweet biscuits—bouillon, at first. 12 people sitting in that small room. Carol and Eric for bridge & tea.

15, Wednesday: Wang Ching-Wei's death reported. Braidwood's "Flight from Warsaw" very good.

16, Thursday: Council discussing illegal use of hot plates, billeting, that $1,000 from "revolving" fund, etc. Missed George's lecture on Christian Socialism but read his notes. Tryout blackout for 10 minutes (total.)

17, Friday: Watched a J. plane catch fire and fall, the pilot descending by parachute. Dick's chilblains already beginning.

18, Saturday: John & I won the debate—That early marriage assists a man's career. We took late side. Hawkins couple lost. Short air raid ½ hr.. 1:30-2 pm. Parcels received. Gifts from 1937 class Lei C Ping.

19, Sunday: A whole day of cooking and nothing else. 2 puddings (Wheat-O-Malt), potatoes, onions, gravy, spread, bacon, etc. scones. Adam Black to tiffin. Complete blackout at 9 pm. Sirens heard.

20, Monday: Received letter from Esther of May 3 — sent via Cairo & Turkey.

21, Tuesday: Sent letters to Dad, Bertie, Nita, Brenda, Cachita, Bernard, Stine, Lei C Ping.

22, Wednesday: Air raid 8 am to 4 pm. Saw a few U.S. planes. Kept indoors all day. Lights on now at 6:30 pm till 9 pm.

23, Thursday: So busy seeing doctors and getting medicine for Betty that I forgot Mrs. Mellor's 11ses party! Council discussion ARP, rebelling, illegal use of electricity, the $1,000 "revolving advance" (decided for eggs.)

24, Friday: Adamson and Lampo came for supper and bridge, Friday:ed eggs on the oil cans. Betty still in bed with cold, complaining of ears.

25, Saturday: Managed to entertain the Meyers four with tongue and pudding cooked on Thursday's chatty. Bridge out-of-doors on a very warm day — 70° in our room.

26, Sunday: In this place — good health — can do. With someone in the family sick — it's awful! Betty still in bed. Paper very short. The bank charges $15 for every page in your account. Preparing for Wilson lecture.

27, Monday:

28 Tues Hillman refused $2,000,000 of onions when we ordered $130,000 worth. Somebody playing pranks on us.

29-30 No entries

DECEMBER 1944

1, Friday: Bitter cold weather descended upon us. Items from Food Pool given to 100 people. 265 contributions.

2, Saturday: Minimum 22°, Maximum 25°. ARC blankets lent to 105 people.

3, Sunday: Busy chatty day – cooking, bath for Betty, etc. The guard stood at the Bodson's door for 40 minutes or more waiting for the girls to finish baths so he could show his photo albums. He's 24. Expects to join the "ambassady" when war is over.

4, Monday: Reference in paper to J. Officers' Military Headquarters – former Foreign YMCA. Parts of Am. plane & Chungking guns on display there.

5, Tuesday: The Japanese have taken down the bronze angel, the wreath & the plate bearing the names of those killed in the last war – Br. Am. Fr. – cenotaph dismantled for scrap metal.

6, Wednesday: Another bitter day – washing in cold water and hanging onto the line! Whew! Rowland lecture on "English Songs & Song Writers" – with illustrations.

7, Thursday: Lectured on "Woodrow Wilson – His Message for Today" in B dining room, freezing the while. Still very cold with wind. 33° in our room when we got up. Council confiscating chatty, looking into well situation. New Comfort money paid at last. Increased to $3,000 per mo. for Oct. Nov. Dec.

8, Friday: Adamson and Lampo came for bridge and supper. Dart upset the bucket of water under our trunks and swished it to the iron stairs. Great Japanese celebrations with supplement to newspaper.

9, Saturday: Bitterly cold still. 32° when we got up at 6:30 am. Roll call at 7 pm so people can go to bed earlier. Choral rehearsal — carols & "Messiah" choruses.

10, Sunday: Supper with Remedios 4. Very good one, too. The chatty cooked potatoes beautifully, then went out before the pudding got on. Differences between Br. & Am. regarding policy in Greece.

11, Monday: Bazaar committee going strong.

12, Tuesday: Bridge with Carol & Eric. J & I 13+. Last Chinese class before holidays. Open Jan. 9. Looked in on "Pygmalion" — Mary's production for the Sophomores.

13, Wednesday: Choral rehearsal. "Wassail Song" ragged, but "Ring Out Wild Bells," a triumph. Heard Earle lecture on "Adventure in Medical Research." Excellent all-camp exhibit of handmade things. Very large number of pictures. Put in my two embroidered maps which interested people.

14, Thursday: Council discussing kitchen reorganization, rebilleting, appointing new Labor & Billeting officers. Two thankless jobs! Reading *Nine Etched from Life* — Ludwig. Shared Claudine Bodson's birthday feast.

15, Friday: Parcels & Bulk supplies due today. They came. Marie Hill and I spoke to Damsgaard about children's gifts (drawing books and pencils wanted) and fruit for puddings. Fresh fruit in our parcels — oranges and apples!

16, Saturday: Air raid all morning till 2 pm. Beautiful sight — those groups of 8 shining American planes. If only they didn't have to drop bombs. Saw the anti-aircraft fire, heard the thuds, our windows rattled, saw smoke. Kiangnan Dock practically destroyed.

17, Sunday: Severe cold continues. 18° & 19° minimum. Chopping frozen cabbage and peeling frozen sweet potatoes, no joke.

18, Monday: Lights out at 9 but in-billets hour extended to 8 pm till Jan. 1.

19, Tuesday: Wrote to Louise Theune, Nita, Sonia, Burnet, Boynton, Stine, Marion Morley, A.E. Women's lavatories failed completely. Now sharing men's on 2 hr shifts till repairs effected.

20, Wednesday: Rehearsed carols all morning and stood in queues all afternoon, first for a flannel blouse (general scramble) then for IRC lard, issued hot in kitchen because frozen. Christmas Tableaux staged by Hawkings.

21, Thursday: Council meeting re IRC donated stocks, IRC rice, failure of water from burst pipes. First Choral Society performance of Christmas music.

22, Friday: Second choral performance postponed because parcels (1348) filled both dining rooms. Many more parcels than last year and Chinese sending things more openly and freely – good sign. 7 trucks came with parcels and fruit for puddings arrived.

23, Saturday: Received 5 Christmas parcels from Kwouks, Beulah Chang, Djao, Leitao, Suenson. Amazing amount and variety of fruit, nuts, biscuits, tins. Made fudge on chatty and cooked supper (chicken, potatoes, peas, pig) for Adamson and Bradford who came for bridge. IRC beef issued. And we drew some bones!

24, Sunday: Vegetable duty followed by last minute stitches and a late tiffin. Grand rush to wash Betty's hair & the floor before carols at 3:45. Christmas Eve service featured children. Various visits with small gifts. Air raid blackout at 8:40. – 3rd challentive (?) night when we'd been promised lights till 9:30.

25, Monday: To church in Dining Room D after breakfast of orange, eggs, bacon, marmalade. Guests to tea: Geo. Osborn, Adam Black, Mr. Mothersill, Lillian Perry. Roast pork IRC rice for tiffin. No Xmas trees in camp except individual decorated branches. Prices stupendous.

26, Tuesday: Visited with Mary between preparations for the general party for children (258) – delicious tiffin with pudding & sauce. Peggy Carter and Winifred Penfold came to tea. "A few pounds of decent gifts and a few tons of excellent wishes for sound health, good luck, a merry Xmas, a Happy New Year" read the card from school staff.

27, Wednesday: After 2 weeks' washing, to the Meyers for bridge and supper. Freddie & Kathleen are choice. I do like them. People put nails in end of logs, intended for barbed wire fence, tied rope at dusk, & at night pull logs into F Block.

28, Thursday: Betty had Jill, Marilyn, Phyllis to tea. Council discussing distribution of IRC beans & rice. Decided to keep for the present.

29, Friday: John up at 5:30 to light chatty in washroom. Cooked all day so as to have supper for Smith and Mothersill. And then burned the pudding, alas! Returned watered peanut butter to canteen for exchange. Strikes in Shanghai. Perhaps no more bread till Jan 4. Already 3 days short.

30, Saturday: Eric & Carol came to play bridge and have supper. Hot water day – (now one in 3) so washing and baths, John fetching the four buckets full. General strike in Shanghai. No bread.

31, Sunday: Quiet day doing vegetables in the morning, visiting with Mary at tea time. Bread ration for last 2 days came in, relieving the situation. No more food coming in till Jan. 4. 15 bags flour distributed this morning. Barbed wire fence going up. Philip collecting plates for the guards to enjoy the two pigs we gave which they've cooked with our coal.

1945

Hoping / Rejoicing

THE YEAR BEGAN WITH A further story about the Korean guard who visited the Belgian family opposite us. On Jan. 2, Mother writes, "Two drunk guards came to the Bodson's where the student guard (aged 24) was hiding because he didn't want to drink. He says it makes him sick."

The bitter winter cold continued and on February 13 Mother writes that we had the sixth snowfall of the season. We all suffered from chilblains, red swellings on our fingers and toes which, when the weather turned warmer, became very itchy. Sometimes the swellings burst and became infected.

Our perennial problem of food, water and fuel shortages persisted, and even worsened. By June 2, we were down to just one meal a day — provided by the Japanese. But we were still receiving parcels from Shanghai and, once again, large shipments of parcels from the IRC arrived. The problem was how to distribute them fairly. In the end, lots were drawn.

Mother spent a fair amount of time cooking on our chatty but she never enjoyed it. The fuel for the chatty was provided by Dick and me: we became expert at finding 'good' pieces of charcoal on the ash heaps beside the hot water stations.

Hope was on the horizon, though, because the air raids by

the Americans became more frequent and more intense. We were instructed to stay indoors but the guards had difficulty in controlling the excited crowds. On January 20 Mother writes: "Worst raid so far. Several U.S. planes circled low over Lunghwa aerodrome and dropped bombs. Much black smoke ascended. One U.S..plane trailed fire and went down. Sight sobered the crowd."

On April 1, "U.S. planes made 3 V's with smoke. Much speculation followed." I can remember seeing the planes writing in the sky and the feeling of elation that followed. Some people said they saw the pilots waving to us when they flew low over our camp.

Reminiscent of 1942, rumors began to circulate as to our future. The General Council made plans "for emergency set up to run camp." People were asked whether they would leave immediately peace was declared or whether they would be willing to stay to help run the camp.

In the meantime, in spite of everything, Mother writes often about the activities that were carried on to keep us going. In the evenings there were lectures, concerts, plays and a quiz. On March 17, she writes, two scenes from "Carmen" were presented – from memory. In June a Gilbert and Sullivan operetta, "Pirates of Penzance", was given. Mother's comment: "Costumes especially successful. Such color and originality!"

After several of the lectures, Mother writes, she had discussions with "Ballard," who also lived in G Block. Little did she know that Ballard's son, J.G., would later make our camp famous with his novel entitled, *Empire of the Sun*. Or that Stephen Spielberg would make it even more famous with his movie of the same name. J.G. was in Dick's class in Lunghwa Academy and in 1945, on Dick's 15th birthday, he invited seven guests to tea, one of whom was "Jamie Ballard." (July 1)

The rumors flying about were not only about our own future but also about the world situation. News could be gleaned from the Japanese-run *Shanghai Times* but, as was learned after the war, there were two secret radios in the camp which were the source of much information. The death of Roosevelt in April was a great shock; Mother was moved by the Memorial Service for him in the camp on April 22, attended by 700, mainly British, people.

On May 8 we learned that the war in Europe was finished. Our happiness was tempered by the questions that arose as to how soon the war in Asia would end, and what would happen to us. By July 29 Mother writes, for the first time, "Ah! is there hope?" Early August was a time of hopes rising and falling but, finally, on Aug. 15, Mother writes: "Swiss took over the camp at noon, it being confirmed that the war is over. Great jubilation..."

The guards departed quietly two days later, the Commandant who had replaced Hayashi, Ohnuki, staying on untill the Allies came. And then began a period of great confusion—relief because of the end of the war but uncertainty as to where we were to go. And when.

I will leave readers to read Mother's diary because she gives a clear picture of that period, which is perhaps not as well known as the actual war stories.

On Sept. 26, more than a month after the end of the war, she and I set off from Lunghwa to an American hospital ship, the USS Refuge (the former President Garfield,) which took a few civilians, along with wounded military people, to Okinawa. There, we were transferred to another hospital ship, the USS Sanctuary, on which we sailed via Guam and Pearl Harbor to San Francisco. Aged twelve, I of course have my own vivid memories of that journey.

Just before we left the camp, there was word of a place on HMS Glen Air, a British ship taking former internees to the U.K. Dick was put on the list and he travelled back to Scotland under the care of friends. He went to a boarding school in Perthshire, the same one that my father had attended, and never returned to China.

My father stayed on in Shanghai for six months to help Medhurst College recover from the war and then he returned to the UK where he was reunited with Mother and me the following summer, 1946.

This is a story mainly set in and about Shanghai and I have therefore ended it on Oct. 28, 1945, when Mother and I reached Dallas, her home.

JANUARY 1945

1, Monday: Grinning guard called out "Happy New Year" at roll call. At 11 am to Miss Teeling's birthday celebration. Freddie, Kathleen, Jill, Ruth came at 2:30 to play bridge and sup. Macaroni cooked on a smoky chatty, Mrs. Suenson's cake, cocoa, fudge. Drinking water short due to lack of coal.

2, Tuesday: High tea with Adamson and Willie Smith, sausages, egg flakes, Xmas cake, scones, coffee. Two drunk guards came to the Bodsons' where the student guard (aged 24) was hiding because he didn't want to drink. He says it makes him sick. New restriction – in billets at 6:30. Roll call 7 pm. Lights out 9. Restrictions lifted when inner fence completed.

3, Wednesday: Bridge with Carol & Eric. Coal arrived only just in time. No hot water today till after breakfast. American parcels due to leave Kobe Jan. 4. Children's chief sport – watching antics of the drunken guards.

4, Thursday: After Council Meeting bridge and tea with Deirdre & John. Out their window watched the spectacle of the arrival of 3 trucks of coal. 42 coolies on the 3. How the foreigners – old and young – did flock to pick up the bits of coal which fell to the road as the coolies unloaded! Women's meeting on lavatory fatigue and monitorship.

5, Friday: A whole day of cleaning shelves and floor with John's assistance. Lavatory fatigue instituted – each woman doing ½ hr per day for one week, then a week off.

6, Saturday: Coffee and cake with Geo. Osborn at 11 in E 107. Mary there and the Aiers, Way and Peter Taylor. Choral preparing for part song concert in Feb. No bread today, reason uncertain – perhaps raid alarms. Guards haven't returned our plates yet.

7, Sunday: Another day of chatty cooking. Nightmare. Orange bread, fudge for Jill's birthday, bacon, etc. Scones!

8, Monday: Awoke to find snow all over the ground. Mary and Mrs. Porter (with needles) came in. Children's clothes, caps, gloves very wet and no place to dry them.

9, Tuesday: Carol and Eric to bridge. Bubbling Well operating on cinders to provide washing water. Now having cracked wheat mixed with maize flour twice a week for breakfast. Millet on Sundays.

10, Wednesday: Opening of school postponed to Monday because of cold. Coal allowance now 60 tons a month.

11, Thursday: Council discussed great variety of matters including barbed wire enclosure nearing completion. IRC rice – not to be distributed. Japanese admit Luzon landing and say fate of their nation hangs on success in Philippines.

12, Friday: Had Adamson and Lampo to bridge and supper. Fie on chatties! Whenever we added coal we were smoked out, impossible to spot soft coal. Headache by night. How I hate the cooking racket – in camp, at any rate. Meat loaf and orange pudding for supper and fried potatoes.

13, Saturday: Power off all day, so John busy with water fatigue. Cleaning of hall and stairs put onto room basis – since no "janitor" can be found. Baxter's lecture on "City of Rams." Choral rehearsal. Insurance company would reckon 30 deaths whereas we've had 16.

14, Sunday: Can't recover so far the plate lent to the guards for their New Year pig. At last thermos refills and containers have arrived in canteen. No cooking this day, but floor mopping and odd jobs.

15, Monday: Have to decide how to spend $50,000 not used for

'F' Block with flags flying after VJ Day, 1945, Lunghwa Camp

'F' Block in 2002 (now the main building of Shanghai Middle School)

children's Xmas. Biscuits or peanuts, perhaps. Desperate for a broom. Trying to make one from dried fire wheels.

16, Tuesday: Bridge with Carol & Eric. Coffee at 11 with Mrs Ranson. Secured thermos refills and basket containers. Chinese class began again. Americans on Luzon. Yamashita's motto: "Fight on to lose on Luzon." Letters to Nell, Elise, Esther, A. Beth, Kwouk, Chang, Chen, Suenson.

17, Wednesday: Spectacular raid with 12-15 small U.S. planes diving low, bombing air fields. Much smoke—Hungjao and Lunghwa aerodromes. Very sudden so guards hadn't time to shoo us in. Walker's lecture on Antarctic. Even that continent claimed by 8 or 10 nations.

18, Thursday: Kept in from 1:30—3:30 pm by air raid signals— local activity. No US planes sighted. Council discussing distribution of 100 lbs bread, penalties for labor shirkers, doctor for G Block. Cooked fruit bread, wheat-o-malt pudding, bacon, peanuts.

19, Friday: Parcels due today. Received letter from Bertie dated March 1944. Burnet married! Maidie and Mac came to have tea & play bridge. We were too late for parcels so had to get them next day. Bean oil lamp sent by students.

20, Saturday: Worst raid so far. Several US planes circled low over Lunghwa aerodrome and dropped bombs. Much black smoke ascended. One US plane trailed fire and went down. Sight sobered the crowd. Shrapnel came into two rooms, breaking windows. Five Chinese were brought to our clinic for treatment—serious shrapnel wounds.

21, Sunday: Addy Black came to tiffin—Cantonese sausages & rice. Winnie & Reg to tea. Made scones on the chatty and then prepared bacon spread.

22, Monday: S. *Times* says IPR—160 delegates—meeting this week in Hot Springs, Va. to consider Pacific problems after the war. Good news! Lights now on 6:30-9:30 pm.

23, Tuesday: Snowy day so I couldn't get the much-needed broom made. John's number lucky in draw, so we could buy a small packet of toilet paper for $92. Betty in bed with a cold.

24, Wednesday: "I Was There" Lectures—Pallis at Sienna, Wanhsien, Nanking. Block nurse came demonstrating many-tailed bandage and asking for donations of cloth for ARP kit. Paper says ILO Conference in London. Wonder if Nell is there.

25, Thursday: 6 trucks brought in 1,000 American parcels! 700 more due on Saturday. Bulk cigarettes and clothes "for Americans." Council discussing air raid procedure, re-arrangement of gardens, procedure during coal deliveries. Betty back to school after cold. Ruthie Meyers got the red bear for her birthday.

26, Friday: Barbed wire gates locked at night for first time. Guards were uncertain which to open so we shuttled back and forth at 8 pm. Japanese Consul General Toyoda visited here. Was in Singapore when J. were managing Italian camps. Adamson and Lampo came for bridge and supper.

27, Saturday: Harvey staged "The Dream of the Lord Marcus Brutus" — very clever cutting of Julius Caesar. Had to wait half an hour for guard to open gate at might. Air raid for short time — must have been false alarm. No planes in sight.

28, Sunday: Mr Nash died Friday night at 6 just after Winnie & Reg arrived at the General Hospital. Mrs Nash not there. They had to spend the night at the hospital. A chatty day. Tea after church with the Rowlands.

29, Monday: At last a quiet day for browsing in library and at home.

30, Tuesday: Spent the morning with Mary, mending & knitting. Bridge & tea with Carol & Eric. Carol still on the subject of American women with dual nationality.

31, Wednesday: Washing had to be done in spite of the rain. Professor's Quiz at night good entertainment. Surprise visit from Yamashita, probably looking for chatties.

FEBRUARY 1945

1, Thursday: Council discussing gardens, private allotments, etc. Chinese class, after attempting to cook on undependable chatty. Russians threatening Stettin (?). Breslau.

2. Fir Mrs Nash's funeral. Winnie & Reg went by taxi $40,000 an hour and went to the Nash home afterward where all the family had tea.

3, Saturday: Bitterly cold. Snow & Ice. Not above 34 in our room all day. Played bridge all the same with Deirdre & John Fee.

4, Sunday: The "London Ambassador" is going away to the Consulate in town. Bade Butterworth farewell with a kiss on each cheek.

5, Monday: The J. are taking every bit of metal. The bars from windows (gym) and gas tank, front gates, leaving openings — all boilers and pipes. Tully's lecture on "Louse."

6, Tuesday: Fall of Manila reported in *Shanghai Times*. Four trucks came bringing the British parcels and Am. bulk supplies (medicine & shoes.) Bridge with Carol & Eric.

7, Wednesday: Special Council Meeting at 11:30 am because monitors felt others had received information as to parcel distribution while they knew nothing official. Gendarmes arrived at 1 pm as scheduled. Teams of men and boys worked several hours opening containers & removing the offensive slogan — "For Victory — Save and Sell this Carton as Waste Paper."

8, Thursday: Early visit to Mary with tumblers on her birthday. Parcels distributed, 2 in the morning, 2 in the afternoon. Betty & I drew one British parcel each (2,4,6,8 terminals). Such joy and delight! Hard to believe we actually possess so much food. British parcels dated London June 1942 intended for Germany. Naturally in rather bad state. "But to think they were sending sugar, tea, jam" — Martin (?)

9, Friday: Adamson and Lampo came to bridge & supper. Had macaroni, with cheese, cooked yesterday, and heated on candle stove. 50% cut in electricity. Lights 7-9 pm only. No corridor or lavatory lights at night. Guards turn switch off at 10 pm, on at 7 am (maybe.)

10, Saturday: Laboring to complete Chinese slippers for John's birthday. Still very cold. North sides of building still have snow which fell a week ago. Attempted a cake with raisins for John's birthday. Mr. Gambling baked it in the kitchen.

11, Sunday: Still on the task of stowing away tinned goods and packing up cigarettes. Too cold for baths. Children upset by too much curry? or else too rich cheese and butter? Strange how quickly we feel satisfied. Coffee with Mary — very good.

12, Monday: Baxters and Adam to tea on John's birthday. Cake shared along the hall. Can't be many more cakes with sugar so short. Meyers sent some crystal heat.

13, Tuesday: Chinese New Year. Snow again! the sixth of the season.

14, Wednesday: Allied Conference at Yalta being reported in press. No hot washing water. Drinking water hours restricted so long queues. Coal gone, burning scrap wood. Commandant says impossible to get coal in Shanghai.

15, Thursday: Council meeting very long. Great concern over finance in view of letter from Swiss to say probably no more comfort allowance. Can the order for a million dollars' worth of eggs stand (5 per head?) Shall we cancel Shanghai milk? Wonder how Nita is celebrating.

16, Friday: Food cart arrived after 3 days' absence but brought no meat and practically no vegetables. Food very hard to get. Mrs Moffatt punished for smuggling in liquor, bribing Chinese fence mender. IRC parcels arrived — only 900 as against the usual 1,200.

17, Saturday: Dorothy Bell sent to Shanghai — Sad Case. Papers announce US task force off Japan bombarding. Sophomores gave a fine concert — variety show. Eric has postponed choral concert in favor of Easter music — Stainer's "Daughter of Jairus" & "Crucifixion." Coal arrived at last or there would have been no Sunday tiffin.

18, Sunday: Bath day for three with the chatty doing all the heating. Coffee at 11 with the Denisons and Adamson. Brief air raid — one U.S. plane sighted by some very high. Corregidor must be in US hands from news items.

19, Monday: Letter from Nell (Aug. 1944 NY) & from Bertie (Jan. '44). Wrote to Nell, Bertie, Nita, Mother, Hsia, Leitao, Djao, Stine. No coal for hot water, so couldn't wash. Lights 7:15-9 pm only.

20, Tuesday: Philip's birthday. Carol & Eric here for bridge. Stan Thornily discussing possibility of G Block lecture group. Dick at last on the list for corduroys.

21, Wednesday: Last eggs — in all probability. 4 per head at $115 per egg. Coal must be kept to 16 baskets per day — 7 to kitchen, 5 to water stations, 2 to hospital, etc. Water hours shortened much to public's inconvenience & disgust. Woodall's lecture on hymns & hymn tunes.

22, Thursday: Council again discussing coal situation, milk and egg situation, boys' dormitory. Lights now 7:15-9:15 pm.

23, Friday: Winnie Nash off to Shanghai hospital again. Hot washing water after a week without, so large washing. Adams & Lampo to bridge & supper. Salmon croquettes & pork & beans. US troops on Iwojima in Bonin Is.

24, Saturday: Pouring rain, so no washing possible. The stack of sheets and bedspreads still waits. Choral Society working Easter music — "Crucifixion" and "Daughter of Jairus." Arranged with Haley to dye some red yarn brown so I can finish B's sweater.

25, Sunday: Drew Lots A,B,C,D for American toiletries: 1 toothbrush, soap, sewing kit, comb, shoe laces & polish, toothpowder. Hurrah! Haley spent ? hours dyeing cotton brown so I could finish the striped sweater. John elected to church committee.

26, Monday: 4 sheets, 2 bedspreads washed at last! Organization....

27, Tuesday: Bridge with Carol & Eric.

28, Wednesday: Haley's lecture on "Story of Dyes."

MARCH 1945

1, Thursday: Early visit to Winifred Penfold on her birthday. Busy preparing Friday supper on chatty. Council discussing dentists's electricity, dogs, etc.

2, Friday: *Shanghai Times* changes to afternoon publication to save electricity — only one sheet. Smith and Mothersill to supper and bridge. John elected secretary of church committee. Last items from Am. parcels drawn for.

3, Saturday: All dogs ordered disposed of to prevent danger of rabies. Men's articles distributed by draw. John got razor, cream, blades. No meat brought by contractor — egg flakes instead 3 oz per head.

4, Sunday: Mary & Philip had coffee & chatted while I finished the garish sweater. Argued with Philip over the proposed lecture in French which he doesn't approve.

5, Monday: Yvette's fruitless trip to town. St. Luke's not prepared to give any medical treatments. Can't even sterilize instruments.

6, Tuesday: Lights 7:15-9:30. Worked on American poetry lecture.

7, Wednesday: Carol & Eric came for bridge & high tea. Opened British meat roll.

8, Thursday: Council discussing Butterworth's boots! Yamashita doing 10 days military training. Jan. & Feb. letters are just going out.

9, Friday: Adamson and Bradford came to bridge & supper 2:30-7:30. Blackout in this area 7:30-8:30.

10, Saturday: Gathered bricks to re-floor our garden hut, now minus its roof due to J. spite. French plays very good. Evans's name proposed for Representative, second term.

11, Sunday: Still very cold—fur coats, hot water bottles. Frost nearly every night this week with thermometer at 35°—38° in our room when we get up.

12, Monday: Exchanged ½ lb tea for 1 jar jam; 4 pots Am cigarettes for one IXL tamale! Bank account 6,700 overdrawn, but 12,000 should be credited today.

13, Tuesday: Maintaining my lead in bridge with Eric & Carol.

14, Wednesday: The Advance Party observed the second anniversary of their advent with a dinner party. All plans made for emergency set-up to run camp—Bond (OC) to be coopted to Executive.

15, Thursday: Council decided to spend only (and last?) available million dollars on toilet paper & eggs (3 per head.) Church youth committee meeting.

16, Friday: Dinner with Adamson and Smith—very pleasant occasion—with both raisin pie and cake—the one he made which lasted, after all.

17, Saturday: Sent Dick to see Cater because of his heaving, now improving. Exchanged 8 pkts of cigarettes for 1 tin brussel sprouts, 1 tin artichokes. "Carmen" (2 scenes) staged by Mooney from memory. No scores available.

18, Sunday: Shanghai milk delivery to be resumed at rate of about $5,200 per month for ½ pt per day. Tried to persuade Marie Hill to stand for Council.

19, Monday: Nominated Lilian Perry for Council. Georgie Fuller's name turned up in the last hour before nominations closed. All sorts of rumors re evacuation, refugees on adjacent fields, etc.

20, Tuesday: No coal, so no tiffin. Delivery arrived in time to cook supper. Lighted chatty for rice & sausages. Had Winifred Penfold to lunch. Usual bridge with Carol & Eric.

21, Wednesday: Wrote to Ruth E., F.A.L., Harriet, Ernest, Jeanne. Lights now 7:15-9:30. Ranson's very learned lecture on "Folklore

& Quackery." "The Men" seem to think fighting will come this way & camp will be affected.

22, Thursday: Hot water for washing this one day in 12. Last Council meeting. I shall feel at sea, in the dark, without that focus I have had for a year. Church youth committee. Sign in huts: "Vote for Georgie and the huts will be Fuller."

23, Friday: Freddie, Kathleen, Jill, Ruth to supper & bridge. Made custard on the oily rags. Parcels arrived (1,135, same as last month.) Huge parcel from J.S. Ling & H.J. Jui via Remedios. Cachita has to move.

24, Saturday: New Council elected.....Still frost at night. Hot water bottle, 5 blankets, down comfort, afghan.

25, Sunday: Another cooking – bathing day. Oh! for a chatty-less Sunday!

26, Monday: "Cross Country" Runs – very good. No boy dropped out. 3 Houses almost equal in points.

27, Tuesday: Bridge with Carol & Eric. New Council elected Harry Orr to executive with Philip & Hoppie. After class to Sherwood's lecture on "Nautical Experiences" (on a sailing ship.)

28, Wednesday: "Other Wise Man" staged by Hawkings – excellent – with Geo. Osborn in lead. Costumes magnificent. Exhaustion after polishing washroom windows, plus cleaning, plus washing.

29, Thursday: One of these awful chatty cooking days. Produced pot roast bacon, & a pudding for guests on Friday. Final rehearsal of "Crucifixion."

30, Friday: Good Friday. Much ado about pork, most people wanting it raw. Thank goodness, our four agree to have it cooked in kitchen. Adams & Lampo to supper & bridge. First performance of "The Crucifixion" 6:50 pm.

31, Saturday: Wedding of Margaret MacKenzie & John Kulesha (Polish American) in Dining Room D, Dean Trivett

RUTH HILL BARR

officiating. Choral Society sang hymn. Second performance of "Crucifixion."

APRIL 1945

1, Sunday: Air raid interrupted rehearsal of choral society at 2:30 pm. "Don't sing." They're bombing," ordered Coward. But it was in Yangtzepoo, not near us. Easter Sunday Church Service, then coffee with Deirdre & John Fee. U.S. plane made 3 V's with smoke. Much speculation followed.

2, Monday: Worst (most effective!) air raid so far 10:30 am. 5 or 6 small US planes bombing aerodromes. Great game hunting shrapnel afterward — plenty scattered over camp. Bridge with Carol & Eric. Rehearsal of "Daughter of Jairus."

3, Tuesday: Sewed & had coffee with Mary in the morning. John spoke on "Problem of Chinese Education" in G Block Series.

4, Wednesday: Paid $2,000 for 20 oz. sugar.

5-6 No entries

7, Saturday: Enjoying *Life & Letters of Walter Hines Page*. Business of clothing growing children is a problem. Jill giving dresses to Betty whose dresses go in turn to Ruth.

8, Sunday: Canidrome has closed. Several hundred greyhounds turned onto city streets — those that wouldn't sell. Paper warns against rabies.

9, Monday: Japanese cabinet changed. Suzuki, premier. Inspected air raid shelter at H made against the grave mounds, their bricks making one wall. Spring cleaning finally accomplished.

10, Tuesday: 950 pounds of tripe brought in. Kitchen manager told contractor, "Anything but pork" and that's what came! Tea party in C Dining Room amid classes for Mrs Baxter on her birthday. Gambling lectured: "From Paddle to Propeller."

11, Wednesday: Meeting of parents to discuss ARP. My duty in case of casualty is to run with 12 towels to downstairs wash room (dressing station.) Lilian Perry entertained Mary, Beryl Macadie, me at bridge & tea, in our quarters. Very pleasant.

12, Thursday: Spent the day cooking biscuits & the like after vegetables. Murray's lecture on "God, Man & History," discussed afterward with Ballard. Betty busy with dancing practices for May Day program.

13, Friday: Rumors of death of Roosevelt. Guards heard it over their radios & communicated. We refused to believe till confirmation received. Bridge with Carol & Eric postponed because Eric busy distributing raw pork, our own pigs slaughtered because not enough food for them. Saw "First Mrs. Frazer. "

14, Saturday: First night air raid. Explosions & sirens, not near us. Newspaper gave tragic news of Roosevelt's death. Truman of Missouri succeeding him. I was bombarded with questions as to vice-president. No one knew who [he] was! Division of opinion as to whether entertainment (play) should have been postponed. Dance was canceled. Had Ruth & Eric Clarke to coffee; Enid & Ted Phillips to tea. Dick cooked the pork.

15, Sunday: Planes overhead last night, explosions which rattled windows, fire in the distance, tracer bullets — at 1 and at 4:30 am. 27 people went off by bus at 8:15 am to visit husbands & relatives in Haiphong Road Camp.

16, Monday: Sad misgivings over Roosevelt's successor. Here's hoping he can rise to the occasion despite his background. Letters to Talitha, Aunt Beth, Roland, Christine, C.L. Boynton, Cachita, Beynon, Stephanie. Philip said my name suggested for librarian.

17, Tuesday: Mary and Philip came to hear Ernest Box on "Attempt at International Cooperation." Ballard and I kept on discussing economic angle and whether the world is better or worse than 1,000 years ago. 30 more American parcels due this week for

"Americans only."

18, Wednesday: Kitchen had to cook fish (a little,) beef and pork and give us 2 meals because no coal has come to enable them to cook tomorrow. Had Adamson and Lampo for bridge and supper.

19, Thursday: Raw food given because coal is exhausted. Had cause to consult Con who prescribed multiple vitamins (American!) Belgian Consul, British and Dutch express to Americans sorrow over Roosevelt's death.

20, Friday: Parcels once more....1,200 +. Went to the Children's Concert — "Out of Pam's Story Book." One gold bar (10 oz) worth 13,000,000 local dollars, then jumped to 18 million, we hear.

21, Saturday: Mary sat and sewed the morning. Bridge with Smith & Mothersill who stayed to supper. Betty rehearsing May Day dances.

22, Sunday: Egg flake sponge cake a flop. Traded 5 cigs for 2 tins DMP meat; 10 cigs for 2 lbs flour. Special Memorial service for Roosevelt. Very impressive — 700 there. 2 minute silence afterward.

23, Monday: A day of self-inflicted misery taking quinine and gravitol. No result.

24, Tuesday: Celebrated Deirdre's birthday. She and John came to tiffin. We played bridge. They provided the 5 o'clock tea. Russell lectured on "Export of Oils & Seeds." Russians in Berlin! Anglo-American forces join Russians at Dresden.

25, Wednesday: 2 tons coal, 5,000 lbs rice on hand for reserve. Some say "for the military when we are moved." Persistent rumors about moving various camps to Yangtzepoo Japanese School.

26, Thursday: Waked up last night by distant explosion which made building rumble and windows rattle. Cooked garden endive and made a successful sponge cake with egg flakes.

27, Friday: Air raid sirens and planes heard at 2:30 am. Adams and Lampo came to play bridge & sup.

28, Saturday: Up went wires and four mosquito nets. Coordinators' show very good indeed. Black night pierced by tracer bullets. Only firing heard — no sirens or planes.

29, Sunday: Church had special "Hymns of Praise" service at night. Kathleen came for a visit so I didn't go.

30, Monday: Gave a lecture on A.E. Robinson & Vachel Lindsay. Mary came and sat the afternoon sewing.

MAY 1945

1, Tuesday: 1 egg each at $125 per egg. The million dollars when finally spent bought only 1 egg & 1 roll toilet paper for the 1,800 people. Bridge with Carol & Eric. Ground too wet for May Day Program. Gates now open till 8 pm so we can come home any time.

2, Wednesday: School had 2nd anniversary tea party on the lawn near the pond. Appropriate speeches. Finished *Life & Letters of Walter Hines Page* — a great book.

3, Thursday: Paper reports Hitler's death. Rather full accounts of San Francisco Conference — editorials, too, playing up differences of opinion. May Day program was excellent — sunny, cool, windy day. Betty in woodland nymphs, hornpipe and maypole dances.

4, Friday: Pork $2,000 a pound (paper.) Japanese offer 1 million CRB for each American airman turned over to them (*S'hai Times.*) (100g gold = $14 million) Child told parent learned about Battle of Bubbling Well (meaning Waterloo.) D. Steeds learned about "our greatest general — Washington."

5, Saturday: All afternoon in garden reading *Story of Philosophy*. Dick busy with melon beds. Lettuce ready to eat. Still sleep under 3 blankets, but mosquito nets are already necessary.

6, Sunday: Determined to read all day but after slim tiffin we were so hungry that I relented and proposed cooking egg flakes, pudding, etc. for supper.

7, Monday: Went to see Mary, sick with a fever, she hopes not malaria. She hasn't learned how to be sick: can't put up with all the visitors and offers to help, gifts of food, etc. Newspaper not in for two days. May be fault of delivery office of *Times*.

8, Tuesday: News brought in that the war in Europe is finished. *S. Times* reports that J. may adopt new attitude if Germany has surrendered; that Yenan is ready to stab J. in the back. Great relief to think of cessation of hostilities somewhere. How well we understand what the Germans now face as to proclamations, registrations, etc. Carol & Eric to bridge as usual. Ballard spoke on "Printing Fabrics."

9, Wednesday: Some people had letters from NY today. Why, oh why, none for me! Children given holiday after George Osborn made appropriate speech at Assembly on the occasion of cessation of hostilities. Deirdre and I had a very frank conversation on philosophy of life, religion, etc. She thinks. Total blackout 9-10 pm. Last month has been one of our most peaceful, with little to interrupt or disturb us.

10, Thursday: Typhoid inoculations. Letter from Bertie sent Dec. 7 answering John's of last May 16. Saw *King John* cutting (called, *Bethink Thee, Hubert*) with George admirable as Hubert, Leslie Thomas as John, Lorna Rogers as Arthur. Discussed with Philip the move of the Chamber of Commerce (heads of firms) to discuss return to Shanghai. John feels it's the same old story of business plowing ahead without including anyone from the missionary community.

11, Friday: Adamson and Lampo—that fine combination—to bridge & supper. On to LMS meeting. Baxter says if possible he, Black and John will go prospecting to Shanghai when we are free. (Actually, he thinks Americans will take Shanghai and will give us orders.) He instructs us to have health exams so as to determine who goes first on furlough.

12, Saturday: Whole Meyers family sick, so they couldn't come to supper. Instead Mary, just up from malaria, & I ate Kathleen's scone and drank coffee at 11 am. Mary back to bed but Philip turned up at tea time. John engaged with Addy, so we talked business and politics.

13, Sunday: Special church service on the occasion of peace in Europe. Admirable effort. George Osborn, luckily, the scheduled preacher, spoke simply and superbly, without a sign of a note. "It is to be regretted that God has again forsaken Germany and given the victory to Britain." Jap. report in *Times*.

14, Monday: Back to school to teach Mary's two classes while she is sick: *As You Like It* in 3A and modern poetry in 5B.

15, Tuesday: John agreed to canvass the Block as to probable procedure when we are free: who will bolt, & who linger? Usual bridge with Carol & Eric. Dart spoke on more auctioneering experiences in Devonshire. All lights dimmed considerably.

16, Wednesday: Cowan's monumental lecture on "March of Time and Thought (Evolution)." Excellent diagrams.

17, Thursday: Taught for Mary the morning, then cooked noodles, sauce, chocolate cake, prunes, nuts, toast, egg flakes—all we could crowd in. John found most men in this block will stay on, not rush out the minute they can.

18, Friday: 22 eggs sent in extra parcel. Hurrah! IRC parcels arrived. Still no peanut butter for us. Butter instead but it doesn't last so long. Meyers four to supper after bridge. Freddie depressed by plasma-quinine and Kathleen worried. Rumor: Americans have landed at Foochow.

19, Saturday: Sick with a fever (102.5) and upset insides. Broke the thermometer, alas. IRC sent in clothes, brooms, toilet paper, brushes, shoes—hurrah!

20, Sunday: Spent the day abed reading philosophy section in *Outline of Modern Knowledge* (Wolf of London), Chinese, etc. Never was anything better than the Campbell's chicken soup we had at night. Special Whitsun Carol Service at Church.

21, Monday: Recovering from fever and internal upset. Oh! the

blessing of health. Baxter's second lecture on Buddhism —
which I had to miss. Wrote to Esther, Ruth P., Nita, Bertie,
Cachita, Stine, Medhurst, Anne MacKeith.

22, Tuesday: Usual bridge with Carol and Eric. Managed to cook
noodles in sausage soup to fill the voids at tiffin.

23, Wednesday: Struggling with fuel problem, only enough to
keep the chatty going a few hours at a time. Children scour the
coal heaps each day to get enough for that day.

24, Thursday: Swedish and Swiss consuls made their 3rd visit.
Council talked freely to them in Yamashita's presence. They
and he (Yamashita) deplore the bad situation with regard to
food. Guides and Scouts Empire Day display (not-so-normal,
of course.) Yamashita present. Murray's lecture "What Is
Christianity?"

25, Friday: Usual bridge with Adamson and Lampo, who brought
a tin of peaches, great treat. Reading *Outline of Modern Knowledge*
(Gollancz) and Durant's *Story of Philosophy*.

26, Saturday: Delicious supper after bridge with Kathleen and
Freddie: ham, tongue, pear, bean salad, coffee cream pie. Philip
sick with jaundice.

27, Sunday: Day of rest and reading. Church at night.

28, Monday: Wretched pickled pork. Have to hold your nose
while eating it.

29, Tuesday: Usual bridge with Carol and Eric. Russell's second
lecture on exports — jade, rugs, ivory, embroideries, etc. Philip
still in bed with jaundice.

30, Wednesday: Bread ration increased, due to lack of rice. Too
much bad bread. Great collection of loaves on table in foyer.

31, Thursday: All the day cooking: scones, biscuits, new potatoes,
egg flakes, almonds, etc. — custard with the last of our eggs.

JUNE 1945

1, Friday: Collected 2 pairs underpants, 1 pr. socks ex Swiss supplies. John, 1 pr. socks.

2, Saturday: Still having only one meal a day—no rice, often no meat. Bread very poor. Spent the day turning blue slacks inside out in effort to improve faded appearance. George Osborn's illuminating lecture on "Alexander the Great."

3, Sunday: Bread now $700 per lb; rice $300,000 a picul; sugar $4,000 a lb; lowest tram fare $150.

4, Monday:

5, Tuesday: Usual bridge with Carol and Eric. Rice now $400,000 a picul. All prices skyrocketing. Sugar $6,000 a pound.

6, Wednesday: Continued friction in the Levant. Excellent performance of "Pirates of Penzance." Costumes especially successful. Such color and originality!

7, Thursday: Big boar escaped, fell in septic tank, drowned! Guards disposed of carcase. How? Murray's lecture on organized Christianity.

8, Friday: Smith and Mothersill to bridge and supper. Lima beans (cooked day before) heated, spam, scrabbled eggs all done on lard stove. Yamashita says no chatties to be used inside.

9, Saturday: Repeated booms and bangs during night and day. Probably bombing at Woosung. San Francisco conference still in session. Spent the day turning blue slacks inside out. What a job!

10, Sunday: A day of quiet, two church services included, Sunday school anniversary service and at night Frank Wood on "Youth and the Church."

11, Monday: Pulled together material and thoughts on "Science and the Problem of Evil" in order to have a further session with Ballard.

12, Tuesday: Had to forego usual bridge due to Eric's being sick. About 70 books, mostly religious, sent by IRC, Geneva, have been censored and delivered by Jap. Further talk with Ballard. He stimulates and also aggravates.

13, Wednesday: Day devoted to cooking: scones, almonds, biscuits, toast, pudding (bread). Murray's lecture on molluscs — "From Cuttlefish to Snail."

14, Thursday: Purchased 8 eggs at $410 each egg. Played bridge with Bodson and Judah, the sharks. Tiffin very slim: salt pork, water bamboo, raw cucumber. Still no breakfast (all this week.) Usually red beans (our IRC stock) at night.

15, Friday: Rice now one million dollars a picul; potatoes $1,000 = a pound; eggplant $1,700 per lb. Every vegetable over $1,000. Meat $6,000; $8,000.

16, Saturday: Addy came to lunch: tinned fish, left over turnips, beans, pancakes fried on lard stove. Says CRB no longer used in Shanghai. Any radio can pick up USA relayed from Okinawa. Winifred P.'s lecture on "Christian and Other Influences in Western Art." She had to talk against heavy rain on tin roof.

17, Sunday: Rainy season good and proper. No sun for 5 days. Betty to Margaret Perry's party.

18, Monday: Alfred and Renée came to announce their engagement, settled the night before. Admirably suited they are though he is about 17 years older. She's 23. They ought to be very happy. Letters to Aunt Beth, Mother, Brenda, Nell, A.E., Jeanne, Stine.

19, Tuesday: Very strong letter sent to Yamashita, J. Consulate, Protecting Powers re food situation — one meal a day, no rice, short bread ration, etc. No news in papers these days — about Pacific area — except India.

20, Wednesday: Renée showed me her ring — a beautiful one with diamonds and sapphires. He's a conjurer — that Alfred. Lecture on Edward Wilson by Goodwin.

21, Thursday: No Chinese class because Matthews is sick, so I used the time on a pillow case for Dick's birthday — one bearing the Lunghwa Academy crest. Cooked all the day ready for supper tomorrow.

22, Friday: Alfred & Maj. to supper and bridge. Very good parcels from IRC and contacts — fresh vegetables included — celery, beans, onions, cucumbers, beets, pears, apples, eggs! Jam & beef from Liu Pa Nie very welcome.

23, Saturday: Saw "The Middle Watch" Sophomore presentation — very good, probably about 20 years old, the play. Coffee with the Goodwins in their shack at 11 am. Cooked the first vegetables! — onions, beans, arranged with Ruby Rudland to cook celery.

24, Sunday: 18 took Cambridge exam — 15 passed — 7 with matric. List posted of tremendous number & range of things sent in by IRC & Swiss — food, clothes, repair materials, kitchen utensils, solder, nails, all and sundry. Dick reports he has 36 tomatoes, numerous melon flowers.

25, Monday:

26, Tuesday: Finally had to bandage the thumb sprained last Friday when a wobbly bench collapsed. Nuisance!

27, Wednesday:

28, Thursday: Drinking water is serious problem. J. Consulate won't service the water truck operated by Chinese contractor. May keep truck here. Drinking pond water, served only at Dew Drop.

29, Friday: IRC has sent eggs — Hurrah — 5 per head — free! Kathleen came in and we drank coffee at 11. Went at night to see Kathleen re Jill and school awards.

30, Saturday: Entertained Alfred and Renée — Bridge and dinner

3-8:30, Frightfully hot. They are a charming couple. Got the supper cooked in spite of chatty difficulties. Betty started her summer job — herding goats.

The goats on the farm, Lunghwa Camp

JULY 1945

1, Sunday: Dick had 7 guests to tea: Roger Phillips, Gordon Biggs, Ian Tulloch, Frank Uhlick, Jamie Ballard, Bill & Buddy Perry. Scorching hot day. Water wouldn't settle in tank due to heat, so threat of no drinking water. Covered tank with matting water in nick of time for tea.

2, Monday: Spent the day recovering from the two parties. Temperature both days 97. Very trying heat.

3, Tuesday: Lilian Perry giving up Labor job after 10 months.

4, Wednesday: Celebrated by having tiffin, Carol, Eric, Patricia coming here: Sausages, macaroni, brussel sprouts, custard made with fresh eggs. Also bridge till 5.

5, Thursday: Great activity noted on Hangchow Road. Cemetery opposite us is becoming some kind of depot. Guns there, 'tis said. Every day, many horses arrive there pulling things in, sometimes out. Looks bad for the future.

6, Friday: IRC sent in meat—1,000 lbs—1,500 lbs tomatoes, cucumbers, potatoes, onions. Bless 'em! and peanut butter. 14 oz per head. Maj and Willie Smith came to play bridge 5:30-8:30, new hours due to heat.

7, Saturday: 3 elderly men arrived from Haiphong Road Camp with the news that the others are being moved to the north—Tungchow? Manchukuo? How sad for the wives left here. Rumor: Chinese army in Hangchow. Death of James Dunlap reported.

8, Sunday: Planned to celebrate the day by entertaining, jointly with Mary & Philip, Kathleen & Freddie. Both Philip and I had fevers, so had to postpone the dinner. Too bad when the

IRC had sent in tomatoes. 5th anniversary for Mary & Philip—Bombay, 1940.

9, Monday: No bridge because of early in billets due to blackout. 4 arrive from Yangchow Camp—young Tully, young MacKinnon, 2 Jamesons. Parents of Tully have been asking his transfer these two years.

10, Tuesday: Reading Longfellow's poems to Betty, Jill, Phyllis. Reports in from the school; Betty given double jump. Her report excellent; Dick's very disappointing. Will he ever wake up and study properly?

11, Wednesday:

12, Thursday: Last session Chinese class—holiday till Sept. 1. Betty received letter from Elizabeth Day, Yangchow, dated Oct. 31, 1944.

13, Friday: Coffee with Peggy Carter to see her portrait by D. Fee. She had a regular Xmas card mailed in Washington, D.C., last Nov. Was I envious! George Osborn and Mothersill came to play bridge 5:30-8:30, the summer hours, for bridge.

14, Saturday: Double anniversary celebration—delayed from 8th. Really delectable salad produced with Mary's help and Mrs. Bodson's mayonnaise. Terribly, miserably hot and drippy.

15, Sunday: Postponed Addy Black's birthday tiffin because of his sore tummy, the heat, etc. I feel worn out with yesterday's exertion.

16, Monday: While we played bridge with Carol & Eric, a hard rain came suddenly, flooded our room so the neighbors had to set to work mopping, moving cases, removing bedspreads, etc. What a muss we had to clear up. Margaret Rowlands back in Labor Office.

17, Tuesday: About 70 planes raided Shanghai at noon. 300-400 casualties—Chinese and Jewish refugees. Billeting Appeal Board met 2:30-4:30 making me late for my birthday tea.

Kathleen & Mary were hostesses; Carol Turner other guest. Bridge and supper — excellent — behind K — with explosions in the distance. Very nice indeed. Gifts — flowers, etc.

* * * * *

Notebook 2

July 17, 1945

A Third Lunghwa Birthday

Kathleen and Mary said come at 4. We adjourned to the rear of K Block right next the outside wire, where it was quiet, cool, green. Chinese farm people came and went along the paths, bent on their endless tasks. One woman shouted out asking if we'd exchange bread for eggs. We must have looked to them to be enjoying a fair degree of luxury, sitting in bright colored dresses, playing a game on a table covered in white, drinking glasses of tea (cool, if not cold.) It was excellent bridge — 8 rubbers — which Kathleen and I won by only a little.

As we played, occasionally we heard an explosion. A few American planes were in the air, evidently dropping bombs here and there. We could see black smoke rising in the city in the distance.

About 6:30 we paused for supper: salad of potatoes, onions, tomatoes, cucumber with sliced cold meat (American tang;) buttered scones; blancmange with pineapple and cookies; coffee (or tea.) It was a delicious meal, served expertly on an ironed green cloth.

Then more bridge till dark — 8:20. I came home bringing flour and vanilla from Mary; honey from Carol. Kathleen had sent canned heat earlier in the day. Mary put the flour into a bag she made out of one of her skirts. We'll eat the flour but the bag will remain.

It was such a happy, peaceful occasion. I had the feeling that we shan't be continuing very long to sit together playing bridge. Perhaps Kathleen will go off to Shanghai under the release scheme. Perhaps conditions are going to be unsettled from now on.

* * * * *

18, Wednesday: Another heavy raid—100 planes—at noon. Box seats by our windows. Peggy Carter here for the spectacle. US Chief in Pacific says must expect raids on all Chinese cities occupied by Japanese. No power, no water—awful in this heat.

19, Thursday: Still my thumb is bandaged; can't wash, can't sew, can't knit—a whole month now. Maj and Willie to play bridge, Friday:ed peas, cooked potatoes, etc for tiffin.

20, Friday: Four days without lights and without tap water. Parcels in, thank goodness—and bountiful supplies from Swiss in lieu of comfort allowance. Vegetables from Community Church. More from B.N. Liu.

21, Saturday: Power and water restored. Betty onto soft diet. Dr. Goodwin says blood count low. Verging on sprue. Swiss say $1 US = $90,000; gold bar jumped from 3 million to 80 million. Bombs small but powerful, hit Naval Landing Headquarters. Civilians killed when houses collapsed.

22, Sunday: Air raid broke up church and Sunday school and sent people scuttling home. Much dive-bombing. The crowd blocked the balcony so I had a hard time frying my fish, issued raw. Adam Black came to tiffin at one when raid was over.

23, Monday: Shoe price "fixed" in Shanghai at $115,000. Another air raid about noon.

24, Tuesday: Another raid about noon. Japanese guards now pay no attention to what we do. They used to stand guard at our doors. Now they stand outside and look—or on the roofs with glasses. Carol & Eric came for bridge.

25, Wednesday: Purchased 2 eggs each at $600 per egg—the last of camp funds except a million dollars kept for petty cash.

26, Thursday: Had the Bodson family of 6 to tiffin—10 of us in all. Everything prepared that morning on a chatty—(their big one, fortunately.)

27, Friday: Renée and Alfred came 6-8:30 for bridge. Winifred Penfold in hospital with malaria. Received IRC jam (?), honey, dates, soap.

28, Saturday: Swiss representatives came to discuss food situation and investigate other needs. Apparently had free access & could talk without Japanese around. Japanese much less strict these days. Got IR shoes 3½ much too big.

29, Sunday: British election results in—Labor government in power. Local papers publish news of ultimatum to Japan with No. 3 item marked: "Deleted by local censor." Such naive psychology! Are they preparing their people gently for an acceptance? Ah! is there hope?

30, Monday: Long queue in a new place—the library for the new American books. 4 boxes of them, sent by International YMCA and Committee for Student Relief. Great boon.

31, Tuesday: Winifred in hospital with malaria.

AUGUST 1945

1-4 No entries

5, Sunday: Mothers' vegetable back on duty. Visited Winifred still in hospital. Mary and Kathleen, too, both with fevers.

6, Monday: Morning devoted to hunting the rodent who pays nocturnal visits. It jumped out the window. Both children on soft diet, with tummy trouble.

7, Tuesday: Winifred still sick and children better. Carol and Eric came at 5:30 for bridge. Two US planes overhead but no raid for two weeks.

8, Wednesday: Concert canceled because of some Japanese anniversary.

9, Thursday: Rumors of repatriation and death of Jap. Emperor, etc. Betty's blood count low 3 million plus.

10, Friday: Ohnuki confirms that Russia has declared war on Japan.

* * * * *

Notebook 2
Sat., Aug. 11
The End (?)
About 8:30 a.m. today the news came that Japan had accepted the ultimatum and fighting had stopped. We were incredulous, of course. Rumors and talk persisted.

In F Block about 10 Evans announced that Ohnuki [Japanese Commandant] was proceeding to town for news. Nothing was official yet. *Ohnuki's car broke down outside the gate so he had to wait till 1 p.m. when the water cart towed his car into town. Ohnuki asked the chauffeur to remove the Japanese flag from the car. (Rather pathetic.)*

Water cart brought back the news that the French in town told them everything was over.

...

Sun., Aug. 12

Before breakfast we heard the latest: the the agreement between the Allies & Japan was signed at 12:15 last night, the Japanese retaining the right to be ruled by their Emperor, to whom the military generals will submit orders.

At 10 a.m. the Block Monitor announced: "The war is not yet over. The only station which broadcast anything about the war was Russia, who said only unconditional surrender would satisfy. Ohnuki and Evans listened to San Francisco and BBC but neither mentioned peace. When the time comes Ohnuki and Evans will go to the Swiss Consulate for the change over. We are still in the hands of the Japanese."

Everybody greatly depressed. Various false reports during the day. Michael Thompson was heard to say to Brian Evamy: "Evamy, have you heard? The war is over again."

Johnny Redland (aged 4) said to Dick: "Is the war over? They won't put Uncle Nuki in prison, will they?" The children like the Commandant, Mr. Ohnuki, and run down the path holding his hand.

Mon. & Tues, Aug. 13 & 14

Still two days with conflicting reports. We don't know why the delay in the official announcement. What are the Japanese waiting for? Two radios in camp — one assembled from parts brought in and parts of a Japanese radio, turned in for repair — hidden under stairs in E Block. Aerial is hidden by a bamboo sun shade.

Martial law in Shanghai, J. soldiers standing with fixed bayonets to keep order. That is best till Chungking and Allied soldiers arrive We understand that Americans are near and could be here in a few days. We keep wondering if the Kwangtung Japanese army won't agree to give up, or if the Japanese army in China, still undefeated, wants to fight on. Such suspense!

Wed., Aug. 15
At breakfast time the word finally came that the Japanese were ready to sign the agreement — rumor. At noon it was officially confirmed and Evans went to town for instructions from the Swiss. Great jubilation!

* * * * *

11, Saturday: Exciting news brought in from Shanghai: War is over, Chinese flags flying. Still unconfirmed at night. Ohnuki went to town but came back without information. Tentative plans for church service; proposed dance not held on roof. Went to take custard (like ice cream) to Winifred, still in hospital.

12, Sunday: Various rumors about agreements signed at 12:15 last night, but no real news. People are very impatient. 13 men went out to buy drink — 3 were caught, 2 stayed away all night. All taken to Bridge House. They reported American pilots there (9 or 10) being horribly treated.

13, Monday: Allies have accepted Japanese surrender, but no confirming answer has come from Japanese. Fears that army in China will not agree & will fight on. People greatly depressed. Wondering why no news. Two radios in camp, one assembled from parts belonging to J. radio.

14, Tuesday: Still waiting for news. Eric was sick, so no bridge. Kathleen & Freddie came to sit in the evening — and speculate. No newspaper for some days now.

15, Wednesday: Swiss took over the camps at noon, it being confirmed that the war is over. Great jubilation. Thanksgiving service at 7 pm out of doors. Six flags were unfurled on top of F. Block—American, Dutch, British, Chinese Belgian, Russian. Entertainments on both roofs till midnight. Clear sky, bright moon; perfect.

16, Thursday: Very moving scenes of reunions as guests arrived by the hundred. Much bartering thru the fence for eggs, chickens, fruit. Crowds of Chinese at the gate. Grass cutters coming in. Peanut Leitao came with messages. Saw Winifred, still in hospital. Supper party with Stella Purchase, Philips, Diacks, Geo. Osborn.

17, Friday: John set off on his first expedition to town. 10 teachers and students arrived from Medhurst soon after J left. Japanese guards departed quietly. Ohnuki staying on till Allies come. Japanese still on guard in Shanghai. Muriel Tu and Mary came; also Miss Chang & Miss Pi. Also Cachita. J. have not signed yet. We cannot leave here to go to Shanghai—(illegible) for this day.

18, Saturday: John found Shanghai a grim, dirty torn-up place and thinks it much better we stay here till things settle. Now looks as if small group of allied forces will land soon to look after prisoners and internees. Will we go from camp to ship for repatriation, we wonder. Beulah Chang and Mr Sone came before breakfast. J.C. Hsia and John after. Sone gave John half a million dollars. John paid $30,000 to ricksha man from end of Ferguson to camp. $11,000 from Hart Road to Bund. One egg costs $4,000. Winifred home from hospital. Chinese cooks installed in kitchen. Party for Matthews. Chinese school authorities came to take over property.

19, Sunday: Made scones because no bread came in. Bakelite workers tried to prevent Jap. taking machinery, couldn't bake bread. Took scones to Ohnuki; very appreciative.

20, Monday: Shelley Shen, with his father and a Dr. Jing, came to visit. They supplied all those IRC parcels for the parcel-less. Also donated $145 million to give each adult in Shanghai camps $100,000 for pocket money.

21, Tuesday: Guests: [names not filled in] Sat with Winifred in the dingle. Soviet film shown out of doors.

22, Wednesday: John off to Shanghai on the water cart.

23, Thursday: American Mission given rousing welcome. I managed tiffin for 28, including 2 Japanese. Major Schoyer (Pittsburgh) at head, says ships for home within a month. Story of their landing at Ta Chang field because of concrete. Jap. didn't know what to do so Americans issued orders for 4 trucks, etc. J. wanted to take them to Gendarmerie, but they insisted on going to the Swiss Consulate.

24, Friday: Mr. Wu walked out all the way. Gourel came and watched me fry Eddie's chicken. Winifred came to lunch. John returned from Shanghai, having had a marvelous time. Stayed with Trock in his other-worldly home.

25, Saturday: 11 Old boys came to spend the morning — 1937 class and 1942. Inspection and photographs. I made fritters early. They brought cakes, candy, etc.

26, Sunday: Crowded into 8:30 am bus to Shanghai. Community Church service just the same dignified, impressive ceremony. Organ good to hear. Y.C. Tu speaking about "Love your enemies." Matthew 5 — and reading Kipling's Recessional. Jap. sentry patrol past windows. Still 40 of them in Church House. Many invitations to lunch. Delicious Chinese food with Mrs J.H. Sun, Mrs Mason Loh there. Mrs Yen came later. She's teaching Sociology in U. of S. Flags everywhere and pictures of Chiang.

27, Monday: Helped to register occupants in categories so that American Mission can help get them out of camp. Most of those with homes reported the Japanese are in occupation. Eddie Pai asked me to help get connection with American drug firm —

local agency. Marguerite Hsia came. Picnic for family at the River. Very pleasant.

28, Tuesday: W.W. Yen, T.K. Ho, Mrs J.H. Sun, K. Chun and others came and present a shield made of flowers from Chiang Kai Shek. They are from the "Shanghai Public Association for Assisting the Rehabilitation of Allied Nationals from Civil Assembly Centers." Family picnic on the high mound overlooking the river. Lovely view across wide water.

29, Wednesday: John and Betty went to town, Betty to visit Stine for a few days. My watch, alas, will have to wait for USA. The hands have rusted away. It would cost too much here. Dripping hot weather, but I packed anyhow. Visit from Hsuan Pao-yuan. Permanent waves half price at the Nanking — about $40,000. Wool sweater $1,300,000. Outport people met and appointed com. to "save them from the BRA."

30, Thursday: Whole day devoted to packing and sorting. A 1939 graduate (whose name I can't read) brought me a pair of silk stockings. Hurray! Very difficult to run the camp. Many leaving. Others don't want to work. We get more food than we can eat. Bread brings about 3,000 a loaf at the gate. Rate maybe $1 = 500,000.00.

31, Friday: Chamber of Commerce & BRA working to get people out and forgetting that some must stay in and camps must be run. Philip Diack has been asked to help the Ch. of Com. in regard to claims for business property and may be going in a week. 12 or more American planes overhead today. 5 transports are lodged on the Lunghwa Aerodrome. Great excitement. Some people have been over to see them. Kathleen says one fashion magazine a year old in town. It costs $10,000 just to look through it. No looking back, either,

SEPTEMBER 1945

1, Saturday: PW Supplies plane flew back and forth over us. What a thrill! A four engined bomber (?). Dick visited the aerodrome where a number of transports have landed. Jap. still on guard. 2 American pilots visited this camp in the evening, against orders. Say they brought magazines for us. Freddie says BRA & Ch. of Com. cannot move fast because Kitagawa won't move fast. Businessmen are taken aback at conditions under new treaty given to Evans in French and translated here by Huckstep. Clocks set back 1 hr.

2, Sunday: With the Hawkings truck to Community Church where there was a record crowd for special Thanksgiving service — 700 and more. 200 from camps were entertained in homes at tiffin. 12 of us at the Hsias. John turned up with malaria, and had to be left there. Lt. Col. Simmonds now head of American Military Relief Mission visited camp. Brought Betty back from Suensons. Peace Treaty actually signed at last in Tokyo Bay on SS Missouri.

3, Monday: Christine Chambers flying to London via Kunming, Rangoon. Tumor on the brain. Gotch may fly to Mayo — growth on nose. American airmen came at night to show movies — news, cartoon, feature (Rosalind Russell in *Blonde Fever*.) They generate own electricity.

4, Tuesday: Magazines brought by Americans have arrived in camp — about 5 copies each of [sentence not finished.] Coffee at 11 with Winifred under the trees. Long chat in the evening with Philip, Mary, Freddy. Kathleen and children in town. Freddy got his house permit & also Philip's — a printed document to put on the door with red, white, blue border. Dick spent the day at the aerodrome.

5, Wednesday: PW Supply planes flew over and dropped drums of supplies fixed to parachutes. Most drums fell outside the camp, and were bashed open, contents lost. We were having a typhoon wind. (illegible) Parachutes were a great prize, of course. Some people were almost injured in their efforts to get to them first.

6, Thursday: Li Djoh-i and Chiu Li-ying came all the way in a carriage—3 hrs it took. Stayed to lunch. General Hayes (British, in charge in China) came here today with some others. Went to Nanking for treaty signing. Found it postponed due to political differences among Chinese, so he took Japanese train & came here. Says we repatriates will all be sent to Manila to be sorted out.

7, Friday: Such excitement over the parachute parcels! 8 times planes dropped 20-25 parachutes. Collecting them was hard task for men. Contents a great treat. Marvelous sight—those multi-colored umbrellas coming down. Australian war correspondent came to speak. John out from town for the night.

8, Saturday: John, Betty and I set off for Shanghai in the 9 am truck. To Scharpf Guenter where I removed from trunks some articles to take to USA. Embroidery thread I simply could not purchase anywhere. Lunch at YM with John & Kenneth Fu. Talked to K.Z. Loh. So much TB among Chinese. Saw Mr Isha (?) of SMC. Tea at Suensons' and on to Li Djoh-i's for the night. Such carnival on the streets! What fine, valiant work Djoh-i has done!

9, Sunday: To Tsai Mo-li's to look into suitcases, on to church where George spoke. Tiffin with Mr & Mrs Mason Loh and also tea when the YW people came: Dr. Yang, Mrs Hsueh, Mrs Tang, Mrs Sun. Supper and the night with Helen Ling. T.G. has gone to USA to represent China on the National Resources Commission to meet men from Br. Russia, U.S.A. etc.

10, Monday: Tried to get around town in the rain without coat or umbrella. Lingered among Helen LIng's lovely things in the shop till 11. Then saw Bacharach. He stayed out for 1 year. Went to Hongkew March 1944. Got job of managing residence in Dec. '44. Left note for Einar Edwards. Spent afternoon collecting things, after lunch at Y with John & Shepherd, and getting back to Lunghwa. Anne MacKeith spent the night. Shooting fray on Ave. Joffre. They say Wang troops resisted the Chungking troops who tried to disarm them.

11, Tuesday: Devoted to taking sulfanilimide and feeling wretched. Betty having malaria, fever 103. Ogden, British consul, spoke. Very realistic, reminding us of sacrifices at home, but he made a poor impression. No humor, no personality, no voice, no graciousness.

12, Wednesday: Rain for three days continuously. Free milk began to arrive—½ pt. per person.

13, Thursday: Household chores. Free bus service instituted by American Mission. Josselyn appointed Shanghai consul.

14, Friday: We hear Empress of Australia has arrived to take away 1,500 British prisoners—probably to Manila. About 1,200 people are still in camp. Only 2 doctors left to look after them. Winifred came for elevenses. Mary came in, too.

15, Saturday: John came back for the night. I've spent the whole week looking after a terrible boil on my face.

16, Sunday: Coffee at 11 with Freddy, Mary, Philip. Diacks move to town in downpour of rain.

17, Monday: Off to town for permanent wave at Pierre's—$135,000 plus tip. Town upside down because a Chinese general for this area had arrived. Joffre blocked off for parade. Big feast at Medhurst for foreigners returned from camp: flags, V's, lights, decorations. Spent night with Li Djoh-i.

18, Tuesday: Went to Hongkew to see the Bacharachs in their "shelter." Lunch with John at YMCA—what a haven it is! Missed the truck and spent a long time trying to get through crowds back to Palace for last truck.

19, Wednesday: We were required to fill in screening questionnaire for War Office, USA. Empress of Australia didn't come here at all. Took people from Singapore and Hong Kong. Internees absent more than 48 hours lose internee status.

20, Thursday: Went in the truck to Shanghai at 2:40. Attended meeting of Sino-American Institute of Cultural Relations at the Tsinghwa Club. Spent the night with Grace and Myra. Eric Bojesen came in with news of how the forces are taking over hotels, etc., so the internees have no place to go. Saw Russian film *Crimean Conference* at Majestic.

21, Friday: Kathleen and Freddy move to town. Made for American and Swiss Consulates to ask re repatriation. Hospital ship goes to USA instead of Manila, Britain. Lunch with Carleton Lacy. Grand to see him! Floods of rain. Couldn't get to YM for bus so took rickshaw through floods to Say Zoong, to catch it there. Saw Einar Edwards.

22, Saturday: Had to take the Bacharachs back on the bus they came on. Dashed off at 2:30 to the Swiss Consulate and there received my "ticket" to the USA and $25 pocket money. Ship supposed to leave about next Saturday, but may have to go aboard on Wednesday. Can it be true? I'll believe it when the anchor is up. Too late to return to camp for parachute committee, so I spent the night with Mary.

23, Sunday: To church where we saw Orrin Magill, in the Intelligence Service. A fine tiffin with Beulah Chang at her sister-in-law's. Too fine—I was desperately sick. Could not return to camp so went back to Mary's for another night. Sakamoto may be able to stay with Millican. The Kwouks have taken Carleton's house.

24, Monday: Back to camp by 8 am bus. Mrs Lent reports Swiss Consulate still gives Wednesday as day to be ready. She and sick husband will be going to Washington. John took his things to town on Baxter's truck. Bought some Bormann prints I like very much. Parachutes distributed, so we have eight gores – ⅓ of a chute.

25, Tuesday: About 11 am announcement was made that the HMS Glen Air will sail on Friday taking repatriates to England, luggage to be ready Wed. am, persons Thurs. Rushed to put Dick on the list. Took him off American list. At 2:30 we were told to have luggage in F Foyer this afternoon for US ship. What a scramble – John came to spend the night and we did a little sorting of things to stay.

26, Wednesday: At 7 am notified to be in F Foyer ready to go at 7:40. Put Betty on ship, then went to have lunch with Ernest Nash, recently arrived from Chungking, at the Metropole. Pouring rain. Back to ship at 4 where I saw Judahs, Susie, Bacharachs. Carol Turner & Bernard Read on board.

27, Thursday: USS Refuge (old President Garfield.) Rather awful ship with no cabins, no public rooms – only wards and dining room. One ward has 60 men. Still we must queue up for everything – regimentation complete. This will be a journey to be endured not enjoyed. But we can buy Coca Cola at certain hours. Mine sweeper ahead using radah (?).

28, Friday: USS Refuge. Stood still a large part of the day to avoid typhoon ahead. Myra and I distributed the 386 tins of tea put on by the Chinese-American Institute of Cultural Relations for all Americans. Played bridge at night with Carol, Bernard, Philip Read. Stretchers everywhere on this ship. Passengers: American 272, British 85, Canadian 27, Chinese 14, Miscellaneous 40.

29, Saturday: USS Refuge. Only thing to do on this ship is to grab a deck chair if you can and sit in it all day long. Lice inspection.

"All patients report to wards for lice inspection." The doctor examined everybody's hair.

30, Sunday: USS Refuge. Still no news of when we reach Okinawa. 5 or 6 days to make a two-day trip! People fainting in "chow line" as the boys call a meal queue.

OCTOBER 1945

1, Monday: USS Refuge — Pacific Ocean. Last night an old man — Harrison crew — died. Found Glen Scott, a Dallas boy, and promised to phone his mother.

2, Tuesday: USS Refuge. Arrived very early at Okinawa, Buckner Bay, (Nakaqu...) (illegible). At least 500 ships in harbor — very impressive. We heard a collision, and saw a man drown just below our ship. At 12:20 told to be ready to leave ship at 1 pm. Packed, stood in wards; were actually told to move out. Then the "evacuation was postponed." Told to go back and resume routine. Army doesn't want us on shore. Navy doesn't want to take us on. Spent night on ship in same hot quarters. Sick sailor brought on. Dead man removed.

3, Wednesday: LCT (Landing Craft Tanks) arrived about 10:20 to take us to the USS Sanctuary. One hour to load patients; 1½ hrs to sail across bay and tie up to ship; settled into Isolation ward by 1:45. Some tiffin about 2:30. Discipline still strict. Not allowed out of wards. "Bunk check" at 9 pm. Piano given by Walton High School students, NY. Face cloths made by Junior Red Cross; bed pockets by Red Cross, Duchess County, NY. 7 decks on this beautiful ship. Nurse closed curtains because couldn't get men off decks. Boys on deck wrote a note asking Betty & Pat if they had sisters 17 and 18 years old.

4, Thursday: USS Sanctuary, Sunset from the top deck is something to remember. This ship is certainly the last word in equipment and convenience, but rules about no visitors, don't go here, etc. mar the pleasure. Small hope of getting our luggage.

5, Friday: USS Sanctuary. Movie for children. Food on this ship not so good as The Refuge. Sent air mail letter to John (70¢) and home (8¢.) Talked to an air corps man from Dallas. Read Saroyan's *Daring Young Man*.

6, **Saturday:** USS Sanctuary. Clocks advanced 1 hr at midnight. Reading *China To Me*—Emily Hahn.

7, **Sunday:** USS Sanctuary Arrived in Apra Harbor, Guam, at 8 am. Army encampments among the palms, jeeps, trucks running everywhere on the shore. We tied up at a new dock. Not allowed on shore. Aircraft carriers, submarines, tugs, transports.

8, **Monday:** USS Sanctuary. Our crowd considerably sobered by sight of 4 rows of ambulances pulling up to gangplank and delivering more than 200 service men on stretchers. So many in plaster casts! Two solid hours it took. 15 navy nurses also came on. A few of crew allowed off, not others. Pulled out of Guam at 3 pm. Captain says San Francisco at 7 am, Oct. 20.

9, **Tuesday:** USS Sanctuary. Reading Van Loon's *Story of the Pacific*.

10, **Wednesday:** USS Sanctuary. Captain doesn't like crew seeing so much of passengers so he specified certain decks for passengers and others for crew. Stood in line an hour and a quarter to make purchases of toothbrushes, etc. in the shop. Captain's order: women must wear shirt waists.

11, **Thursday:** USS Sanctuary—homeward bound. Captain disgusted with behavior of some women passengers. Issued order that women must wear shirt waists with their shorts or slacks. Wives of some Harrison men misbehaving.

12, **Friday:** USS Sanctuary. Days seem very long and uneventful. Meal hours—7—11—4.15. "All galley corpsmen lay down to the mess hall." Ship's orders changed. We go to Pearl Harbor. News from Frisco coming over radio.

13, **Saturday:** USS Sanctuary. We had two Saturdays, Oct. 13— having crossed the International Date line. Clocks advanced 4 hours already; four more to advance before San Francisco. Read

Wescott's *Apartment in Athens.*

14, Sunday: USS Sanctuary. Very suitable church service. Enjoyed Dobie's *A Texan in England.* Writing letters for Honolulu.

15, Monday: USS Sanctuary. Talked to the Chaplain—Phi Beta Kappa from Duke, knew Sid Anderson. Only 26.

16, Tuesday: USS Sanctuary. Arrived in Pearl Harbor, Hawaii, at 9 am, sighting land about an hour earlier. On the dock people with lei's, reporters, band. One man brought on 40 newspapers and gave them out. About 20 passengers got off. We took on men who flew from U.S.A.—immigration, customs, war crimes attorneys. Grand view of air field and army post—air craft carriers, cruisers. We were interviewed at night by the inspectors, ready for San Francisco. Gave Betty one year.

17, Wednesday: USS Sanctuary. Captain has ordered all engines used to the full. Now traveling 18.25 knots an hour and should reach the Golden Gate at 5:25 Oct. 21—Sunday next.

18, Thursday: USS Sanctuary. Had a talk with one of the crimes attorneys about Japanese in America.

19, Friday: USS Sanctuary. Captain announced receipt of radiogram instructing him to reach San Francisco Mon. morning not Sunday night. Harbor full of ships there for Navy Day.

20, Saturday: USS Sanctuary. Long dull days these are. Cooler now on deck.

21, Sunday: USS Sanctuary. Last day on board. Hurray! Due tomorrow early. Many people sick on board very suddenly because of some food poisoning. Talked to Rhodes Baker, Jr.

22, Monday: The Sanctuary docked at Pier 7, 8:30 am. Dad and Ann there to meet us. Eleanor Breed & Mrs. Hunter came aboard. Took 6 hours to get off the ship. Even then trunks not released. Went to spend the night with Connie—Mrs Albert Wright in Piedmont. Beautiful home and splendid view. Train tickets hard to get. Reserved 1 upper for Thursday.

23, Tuesday: Spent clearing baggage, securing accommodation for 2 nights (YWCA;) purchasing Santa Fe ticket to Dallas. Waiting in lines, traveling distances. Letters & telegram from Marion Witt, Florence Pierce, Nita ($25, too), Viola, Louie, Lois Ruth, Ruth. Staying at a YW is a treat. It feels like home. Called Mamie Barrett.

24, Wed Shampoo, trips to Red Cross, Western Union, etc. Tiffin at Women's City Club with Peggy & Eddie Wise and Mr and Mrs Read. Then meandering with Betty. I have fallen in love with San Francisco all over again. Called Roland van den Berg, Jane Ward, Julian Arnold.

25, Thursday: Left San Francisco for Dallas. Sent letter to John by Eddie Wise. One upper berth not very big for two people.

26, Friday: Managed to get two meals in the diner by waiting hours in queues.

27, Saturday: Lunched at a Harvey House at Clovis, N. Mex. Train about 6 hours late.

28, Sunday: Arrived in Brownwood at 6 am. Took bus to Fort Worth where Ruth, Irene, Esther, Nancy, Mac met us. Good to be home.

* * * * *

End of 1945

"Good to be home," Mother wrote on Oct. 28, 1945.

To save space in this book, Nov. and Dec., 1945, have been omitted because they tell mostly of her visits to friends in the USA not seen for many years. She visited Nita in Williamsburg and saw many other ex-Shanghai friends in New York and Washington, DC.

   She was asked by several organizations to speak about her wartime experiences and, of course, she reported to the YWCA, her original employer in China. She also went to the headquarters of the American Red Cross to thank them in person for the parcels we had received in Lunghwa.

I was left in Dallas with her family and it was then that I got to know them. I became a Freshman in my mother's Dallas high school where I even had some of her former teachers. Aged twelve, short and skinny after emerging from a Japanese internment camp, surrounded by glamorous Texan teenagers, this was one of the great culture shocks of my life.

As recounted in the Foreword of this book, in 1946 Mother and I returned to Shanghai with my father. The rest is another story.

* * * * *

AFTERWORD

Notebook 2 Statistics
1725 Occupants
270 Children under 16
According to occupations –

Customs 70
S.M.C. 100
Outport missionaries 100
Shanghai people 600
Others – business people 855
with home ties

In 1945, 600 of the internees in Lunghwa CAC were "Shanghai people;" in other words, they had no other home. Today, more than 70 years later, I am, to my knowledge, the only British person born in Shanghai in the 1930s still living here in my hometown, Shanghai.

GLOSSARY

CHINESE WORDS USED in the text. The spellings in brackets are those used in China today.

fa pi (*fa bi*) Name of currency in use in Shanghai in 1941

feng lu (*feng lu*) Charcoal stove

mien (*mian*) Noodles

mow (*mu*) A Chinese area unit = 0.1647 acre or 797.3 sq yd

pa pao fan (*ba bao fan*) Eight Treasure Rice. A sweet Chinese dessert made of glutinous rice and other ingredients such as dried red dates, lotus seeds and assorted nuts.

pai lou (*pai lou*) A decorative arch

pao chia (*bao jia*) An old administrative system organized on the basis of households, each jia being made up of ten households.

tsung tzu (*zong zi*) A rice dumpling made of glutinous rice stuffed with different fillings, sometimes savory, such as fat pork, and sometimes sweet, such as red bean paste. Traditionally eaten at the Dragon Boat Festival on the fifth day of the fifth month of the lunar calendar.

PEOPLE

Family

Ruth Hill Barr - (diarist) my mother, b. July 17, 1903, in Dallas, Texas, U.S.A., d. July, 1990 in Scone, Perthshire, Scotland
John Snodgrass Barr - my father, b. Feb. 12, 1900, in Glasgow, Scotland, d. 1970, Scone, Perthshire, Scotland
John Richard Barr (Dick) - my brother, b. July 1, 1930, in Shanghai to Marie Raffo, an American missionary who was my father's first wife. She died in childbirth. Dick died of a sudden heart attack in Dec., 1974, in Edinburgh, Scotland. Dick's son, Graham, b. Aug. 16, 1966, is now an epidemiologist at Columbia University, NYC. He and his American wife, Kristen, have two children, Maya, b. Oct. 4, 2004, and Iain, b. May 25, 2006. They have visited us in Shanghai.
Margaret Elizabeth Barr (Betty) - b. April 8, 1933, in the Country Hospital (now Huadong Yiyuan) in Shanghai. Married Wang Zhengwen (George) Aug. 1984 in Shanghai.

Dallas, Texas

Pearl Porter Hill	my grandmother
James R. Hill	my grandfather
Esther Hill	my aunt (Mother's younger sister)

Scotland

Robert Barr - my uncle (Father's elder brother, "Bertie")
Margaret Cairns Barr - my aunt (Uncle Bertie's wife. "Meg")
They lived on a sheep farm named "Drumloist" near Callander, Perthshire.

Friends

Adams, Barbara - An American, wife of a wealthy Scottish businessman. In later years she, like Mother, lived in Perthshire and they celebrated Thanksgiving together many times. (Jan. 20, 1942)

Ballard, Mr. - It seems that Mother enjoyed discussions with Mr. Ballard who lived, like us, in G Block. His son, "Jamie", (i.e. J.G.,) was invited to Dick's 15th birthday party in our room. He later made Lunghwa famous through his novel *Empire of the Sun*. (Sept. 2, 1943)

Barnett, Eugene & Bertha - Eugene came to China with the Y.M.C.A. They had three sons, Robert, DeWitt and Doak and a daughter, Gene. DeWitt was a good friend of mine in Hong Kong in 1972. Together, we watched on a small black-and-white TV Nixon and Zhou Enlai shake hands in Beijing. I am still in touch with DeWitt's son, James, and a grandson, Chris. (Jan. 30, 1941)

Baxter, Mr. & Mrs. - Mr. Baxter was the leader of the London Missionary Society (LMS) group in Shanghai. (Jan. 2, 1941)

Box, Ernest - Ernest was an LMS missionary in the interior of China. The family lived two doors from us in G Block and Phyllis, one of their two daughters, became my good friend. (May, 29, 1943)

Butler, Rosa May - She was a teacher of Music at McTyeire School for Girls (now No. 3 Girls' School) on Edinburgh Road (Jiangsu Lu) not far from our home on Yu Yuen Road. (Feb. 4, 1941)

Byrd, Juanita ("Nita") Mother's close friend - and bridesmaid. She served with the American Baptist Foreign Missionary Board for more than seventeen years, teaching English at the University of Shanghai. In 1946 she married Claude Huang, a former student, and they later went to the U.S.A. to live. (Jan. 1, 1941)

Carter, Peggy - Peggy Pemberton-Carter has written a book about Lunghwa entitled *A Curious Cage*. In it can be found details of her unusual life before, during and after the war. In the camp she became a good friend of Mother's.

(June 5, 1943)

Chang, Mr. & Mrs. T.T. - Chinese friends of Mother's. (April 13, 1941)

Chun, Mrs. (Miss Yang) - A Chinese friend of Mother's. (April 13, 1941)

Deng, Cora - A leader in the Chinese Y.W.C.A. I met her in Shanghai in the 1970s and 1980s. (June 9, 1941)

Dent, R.V. - He was a descendant of one of the wealthiest British merchant firms active in China during the 19th century. They were, of course, associated with opium. This Mr. Dent was a musician and later, in 1949 and 1950, I went to his home at the corner of the present Shaanxi Nan Lu and Nanchang Lu to have piano lessons. His student, Margaret Yuan, gave me lessons on the pipe organ in Community Church on Avenue Petain (Hengshan Lu) and in the Anglican Cathedral, Holy Trinity. (Jan.21, 1943)

Diack, Philip & Mary - They became good friends of my parents in Lunghwa Camp. Mary worked with Mother in the Labor Office and Philip was on the General Council with her. (Nov. 2, 1943)

Dunlap, Dr. Sandy - An American ENT specialist in Shanghai. I visited him often in my childhood. (Jan. 6, 1941)

Eggo, Christine - She was a good friend of mine in the Public School for Girls. Her family lived in our lane on Yu Yuen Road. Her father worked in the British Consulate. (1941)

Estes, John - Son of Ruth Estes, a good friend of Mother's who lived in Waxahachie, Texas. The two Ruths first met at Glen Rose, a summer resort near Dallas. I am still in touch with John. (Feb. 7, 1941)

Farquharson, Dr. & Margery - Dr. Farquharson, an LMS medical missionary, died of typhus, a reminder to us today that in those days diseases such as cholera, typhoid and typhus were rampant.

Fee, John & Deirdre - They were, I think, Irish Presbyterian missionaries. Deirdre was an artist. The drawings of Lunghwa in this book are by her. (May 18, 1943)

Fukuda, Mrs. - A Japanese friend of Mother's. (1942)

Hardie, Joe - A young LMS missionary who "disappeared" in 1942, thereby causing much trouble. (Jan. 24, 1942)

Hinder, Eleanor ("Nell") Australian - Chief of the Industrial and Social Division of the S.M.C. from Jan., 1933, to Aug., 1942, when the Japanese occupation of Shanghai forced her repatriation to Britain. (Jan. 27, 1941)

Hoenigsfeld, M. - A German Jewish friend who lived in the ghetto in Hongkew (Hongkou). (Jan. 22, 1941)

Kucej, Sonia - A Czechoslovakian friend of Mother's. (1942)

Lampo, Alfred - A Belgian banker. He came often to our room in Lunghwa to play bridge with my parents. Later, he became engaged to Renée Bodson, one of the daughters of the Belgian family who lived across the hall from us. (1943)

Leitao, Cachita - A Portuguese friend who, coming from a neutral country, was not interned. She kindly sent food parcels to us all through the war. (Jan. 4, 1943)

Ly, Dr. J. Usang - A former President of Shanghai Jiaotong University. He happens to be one of my parents' many Chinese friends whom I especially remember. (Jan. 13, 1941)

MacKeith, Anne V. ("Mac") - An LMS missionary who in 1942 studied Japanese with Mother and, in the 1960s, was a colleague of mine at Ying Wa Girls' School in Hong Kong. (May 28, 1941)

Meyers, N.F. ("Freddy") & Kathleen - Jill Meyers was my good friend in primary school, Ruth her younger sister. Through them, my parents became acquainted with their parents. Freddy had come to Shanghai in the 1920s from Melbourne and was an import-export merchant. Kathleen, like her mother before her, had been born in Shanghai, i.e. she was a real Shanghailander.

These names reappear many times in the diary, especially during our time in Lunghwa Camp. I am still in touch with the next generation of the family, Jill's children - Martin, Isabelle and Cathy Griffiths. (1941)

Nance, Dr. - An American doctor whose parents had been missionaries. I am still in touch with his son, Walter, through the Shanghai American School Association. (Feb. 14, 1941)

Nash, Ernest and Ann - Ernest was a Shanghailander and we knew his mother who was universally known as "Mother Nash." Ernest and his American wife, Ann, helped my father look after his infant son, Dick, after the untimely death of Marie Raffo in childbirth. (Feb. 12, 1941)

Osborn, George - An English Methodist missionary who became the Head of Lunghwa Academy. (Mar. 21, 1942)

Packard, Ruth - A Y.W.C.A. friend who returned to Shanghai from the U.S.A. in 1941. (May 8, 1941)

Penfold, Winifred - Headmistress of the Cathedral School for Girls before the war and of the Shanghai British School after the war. (Sept. 6, 1943)

Read, Bernard - An LMS missionary who worked at the Henry Lester Institute of Technical Education on Avenue Road (Beijing Xi Lu). (May 14, 1943)

Robinson, Louise ("Bobby") - She was, I think, the Principal of the McTyeire School for Girls on Edinburgh Road (Jiangsu Lu). (Feb. 4, 1941)

Sadler, Brenda - Mother's English friend in England. (Apr. 6, 1941)

Sakamoto, Mr. - A Japanese friend of Mother's. (1941)

Service, Jack - An American Foreign Service officer who was later hounded by Senator Joseph McCarthy for being too pro "Red China." (1941)

Small, A.E. & Barbara - A.E. was an LMS colleague of my father's and Barbara was a good friend of my mother's. Shirley, their daughter, who was my age, died of polio on Nov. 6, 1940. She was buried in the cemetery on Bubbling Well Road and I think of her when I go to the present-day Jing'an Park. Martin was their son; I am still in touch with him. Mary, another daughter, died young because she had an enlarged heart. (Jan. 29, 1941)

Smith, A. Viola ("V") An American solicitor and trade commissioner, a lifelong friend of Nell Hinder. (1941)

Suenson, Stine -A Danish friend I met first in the primary school of the Public School for Girls on Yu Yuen Road. Her father was born in Shanghai but was sent to Denmark at the age of eight to be educated. After graduation as a civil engineer, he returned to Shanghai and started his own company. His main interest was in entomology and he traveled to many remote places in China to collect insects and beetles. Stine was born in Denmark but was brought to Shanghai at the age of two-and-a-half. I am still in touch with her and she remembers her mother baking cakes for us in Lunghwa. She has five children and lives near Stockholm in Sweden. (Mar. 15, 1941)

Tagawa, Mr. - A Japanese friend of Mother's. (Sept. 15, 1941)

Theune, Louise - Mother's German friend in Berlin. (Apr. 4, 1941)

Turner, Eric & Carol - Carol was one of the few American women in Lunghwa Camp. She and Mother celebrated American holidays such as July 4 together. Carol and her daughter Patricia, a little younger than me, sailed across the Pacific Ocean in an American hospital ship with Mother and me after the war. (May 16, 1943)

van den Berg, Roland - My brother, Dick's, good friend who lived in a tall building in a nearby lane on Yu Yuen Road. His father was Consul at the Consulate General of the Netherlands in Shanghai from 1924 until December, 1942. He was put under house arrest by the Japanese and left for Lorenzo Marques with the exchange of diplomats. Roland himself was later Ambassador of the Netherlands, first to South Korea (1979-1982), then to China (1986-1992) and finally in Japan (1992-1995). I am still in touch with him. (Feb. 22, 1941)

van Hengel, Jeanne - An American Y.W.C.A. colleague of Mother's. (Mar.. 14, 1941)

Wise, Eddie - An American friend who was, I think, a journalist. (Jan. 18, 1942)

Yang, Mae / May - A Chinese friend who asked Mother to coach her in English and history. (Jan. 5, 1942)

Public Figures in 1941-1945

Chiang Kai-shek - President of the Nationalist Government before the founding of the People's Republic of China.

Wang Ching-wei - Leader of the puppet government in Nanking in 1940.

Roosevelt, Franklin D. - 32nd President of the United States. He made the decision to declare war on Japan in December, 1941.

Truman, Harry S. - 33rd President of the United States. He made the decision to drop the two atomic bombs on Hiroshima and Nagasaki in early August, 1945.

Hirohito, Emperor - Emperor of Japan from 1926 to 1989. On August 15, 1945, he made a surrender speech which was broadcast to the Japanese people by radio.

BOOKS MOTHER READ

1941

1. *Testament of Friendship* Vera Brittain
2. *The Family* Nina Federova
3. *Where Do We Go From Here?* Harold Laski
4. *Unser Kampf* Richard Acland
5. *War Time Letters to Peace Lovers* Vera Brittain
6. *Victories Without Violence* Ruth Fry
7. *Faith for Living* Lewis Mumford
8. *Mrs. Miniver* Jan Struther
9. *The Defenders* Franz Hoellering
10. *Sapphire and the Slave Girl* Willa Cather
11. *My Name is Aram* Saroyan
12. *Thrice a Stranger* Vera Brittain
13. *Pilgrim's Way* Lord Tweedsmuir
14. *Here I Stay* Elizabeth Coatsworth
15. *The White Cliffs* Alice Duer Miller
16. *Tragedy of France* André Maurois
17. *There Shall Be No Night* Robert Sherwood
18. *Under Fire* A.M. Chirgwin
19. *H.M. Pulham, Esq.* J.P. Marquand
20. *The American Presidency* Harold J. Laski
21. *Maria Chapdelaine* Louis Hémon
22. *The Good Shepherd* Gunnar Gunnarsson
23. *Random Harvest* James Hilton
24. *A Mother Fights Hitler* Irmgard Litten
25. *Our Future in Asia* Robert Aura Smith
26. *Why Britain is At War* Nicolson
27, *Dawn Watch in China* Joy Homer
28. *Ambassador's Diary* Dodd

1942

1. *England the Unknown Isle* Paul Cohen-Portheim
2. *Junior Miss* Sally Benson
3. *Toward Freedom* Jawaharlal Nehru
4. *Kabloona* de Poncius
5. *So This is Glasgow* Gulliver
6. *Report on England* Ralph Ingersoll
7. *Europe in the Spring* Clare Boothe
8. *Combat at Midnight* Hermann Hagedorn
9. *Christian Faith & Democracy* Gregory Vlastos
10. *Keys of the Kingdom* A.J. Cronin
11. *Black Lamb Grey Falcon* Rebecca West
12. *And Tell of Time* Laura Krey
13. *Social Salvation* John C. Bennett
14. *Seven for a Secret* Mary Webb
15. *Imperialism & World Politics* Parker Moon
16. *God is My Adventure* Rom Landau
17. *Precious Bone* Mary Webb
18. *Mein Kampf* Adolf Hitler
19. *The Problem of India* Shelvankar
20. *Mandoa, Mandoa* Winifred Holtby
21. *Leaves from a Greenland Diary* Ruth Bryan Owen
22. *The Laurels Are Cut Down* Binns

1943

(Lunghwa CAC)
1. *Fame is the Spur* Howard Spring
2. *Roosevelt* Ludwig
3. *Straight and Crooked Thinking* Robert H. Thoules
4. *The Zeal of Thy House* Dorothy L. Sayers
5. *Gaudy Night* Dorothy Sayers
6. *Building a Cottage* Esther Meynell

7. *Moral Man & Immoral Society* Reinhold Niebuhr
8. *Letters from Women of Britain* Brown, Struther et al
9. *These Hurrying Years* Gerald Heard

1944
(Lunghwa)
1. *The Small House at Allington* Anthony Trollope
2. *Jane Eyre* Bronte
3. *Sense and Sensibility* Austen
4. *Swann's Way* Marcel Proust
5. *Changing Governments & Changing Cultures* Harold Rugg
6. *Prince Otto* R.L.S.
7. *Master of Ballantrae* R.L.S.
8. *The Brontes went to Woolworth's* Rachel Ferguson
9. *English Saga* Arthur Bryant
10. *The Windsor Tapestry* Compton MacKenzie
11. *Nine Etched from Life* Ludwig
12. *Grey Steel* Smuts

1945
(Lunghwa)
1. *Erewhon* Samuel Butler
2. *Poland* Rosa
3. *Life & Letters of Walter Hines Page* Hendrick
4. *Story of Philosophy* Durant
5. *Life of an Ant* Maeterlinck
6. *Song of Years* Bess Streeter Aldrich
7. *The Story of the Bible* Bowie
8. *God* (Two above sent by World Com. YMCA, War Prisoners Aid)
9. *Native American* Ray Stannard Baker (David Grayson)

RUTH HILL BARR

USS Refuge
10. Pacific Charter Hallett Abend

USS Sanctuary
11. The Daring Young Man on the Flying Trapeze William Saroyan
12. China to Me Emily Hahn
13. The Devil & Daniel Webster Benet
14. The Human Comedy Saroyan
15. Apartment in Athens Glenway Wescott
16. The Story of the Pacific Van Loon
17. A Texan in England J. Frank Dobie
18. Texas: A World in Itself George Sessions Perry

Notebook 3

NOTICES

LUNGHWA CIVIL ASSEMBLY CENTRE
UNNUMBERED NOTICES POSTED
MARCH 17 to April 26, 1943

(1) Preliminary Information and Advice to Camp Occupants
(2) Camp Services
(3) Discipline (Don't purchase through the fence)
(4) Protection of Trees. Dormitory Shelves (Don't put heavy things on shelves)
(5) Red Armbands (Don't wear but keep)
(6) Cleaning Equipment (Buckets, brooms, mops, etc. issued to various buildings)
(7) Occupation of New Buildings (Don't drive nails. Don't write on walls.)
(8) Gardening (All plots being used to serve children and invalids)
(9) Warning — Dangerous Places (Ponds, wells, pits, ruins, etc.)
(10) C.A.C. Services (Baggage, etc.)
(11) Medical Services (Clinics, etc.)
(12) Meals Seating Arrangements beginning 6 April
(13) Discarding Packing Materials (Don't do it)
(14) Regulations of the C.A.C. (All must read separate sheet)
(15) Supplementary Rations for Children (Soya bean milk, fruit, etc. for those who pay)
(16) Area Out-of-Bounds
(17) Meals Temporary Seating Arrangements from April 10
(18) Danger to Children (Flat Roofs of E & F Blocks out of bounds)
(19) Repairs to Watches and Clocks

(20) Lights Out (Must stay out 10:30 – 5)

(21) Meals New hours and seating arrangements from April 14

(22) Outgoing Letters (One a month permitted)

(23) Laundry – Provisional Scheme (Large articles only)

(24) Lighting of Fires (Not permitted)

NUMBERED NOTICES
BEGINNING APRIL 26, 1943

1. Shoe repairs
3. Children's Meals — Age Limit
4. C.A.C. Charges — Personal Accounts
7. Entertainments, Amusements, Games
8. Control of Children
9. Kitchen Fatigue Duty
10. Passports Must be turned in by Assembly 24 and all those transferred from Ash Camp and Yu Yuen Road.
11. Shelves / Wood Pile / Materials
12. Ex-S.M.C. Employees Finance Matters
13. Issue of New Ration Cards to No.
15 Assembly Group
14. Commandant's Inspection
15. Boundary Road (May be used in daylight hours)
16. Soya Bean Milk (for children, invalids)
17. Married Status of Women (Those widowed or divorced from British husbands)

May 1943
18. Medical Services
20. Live Stock (Can anyone donate?)
21. Protection of Gardens
24. Eggs

27. Menus and Cooking
28. Flat Roofs of Blocks E & F
29. Smoking in Dormitories
30. Issue of Special Food (Must be paid for by individuals)
31. Camp Services
32. Meals and Ration Cards
33. Meal Arrangements and Ration Card Numbers
34. Appropriated Equipment
35. Loan Service
38. Laundry — Extension of Facilities
40. Lost Property
41. Barber's Shop for Men
42. Canteen — Extension of Facilities
43. Inoculations
45. Newspapers (Will not be delivered to individuals)
46. Meal Arrangements and Ration Card Numbers
47. Statement of Cost of Eggs, Fresh Vegetables and Fruit Purchased locally and supplied to members of this Centre.
48. International Red Cross Letter Forms
49. C.A.C. (Civil Assembly Centre) Services Department
50. Medical Services

51. Typhoid Inoculation Charges for Medicines, etc.
52. C.A.C. Bank
53. Dental Services (Begin Mon May 17, 1943)
54. Visits to Hospital Visits to Sick Relatives
55. Transfers from Ash Camp
56. Issue of Drinking Water
57. Lost Property
58. Drinking Water (45% of ration only – trucks broken down)
59. Meal Arrangements Assembly 27
60. Notices Concerning Games etc.
62. Soya Bean Milk
63. Outgoing Mail
64. Drinking Water (New Regulations)
66. Meals (Punctuality and Disregard of Seating Arrangements)
69. Use of Electrical Equipment (No irons in rooms)
73. Meal Arrangements Suggestions for Improvements.
76. Shower Baths for Men
78. Removal of Wood
79. Canteen – New Procedure
80. Malaria – Use of Mosquito Nets
82. C.A.C. Finance Monthly Comfort Allowance (First available – sign for it up to June)
83. C.A.C. Police Matters

June 1943
84. Prevention of Hongkong Foot
85. Repairs to Watches etc. (Here and in Shanghai)
86. Sale of Empty Tins
87. Personal Services (Hair Washing, Massage, etc)
88. F.C.L. & H.H. Jam Jars (Return 12 oz size to Canteen)
89. F.C.L. & H.H. Jam Jars (Jars will not leave camp. This will mean cheaper jam and marmalade.
90. Theft of Plants and Garden Produce
91. Malaria – Use of Mosquito Nets
92, Mon thly Comfort Allowance Belgian Nationals
93. Mosquito Nets (Additional Orders may be placed in Canteen)
95. Personal Services (No more washing of clothes)
96. Welfare Fund (Donate your Small Money)
97. Rations of Hospital Patients (Cannot be drawn in Dining Room)
98. Control of Children (Rules for Children)
100. Wives of Husbands in Haiphong Road Centre (Register in Office)
102. Use of Window Sills (Don't place bottles, heavy objects on them)
103. Deposit of cash (All must be

turned in by June 15.)

104. Dining Room Trays

105. Block Representatives (Those elected posted)

106. Billeting — Basic Plan

107. Extra Bread Ration for Children Aged 9-17.

108. Appeal for Sharpening Steels for Butchers

110. Theft of Bread Box from Dining Room.

111. Personal Services

113. Mr. Hayashi's Lost Wallet

115. Meal Arrangements

116. Out-Going Letters

117. Empty Tins (Be Sure to turn in)

118. Hospital Kitchen Appeal for Equipment

119. C.A.C. Finance Deposit cash by June 22.

120. Medical Cases (Those returning from Shanghai report to Dr. Paterson)

121. Meals Unpunctuality and Disregard of Seating Arrangements

123. Regulations regarding Return to Billets

126. Lunghwa Academy Summer School

128. Canteen

129. Domestic Mail

130. Meal Arrangements (Suggestions for Improvements)

131. Welfare Fund (Donate your small money)

132. Dental Clinic

133. Men's and Women's Shower Baths — Change in Procedure

134. Shoes for Men, Women, Children Samples — orders

July 1943

135. Shacks and Sun Shelters (Private ones must be dismantled since block ones erected)

136. International Red Cross Parcels (1 per month permitted)

137. Office Hours

138. Outward Mail

139. Out-Going Letters

140. Electric Lights (Don't replace bulbs. No extensions allowed)

142. Fire Precaution Safety gangways in corridors must be 3 feet.

143. C.A.C. Financa Monthly Comforts Allowance

144. Non-British Dependents in Shanghai (Funds may be remitted)

145. Washing and Ironing (No more accepted by Personal Services)

146. Laundry — New Service Opens July 5.

148. Visit of Swiss Consul General and Swedish Consul General on July 6.
149. Lunghwa Centre Hospital – Visiting Hours 3-5 pm.
151. Visits to Sick Relative in Shanghai
152. Transfers to other C.A.C. Centres (Those wishing to transfer should apply)
153. Afternoon clinics – Change of Hours
154. Passports of Assemblies No. 27 & 30 (Hand them in)
155. Transfers to Other Centres (Only those centres in Shanghai)
156. Kitchen Administration
157. Shower Baths (May have one every day)
158. Comforts Allowance Belgian Nationals
159. Personal Services Knitting Section (Have you any wool? Will you knit for others?)
160. Showers – Use by boys. (Certain hours. Don't use too much water.)
161. Comforts Allowances
162. Cheques on accounts with Banks in Shanghai (Can draw)
163. Removal of Bricks (Don't take them)
164. Laundry – Suspension of Facilities (to relieve congestion)

165. Removal of Sand
166. Washing Water New Approach to Pond
167. C.A.C. Police
170. Equipment for Kindergarten
171. Use of Kitchen by Unauthorised Persons.
172. Information Regarding Mails, Cables, etc.
173. Report on Recent Billeting Difficulties with Room E. 303.
175. Parcels for Hospital Patients
176. C.A.C. Bank Transfers
177. Issue of Wheat Flour (2 lbs.)
178. Malaria Prevention Use of Mosquito Nets
179. Sun Blind Orders
180. Visit of Apostolic Delegate
182. Whooping Cough
183. Married Status of Women
184. Memorandum Constitution & Rules
185. Outward Mail
186. Adult Library
187. Passports Amoy Assembly and Assemblies 30 & 31
188. Labour Department
189. Boiled Drinking Water
190. Election of C.A.C. Representative
191. Election of General Council
192. Doctors' Visits

RUTH'S RECORD

August 1943

193. Conversation with Persons
Outside the Boundary (Not
permitted)

194. Library

195. Election Committee

196. Council Election

197. Suggestions Box

198. Theft of Garden Produce

199. Laundry Arrangements

200. E.G. Byrne—Deceased Effects to
be sold at auction

201. Empty tins

203. Tap Water Supply

204 Kitchen and Dining Hall
Management

205. Commandant's Inspection

206. House Monitors

207. Regulations Regarding Messages
and Shopping

208. Danger to Children

209. Outward Mail

210. C.A.C. Finance and Expenditure

211. The Typhoon of August 11.

212. Laundry transferred to C East

213. Meals—Serving Arrangements

214. Labour Vacancy—Typewriter
Repairs

215. Sports Ground

216. List of Divine Services Aug. 15

217. Boot and Shoe Repairs

218. Publicity (See Special Bulletins)

219. Comforts Allowance Sign for
July—August

220. Canteen—Closed today due to
structural alterations

221. C.A.C. Finance Monthly Comforts
Allowance

222. Appeal for Used Gramophone
Needles and Flower Seeds

223. Assemblies of 23rd July, 30 July, 9
Aug. Accounts

224. Election of Council Ballot Papers

225. Lunghwa Polytechnic—
Afternoon & Evening Classes

226. Election of C.A.C. Representative
and General Council Ballot Papers

227. Adult Library

228. Shoe repairs

229. Lunghwa Church and Sunday
School (Aug. 22)

230. I.R.C. Parcels (Save string and
Other Packing Materials)

231. Danger to Children—Castor Oil
Seeds

233. Visits to Sick Relatives (Those
in Shanghai must send medical
certificates before occupants may
visit them.)

234. Outgoing Correspondence
(Confine correspondence to
personal and general matters.
Exception was taken to "Dances
every night" and "We stew in

304

every way in the dining room.")

235. Rumors of Exemption
(Exemptions not imminent)

236. Outward Mail—September
Schedule

237. I.R.C. Parcels (Return boxes to
I.R.C.)

238. Auction Sales—Weekly for
clothes, food, anything

239. Labour Shortage (Workers needed
for canteen extension and bean
milk.)

241. Passports—Assemblies No. 30,
31, 32.

242. Comfort Allowance (Trying to get
increase due to high prices, but
occupants must live within their
allowances.)

243. Occupants with Relatives in
Shanghai (Those with wives
or blood relations report to
Commandant. Record purposes
only.)

244. Church of England Service

245. Coal for Private Cooking
(Occupants may collect only used
fuel from ash heaps, not real coal.)

246. Outgoing Cables (Only important
ones received by Japanese.)

247. Special Red Cross Letters (for
Repatriation ship—2 per family)

248. Meal Hours

249. Bank Accounts (Don't spend more
than you have.)

250. Special Red Cross Letters (1 per
person for Repatriation ship)

September, 1943

251. Special Church of England
Services

252. Lunghwa Academy—Opening of
School—Autumn Term 1943

253. Personal Services—Legal Advice
(Wills, etc.)

254. Dancing on E & F Roofs (Only
on certain evenings. E—Tues &
Thurs, F—Mon, Wed, Fri)

255. September Comfort Allowance

256. Distribution of Flour—2 lbs

257. Meals on Thursday, 9th Sept.—
Only stew, due to kitchen repairs.

259. Kitchen Management

260. Southwest Extension—Out of
bounds

261. Inoculation and Vaccination
(Early for American & Canadian
repatriates)

262. Resignation of Tinson from
kitchen (Council resolution)

263. Out of Bounds—Warning
(No one allowed in gardens of
Japanese guards' residences)

264. Subscription Lists (not allowed)

265. Kindergarten and School Charges

(Further consideration of fees)

266. Appeal for Gifts of Rope (to tether goats)

269. Repatriation—Names of those leaving Sept. 20

270. Use of Assembly Hall (Apply to certain gentleman)

271. Issue of Drinking Water—Only from Dew Drop Inn & Waterloo

272. Japanese Language Classes—Resumed Sept. 20

273. Lunghwa Polytechnic—Afternoon & Evening Classes

276. Transfers to and from the Weihsien C.A.C.

277. Synagogue Services—Jewish New Year and Day of Atonement

278. By-Election for Gen'l Council (to fill vacancy of Capt. Smith, repatriated)

279. Canteen Sales of Footwear and Overalls (Limited to heavy workers)

280. By-Election for General Council—Nominations received

282. Outward Mail—October Schedule

283. Clinic Hours

284. Out of Bounds Warning—Boundary Walk out of Bounds (due to escape of Conder)

285. Roll Call and Lights Out—Roll Call to be taken at 8:30 am & 8:30

pm by Jap. gendarme. Remain in billets till 9. (due to escape of Conder)

October, 1943

286. Meal Hours (changed due to new roll calls—due to escape of Conder)

287. Repatriation (Those not wanting to go see Gardener)

288. By-Election—Oct. 1 & 2—Change of times for Ballot (due to new roll call, escape of Conder)

289. Playing with Bows & Arrows (forbidden)

290. Out of Bounds Warning—Road near New Area

291. Empty Tins—Collected in "D".

292. Entertainments Committee (named)

293. Comfort Allowances (Don't spend more than you have.)

295. Cultural Activities (Meeting of those interested in Literary, Debating, Scientific & Engineering subjects)

296. Outgoing Letters—Additional Facilities (2 answers per mo. allowed)

299. Mosquito Nets (Continue to use them.)

300. Official Time (Consult Assembly

Hall clock)

301. Comfort Allowance (To be increased to $1,200 retroactive for Sept.)

302. Hospital Expenses – Hope to get these paid by advance from Swiss for governments, so – $323,100 paid by Hayashi to Country Hospital)

303. Clothing Stored in Shanghai – Possibly can be brought. Put in request for anything urgently needed for use in the Centre.

304. C.A.C, Mon thly Comfort Allowance (Sign for Nov. and Dec.)

Visit of Wives, etc to this Centre

a. Legal wives of Asiatic origin

b. Legal wives / husbands who are neutral

c. Wives exempt because of marriage subsequent to Dec. 8

d. Legal wives exempted to care for sick

e. Parents or close relatives of minors with no parents here.

306. Personal Services (Massage 9 – 12 daily) (Lost Property will be sold if not called for.)

307. Office Hours

308. Vaccination & Inoculation (For those who have missed)

309. Outward Mail – October Schedule (amended)

310. Personal Services (Pedicure – Ladies only)

311. Revised Dining Room Arrangements

312. Transfer of Pootung Bank Accounts

313. Road Name Competition

314. Community Fund

315. Personal Service – Darning and Mending

316. Distribution of Flour

317. Dancing, Music, etc. (Must have Commandant's approval – stop at 9:30.)

318. Hospital Expenses for Belgians (Will be met by Swedish Consulate)

319. Lost Property

320. Outward Mail – November Schedule

321. Appeal for Trained and Volunteer Nurses

November, 1943

322. Comfort Allowance – Reduced from $1,200 to $1,000

323. Injuries Received while on C.A.C. Duty (Cost up to $500 will be borne by C.A.C.)

328. Road Name Competition Results

329. Labour Office—The undernoted appointments have been made and will be effective as from Nov 10: Labour Officer—J.A. McKinney Assistant Labour Officer (Women)—Mrs. R.H. Barr Assistant—Mrs. M.K. Diack

330. Domestic Water Service Restrictions—One compressor being repaired. Water off 3 hrs. per day.

331. Time of Breakfast—8 am

332. Comfort Allowance—Nov. credited

333. Electric Heaters—Wanted for Hospital

334. Coal Consumption—Block Stoves & Showers on Thurs.

336. Coal Consumption—Showers—Hours for Thursday

337. Comfort Allowance—Alteration of Vouchers

338. Coal Consumption—Allotments to various depth.

339. Transportation Charges—$25 per trip

Commandant's Notice 11
Unlawful employment of Physical Force—liable to 10 yrs. imprisonment

340. Medical, Dental & Similar Expenses (Swiss will pay up to Nov. 5. Sign)

341. Bank Transfers (Not less than $100)

342. Clothing Orders recently placed with Canteen

343. Shoes, Clothing & Bedding (If urgent, Council will try to get Swiss to pay)

345. Chatties (may not be used inside)

346. Mosquito Nets (no longer needed)

347. Kitchen Equipment—Butcher knives & oil stone needed

348. Cracked wheat gruel—Served only in Dining Room D, not at hospital to invalids)

349. Comfort Allowance—Dec. may not be received till Dec. 15

Commandant's Notice No 13
Swiss Consulate has suspended comfort allowance.

350. Hot Water Services—Hours -

358. Vegetable Gardens—Appeal for Volunteers

359. Outward Mail—Dec. Schedule

360. Lunghwa C.A.C. Hospital Charges—$15 per day

361. Secretarial Appointment

362. Empty Tins (No facilities to transport)

366. Mincing Machine (disappeared from kitchen)

369. New Territory Out-of-Bounds

372. Bread (None delivered on Jan.1,2,3)

374. Bank Transfers

376. Christmas Post Office for Children

378. Radio Messages to Australia

379. Issue of Flour

380. Discarded Footwear (Give old shoes to repair depot)

384. Menus for Xmas Day: Bkfst Cracked Wheat, Tea Tiffin Sweet & Sour Pork, Rice, Cabbage, White Rice & Raisin Pudding Supper Braised beef, Vegetables, Rice

388. Theft from Farm (14 chickens, 1 gosling)

392. Theft of Buckets from Children's Kitchen

395. Blocked Salaries (J. will try to secure release)

398. Alcoholic Liquors (Must not be brought in or bought)

January 1944

400. Women's Vegetable-Preparation Fatigue

413. Splitting Axes (Needed by kitchen—loan)

417. Constitution & Rules (Committee appointed to receive various plans)

419. Appeal for Welfare Funds

423. Fresh Milk (63% increase in cost)

425. Transfers to Weihsien (applications)

426. Women with bonafide neutral or stateless common law husbands in Shanghai may apply for exemption.

427. Loss of Farm Property (Water proof cover for Cow)

429. Letters to Weihsien (must be in by Jan. 29)

February, 1944

436. Theft of Bread (100 loaves)

437. Meat Ration (reduced 30%)

438. Unidentified Letter from England

439. House Monitors

441. Family Cubicles (will be arranged)

442. Matzos (Jews may obtain them for Passover)

444. Labour (Those who won't work will be deprived of Canteen, Welfare, Education, Entertainments, Sports, Library)

445. Amendments to Constitution

447. Referendum on schemes A, B, C, D to amend constitution)

448. Collection of Empty Tins

451. Letters to Civilian Internees in

Philippines (Ordinary messages not possible; For Special, apply)

452. I.R.C. Donated Supplies

460. Special Police (100 men)

461. Disciplinary Courts (Set up, 3 judges)

463. Theft of C.A.C. Service Gear (wheel & tyre of truck)

469. Election of C.A.C. Representative and General Council

March, 1944

471. Lunghwa Polytechnic (classes, etc.)

475. Registration of Australians or those with dependents there.

476. Appeal for old shoes

477. Dire Need Clothing (those who registered last Nov. collect)

500. Police Regulations

April, 1944

502. Departmental Heads – appointments

504. Vegetable Garden Allotments

506. Danger from Stray Dogs

508. I.R.C. Supplies (April 6, 1944) – 1840 Parcels from American Red Cross

Summons to Skinner to appear in Court for stealing 28 lbs pork.

511. Theft of Man-Hole Covers

512. Book Binding Materials & Care of Books

514. Fresh Milk (increased cost by 65%)

517. Supplies (Draw for odd lots of American parcels)

518. Letter from Jost of I.R.C. listing clothes and drugs from America

519. Malaria prevention

524. Spectacles and Watch Repairs

524. A. Rations (Meat cut further by 20% bringing it down to 3½ oz per day or about 2 oz. edible meat. 50% of original ration.)

525. American Red Cross – Women's Supplies – List of American women – by passport and by birth

527. Control of Children

527.A. Death of Miss Isabella Smith

528. Malaria Prevention – Mosquito nets must be in use by May 1.

May, 1944

539. "Dire Need" Clothing and Shoes

540. Vegetable Preparation

542. Public Health Regulations

544. Bathing in Ponds (dangerous)

546. May 10 – Donations to American Nationals – CRB $2,535 donated by repatriates on Teia Maru for American inmates here.

548. Final draw for A.R.C. goods

552. Fresh Milk — $515 per ½ pt

553. Outward Mail regulations

563. A.R.C. Toiletries — Results of
Draw

569. Commandant says all tools must
be handed in to depot heads &
locked at night)

570. Dining Room Service
(Explanation of "Seconds".)

572. Malaria

June, 1944

574. Mattresses (Commandant wants
list of those using mattresses
belonging to people who have
repatriated or left.)

575. Draw for A.R.C. Women's Clothes

583. Music and Singing — Only in
Blocks, not after lights out

585. Registration of Australians, New
Zealand, South African subjects.

589. Visits of Relations to the Centre

593. Distribution of A.R.C. Shoes

594. A.R.C. Clothing and Toiletries —
"Seconds" Draw

602. Comfort Allowances $3,000 per
mo.
Official rates = £1 = 94.23
U.S.$1 = 23.42

July, 1944

617. Declaration of Retention of British
Nationality
Persons born abroad on or after
Jan. 1, 1915, of fathers, natural
born Br. subjects, but not born
within His Majesty's allegiance,
do not acquire Br. nationality
unless registered at Br. Consulate
or registered. They must
within one year of becoming
21 assert his Br. nationality by a
Declaration of Retention.

621. Disciplinary Court — Action
against Mrs. P. for destroying
rations and creating disturbance
in dining room.

623. Comfort Loans — Swiss will
advance funds for Hospital —
Medical diet, etc.

624. Comfort Loans — American
Nationals — Exchange rate will be
fixed later.

626. Cotton Socks and Stockings — A
few I.R.C. ones (Black) available

627. Theft of Melons

634. Letters from Haiphong Road
Camp

637. Donations from Swiss Consulate
General — Peanut butter, Maltose,
Salmon, Beef, Pork, Sugar, Rice,
Cracked Wheat flour

638. Shoe Repairs

639. Goats — must be allowed to graze. Garden plot holders don't frighten them in driving them away.

641. Black Out — Aug. 9 — Striking matches, smoking cigs near windows prohibited.

647. Referendum No. 3 — Change of Constitution

648. Lost Books

August, 1944

Election of C.A.C. Representative

655. Application for Exemption — Women of neutral or stateless birth who acquired enemy nationality thru marriage before Dec. 8, 1941, and who are widowed, divorced or separated may register for exemption.

656. Application for Exemption — Enemy nationals by birth married to neutral or stateless husbands after De. 8, 1941, may apply for exemption. Parents or guardians of children 10 and under who have a responsible guarantor in Shanghai may register.

658. Disciplinary Court — Belgian subjects now subject to court, not to their consul.

659. Cables per I.R.C. — Only emergency ones can be sent.

660. Out-of-Bounds Warning

661. Donations from Swiss Consulate General — Food & Clothes

(Here occurred the escape of 3 occupants)

662. Relaxation of Restrictions — Can leave billets on Tuesday at 7 Breakfast and Canteen restored Letters restored. Roll call by guards at night & in am.

666. Careful Use of Tap Water

667. Tap Water — Hours of Supply

669. Escapes — Council considers the duty of each occupant is to the community as a whole and as the suffering which the community will have to bear as a result of further escapes will greatly outweigh the benefits of freedom which may accrue to the few, it is the clear duty of each individual to suppress his or her desire to escape. The Council also urges upon all occupants their responsibility to use their personal influence to discourage other occupants from planning or attempting to escape.

September, 1944

671. Distribution of Donated Shoes (to those who registered)

686. Articles Received from Swiss Con. General — Clothes, Shoes, Toothbrushes, etc.

687. I.R.C. Parcels — Articles Missing

689. Visit of Swiss Consul-General (Sept. 29)

692. B. Welfare Fund — Occupants of non-recognized status — sign for loans

694. Distribution of Sweatshirts & Shoes

October, 1944

696. Tap Water Control

698. Rebilleting Arrangements — Married couples wanting cubicles register today.

699. Collection of Empty Tins & Bottles

700. Fumigation Chamber (in operation again)

701. Water Supply (Change of Hours)

702. Fresh Milk

703. Cash for patients in Shanghai hospitals

706, Sundry Information - Chatties allowed Tues, Th, Saturday:. 11-6 Supper — 4:45 Don't leave billets till 7 am.

711. Hot Drinking Water Service

714. Return of Baskets Lent for Billeting Moves

717 Fresh Milk — Increase in Price $1,050 to $1,800 for adults $900 to $1,600 for children

November, 1944

719. Seeds and seedlings for Private Allotments

721. Male Volunteer Vegetable Cleaners

722. Donation of Supplies — 200 persons received parcels this year; those willing to donate good please hand to Block Monitor.

723. Loan Notes for Hospital Diet & Eggs

727. Blankets (125 A.R.C. blankets will be issued on loan. Register.)

729. Rat Poison — Please donate.

730. Unauthorized Use of Electrical Appliances (Hot plates, irons, etc. — users will be taken to Court).

734. Air Raid Precautions — Signals, etc.

736. Christmas Gifts to Haiphong Road — Hoped to arrange for delivery of small parcel to husbands.

738. Bank Stationery — $15 per page of accounts charged to depositors.

743. Appeal for Donation of Rags (for kitchens)

745. Illegal Use of Force—Mr. Calder assaulted Mrs. Gladhill. Settled by Ex. Com.

749. Theft of Amplifier Fittings

751. Men's Corduroys

December, 1944

753. Shanghai Shoe Repairs

755. Drinking Water Service

757. Roll Call & Return to Billets—Extension to 8pm during holidays.

759. Electric torches (Must be surrendered except by authorized persons.)

761. Disorderly Behavior—Ex. Com. investigated complaint (he was drunk) and sentenced him to lavatory and corridor fatigue for one month.

762. Goods Received from Swiss Consulate—Toilet paper, soap, food, etc.

764. Reserved Ash Heaps—Refrain from taking ashes from certain piles at Dew Drop & Waterloo so as to provide ashes for hot washing water.

767. Baking of Cakes—Kitchen will bake on Sunday, Dec. 24. Register.

774. Air Raid Warnings—Signals After Dusk

775. Occupants of Irish Nationality—Free-State Citizens please register.

January, 1945

Message from Ex. Com. of I.R.C., Geneva, to Prisoners of War and Interned Civilians of All Nationalities

785. Loan Notes on Swiss Consulate—New Procedure

787. Misuse of Electric Current (Hot Plates)

788. I.R.C. Parcel Containers—Please turn in in B Dining Room. $10 per carton paid

789. Pig Swill (Don't put glass, etc. in)

790. Warning Against Eating Raw Vegetables

792. Air Raids—Even if no signal, return to billets or take cover at once.

793. Adult Footwear

795. Important Notice—Camp Labour Penalties for those who don't work - Withdrawal of Canteen Issues of cigarettes, tobacco, sweets, and of foodstuffs produced in Center, exclusion from Library facilities, non-admission to Camp Entertainments, non-participation in Educational & Sports activities. Freezing of

Bank accounts for all purposes
except purchase of Canteen
foodstuffs. No hot washing,
water, clothing, shoes, shoe
repairs. Posting of names on
Notice Boards.

799. Outward Mail

800. Air Raids—Precautions against
Injury (Last Sat. 5 Chinese injured,
one fatally, within a mile because
they failed to take cover.) Keep
away from windows.

801. Out-of-Bounds Area during Coal
Deliveries (to prevent people
snatching off trucks)

802. Separated Families—
Commandant wants information
about

  1. Wives with husbands in
Haiphong Rd.

  2. Those whose husbands or
wives are exempt by reason
of their having been married
after Dec. 8.

  3. Occupants whose husbands,
wives or children under adult
age are exempt on account of
their Asiatic origin.

  4. Occupants having husbands,
wives or children in other
camps (including Prisoner of
War camps) in Hong Kong

and China.

  5. Families separated by other
reasons.

803. Meeting of Belgian Nationals

804. Roll Call in Evening—Will be
taken by Monitors except in E.
Block.

805. Inner Fence Gates Instructions

807. Tooth Powder—Swiss sent a little.
Only for those genuinely in need.

808. Distribution of Adults' Winter
Pyjamas.

February, 1945

810. Adult Footwear

811. Theft of Vegetables—Mrs. R.
Goldenburg

813. To Occupants of Australian,
New Zealand, South African
Nationality

815. Malpractice—Referring to 811.
Names will be posted and
penalties imposed.

816. Shoes

817. Men's Socks

818. Conservation of Food Supplies

819. American and British Gift Food
Parcels
  A.R.C. 1,628 big parcels of 4
units = 6512
  B.R.C. 120 " 6 " = 720
  Draw to see who gets Br. parcels.

820. American and British Red Cross Parcels—List includes food, medical supplies, men's wool clothing, shoes, shoe repair kits, cigarettes. Br—food, 3 cases men's shoes.

821. Adult Boxing Classes

823. Sale of Eggs (even those without money may have).

824. Gardens—Private Allotments—Locations

825. Am. & Br. Red Cross Parcel Containers—Occupants don't take away from D.R.

828. A.R.P. Organization and Procedure

835. Bugle Calls—7 am, 8:50 am, 6:50 pm, 8 pm, 8:20 pm

836. Dental Clinic—Hours of electricity allowed

837. Coal Shortage—Emergency Arrangements

838. I.R.C. Letter Charges—$50—Replies $30

839. Distribution of Shoes, Clothes

841. Am. & Br. Red Cross bulk Supplies—Lists

March, 1945

847. Theft of Community Property (Coal from Water Stations)

848. Prevention of Rabies—Regulations regarding Dogs.

851. Liver Injections—Several patients in great need. Those willing please donate.

855. Theft from Baggage in E Block (Shoes, A.R.C. parcel)

856. Lettuce Seedlings

857. Grass Burning—Lighting fires forbidden. Apply to P.H.D. (?)

862. Theft of Vegetables—Workers report to team leaders immediately so investigation can be made on the spot.

863. Fresh Milk—$5,400 per mo for ½ pt per day.

864. Issue of Clothing and Footwear

865. Appeal for Worn-out Gum Boots

866. Manure for Garden Plot Holders

867. Danger of Sitting Near F Block—Heavy lumps of cement are falling from facing of building.

868. Repairs to Spectacles

870. Supplies from Swiss Consulate—brooms, saucepans

871. Letter from I.R.C. Committee (regarding safety of relatives in Hong Kong)

872. Digging of Holes and Ditches—Forbidden because of breeding mosquitoes.

873. Tap Water Service during Air Raids

875. Camp Labour—Penalties applied

to Gladhill who refuses to work.

878. Hot Washing Water Service —
Hours of issue and days

880. Exchange and Mart — Restriction
of Activities.

881. A,R,P, Appeal for Canvas (to
make shoulder straps for stretcher
bearers)

889. Lost Property

April, 1945

890.. Mosquito Nets (must be in use by
May 1).

892. Bathing in Ponds (prohibited)

895. Letters from Belgian Consul, Br.
and Netherlands Communities
expressing condolences to
Americans because of Roosevelt's
death.

896. Memorial Service (for
Roosevelt) — April 22 — 10:30
am. Last Post sounded at 11:30,
followed by 2 minutes silence.

898. Supplies from Swiss
Consulate — 513 straw hats, soap,
stationery, medical supplies

899. Shanghai Land Title Deeds — Must
be surrendered at once.

901. Return of A.R.C. Blankets

903. Straw Hats

905. Out-of-bounds — Japanese
residences

906. Adult Library — Appeal for flour
to make paste and cloth to rebind
books

907. Anti-Typhoid Inoculation

908. Shoe Repairs

909. Theft of Split Bamboos

May, 1945

913. Closing of Inner Gates (open till
8 pm)

914. A.R.P. Organization

915. Belgian Occupants — Comfort
Loan

917. Malaria Prevention

918. Finance and Comfort Loans —
Feb. — March received — $3,000
per mo., Swiss Consulate funds
exhausted.

919. Yu Yuen Road and Columbia
Country Club Camps —
transferred to Yangtzepoo.

921. Comfort Parcels — I.R.C. will try
to send to those with no contacts.

922. Exchange and Mart — Closing

928. Radio Messages to Australasia

930. Supplies from Swiss Consul

933. Visit of Swiss and Swedish
Consuls General & I.R.C.
Representative

934. Removal of Wood from
Assembly Hall

935. Meals — Temporary Rice Shortage

937, F. Block Roof—Can use from
6—7:30 pm.

940. Shoe Repairs—Appeal for
Volunteer Labour

941. Vegetable Gardens—Appeal for
Volunteer Labour

942. Hot Drinking Water

944. Malaria Prevention

945. Food Situation—grave shortage

947. Return of Medicine Bottles

June, 1945

949. A.R.P. Instructions for Audiences
at Concerts, Lectures

951. I.R.C. Letters—Cancellation of
Fees

952. To Occupants of Unrecognized
Status

953. Overdrafts

956. Gambling Debts—Bank will not
make transfers

958. Shanghai Milk—$325 per day
for ½ pt.

902. Typhoon Precautions

963. Empty Bottles & Cartons

964. Outward Mail

965. Cholera Injections

966. Appeal Appeal for Literature on
Careers—Needed for adolescents

968. Anti-Vermin Fumigation—Can't
undertake till chamber repaired.

July, 1945

969. Tap Water & Drinking Water—
Economy necessary

975. Rumours of Transfers from
Lunghwa

978. Grass Cutting for Haymaking—
Volunteers needed.

981. Release from Civil Assembly
Center—On account of acute food
situation details needed of all
women, children under 18, mean
over 65 who have outside support
with relatives or friends.

983. Supplies from Swiss—Food, soap,
insecticide

985. Rinsing & Washing Clothes at
F Block Pond—Keep to certain
spots to avoid congestion while
water is being drawn for general
purposes. Tap water off for 4 days
due to air raid.

988. Garden Produce—Tomatoes &
Melons

989. Water Emergencies Resulting
from Raids and/or Other Causes

990. Visits of Relatives—Husbands,
Wives, blood relatives—will be
arranged.

991. Red Cross Relief Shipments—
Letter from I.R.C. saying that
so-called American parcels were
provided jointly by American,

British, Canadian, Australian, East India Red Cross.

993. Air Raid Precautions – Evacuate roofs.

995. Rat traps – Return borrowed ones.

996. Loss of Library Book – Concise Oxford Dictionary – Taken from Library.

August, 1945

1000. Record of Donated Property – Submit list of articles donated.

1002. Haiphong Rd. Camp – Men have arrived near Peking.

1003. Outward Mail – Envelopes Not required.

1007. Discarded jFootwear & Shoe Repairs – Collect shoes in repair dep't by Saturday. (Shop about to close with the war.)

14 Aug, 1945 [All the following written in pencil.]

1005. Dental Clinic – All appointments canceled.

1009. Supplies from Swiss

1010. Camp Regulations & Arrangements – Jap. guards withdrawn

Thanksgiving Service & Flag Raising 7 pm – Aug. 15

1011. Lights Out – 11 pm!

1012. Donation from General Dai Li -Candies & Cigarettes

1013. Warning – Internees should not go to town. Several undesirable happenings in town.

1014. Library (winding up)

1015. Anhui Evacuees – Whereabouts now available.

1019. Auxiliary Police – Night Duty

1021. Library (reopens)

1022. Unauthorized coolies not allowed to enter camp.

1023. Registration for Evacuation – Information for American Mission

1025. Notice for Belgian Internees

1026. Repossession of Homes

1028. Abolition of Daylight Saving Time

1030. Compradore Shop (Closes at 7:00)

1033. Housing – Japanese new Enemy Property Commission advises which apartments can now be reoccupied & which are still in use by Naval & Military people.

Internee Status – Those who left camp between Aug. 11 and Sept. 16 lose their internee status.

Notice No. 17 – Married Status of Women

We have been requested to provide information concerning women occupants of this Centre under the following headings:

1. Women who have common law husbands of Japanese nationality.
2. Women legally married to Chinese nationals where the wife has both British and Chinese nationality.
3. Women formally married to Chinese nationals but without legal Chinese national status.
4. Women legally married:
   a) To neutrals subsequent to 8th Dec., 1941, according to the law of the state of the said neutral where dual nationality obtains because the wife has been unable officially to relinquish her British status.
   b) To stateless Russians
5. Women who are neutral or Russian by birth
   a) Who have been separated from their husbands for an appreciable time
   b) Who are divorced from their husbands
   c) Who are widows
6. Any complicated or involved status not covered by the above headings.

Will those who qualify under any of the above headings please address a letter to Mr. Bates, C.A.C. Representative, and send their letters to the Office, Room 110, Block F. marked "Married Status—Confidential."

[Inside back cover of notebook]:

Deaths

1. Isabella Smith
2. J. Hanson Kahn
3. Godfrey Pearson
4. Mrs. Reeves
5. Mrs. Huber
6. Pamela Orchin
   Mr. Gibson
   Mr. Bruce
   Mr. Fabian
   Mr. Souza
23 deaths to Aug. 13, 1945

For Further Reading

Abkhazi, Peggy - *A Curious Cage - A Shanghai Jounrnal*, 1941-1945, Victoria, B.C,, Canada: Sono Nis Press, 1981

Ballard, J.G. - *Empire of the Sun*, London: Gollancz, 1984

Ballard, J.G. - *Miracles of Life - Shanghai to Shepparton*, London: Fourth Estate, 2008

Bickers, Robert - *The Scramble for China - Foreign Devils in the Qing Empire 1832-1914*, London: Allen Lane, 2011

Collar, Hugh - *Captive in Shanghai - A Story of Internment in World War II*, Oxford: O.U.P., 1990

Earnshaw, Graham - *Tales of Old Shanghai*, Earnshaw Books, 2008

Leck, Greg - *Captives of Empire - The Japanese Internment of Allied Civilians in China, 1941-1945*, Bangor, PA: Shandy Press, 2006

Mitter, Rana - *China's War with Japan 1937-1945 The Struggle for Survival*, London: Allen Lane, 2013

Read, Elfrieda - *Congee and Peanut-Butter*, Canada: Oberon Press, 1990

Wang, George & Barr, Betty - *Between Two Worlds - Lessons in Shanghai*, Shanghai: Old China Hand Press, 2004

Wang, George & Barr, Betty - *Shanghai Boy Shanghai Girl - Lives in Parallel*, Shanghai: Old China Hand Press, 2011, revised

ACKNOWLEDGEMENTS

AT ONE OF OUR early lunches to discuss this book, Graham Earnshaw, my publisher, told me if we did things in a certain way then "Robert's your father's brother." I stared at him.

"How did you know that?" I asked, having only just sent him a document giving my family tree.

"I only meant 'Bob's your uncle'," was his response.

From that time on, we got on well and the result is this book.

Since I am of a certain generation, I needed all the technical help I could get. Mr Bian of Earnshaw Books and many others helped me to push the right buttons on my computer.

The following people have helped me in a variety of ways: James Barnett, John Estes, Mimi Hollister Gardner, Martin, Isabelle and Cathy Griffiths, Harold and Ann Hindle, Keiko Itoh, Sachiko Yamanouchi Itoh, Martin Small, Stine Suenson and Roland van den Berg. The last two were my childhood friends in Shanghai.

My Study Group in today's Shanghai asked many relevant questions and made suggestions when I presented this diary to them as a work-in-progress. They helped me along the way.

Special thanks go to Sven Serrano, a history teacher at Shanghai High School, International Division, who provided the information about Mr Hayashi, the first Japanese Commandant at Lunghwa Civil Assembly Center.

George Wang has encouraged me for years to get this project done. My thanks go to him.

Betty Barr
Shanghai
July 2016

ABOUT THE AUTHOR

 **Ruth Hill Barr** was born in Dallas in 1903 and graduated from Columbia University in New York before moving to Shanghai where she worked with the International YWCA and married a Scottish missionary teacher, John Barr. After release from the Lunghwa internment camp at the end of the war in 1945, Ruth and her husband returned to Shanghai in 1946 and lived there until 1952. They then moved to Hong Kong until 1965 when they retired in Scotland. Ruth died there in 1990. Their daughter Betty still lives in Shanghai.

www.ingramcontent.com/pod-product-compliance
Lightning Source LLC
Chambersburg PA
CBHW011233120626
46549CB00009B/3259